Financial Reforms in Modern China

Financial Reforms in Modern China

A Frontbencher's Perspective

Sun Guofeng

palgrave
macmillan

FINANCIAL REFORMS IN MODERN CHINA

First published in 2015 by
PALGRAVE MACMILLAN®
in the United States—a division of St. Martin's Press LLC,
175 Fifth Avenue, New York, NY 10010.

Where this book is distributed in the UK, Europe and the rest of the world, this is by Palgrave Macmillan, a division of Macmillan Publishers Limited, registered in England, company number 785998, of Houndmills, Basingstoke, Hampshire RG21 6XS.

Palgrave Macmillan is the global academic imprint of the above companies and has companies and representatives throughout the world.

ISBN: 978–1–137–50346–6

Library of Congress Cataloging-in-Publication Data

Sun, Guofeng, 1972–
Financial reforms in modern China : a frontbencher's perspective / Sun Guofeng.
pages cm
Includes bibliographical references and index.
ISBN 978–1–137–50346–6 (hardcover)
1. Finance—China. 2. Monetary policy—China. 3. China—Economic policy—1976–2000. 4. China—Economic policy—2000– I. Title.

HG187.C6S8533 2015
332.0951—dc23 2015005591

A catalogue record of the book is available from the British Library.

Design by Newgen Knowledge Works (P) Ltd., Chennai, India.

First edition: August 2015

To my wife
Fang Li

Contents

Illustrations

Figures

Tables

Preface

Most developing countries undertake financial reforms when there are varying degrees of problems in their financial systems and financial institutions. Although China starts its financial reforms under the similar conditions as other developing countries, it is in the course of transition from a planned economy to a market economy, faced with the task of maintaining a steady and fast economic growth. This requires the integration of China's financial reforms with financial management, entails systematic and sophisticated reforms ahead, and meanwhile means coordinating the reforms as a whole, weighing the pros and cons, and achieving mutually reinforcing effects while emphasizing the key area. Therefore, a systematic study of the issues in China's financial reform is of great theoretical and practical significance.

Sun Guofeng had developed his independent thinking and opinions on major theoretical issues. After graduation, he has been working for many years in the Monetary Policy Department of the People's Bank of China, which is the forefront of China's macrofinancial management and monetary policy operations. He participated in the design and establishment of the interbank bond market, the launch of open market operations, the reform of the RMB exchange rate regime and other major financial reforms, and had a profound insight and pioneering studies on the reforms of monetary policy and financial markets. He values and conscientiously studies the mainstream monetary theories but never blindly follows the established textbook theory. His new theory of money creation, which he has studied earnestly and tested through monetary policy operations for years, is important to the development of monetary theory and the current policy practice.

This book, as a collection of articles written by Sun Guofeng, focuses on the financial reforms, and proceeds to discuss money market, bond market, foreign exchange market, and stock market. His knowledge and capabilities are demonstrated in this book. These papers are written from the perspective of an informed observer to offer readers a side view of the vigorous financial reform of China and also provide discussion topics to concerned researchers of China's financial reform for them to broaden their mind and serve as a reference for decision-making. This book contains the fruitful results of the author in the frontline with independent thinking.

With the development of economic globalization and reforms, the financial sector of China is confronted with more complicated and graver challenges. The Fifth Plenum of the 17th Central Committee of the CPC proposed to deepen the financial system reform, which is also an important consensus reached upon reflections on the international financial crisis. In the course of financial reform, we need to open up our mind and conduct thorough research in a practical manner on issues as how to properly deal with the relationship between reform and management, how to coordinate the pace of reform in all aspects and how to realize the reform in a way that renders optimal results for all.

The theories and views in this book are just the author's opinions, which have yet to be examined, analyzed, and discussed to a full extent. I hope that Sun will keep up his efforts, and others with insights and vision will take part in the research of China's financial reform and explore relevant issues from different perspectives to facilitate China's financial reform and accelerate its economic transformation.

Shang Fulin
(Chairman of China Banking
Regulatory Commission)

Introduction

I have been working at the Department of Monetary Policy in China's Central Bank since 1996, designing and conducting with my colleagues the reforms of the money market, interbank bond market, and foreign exchange market of China, as well as taking note of the development of the stock market. From a frontbencher's perspective, I have been pondering on the theoretic framework and the path to take concerning China's financial reforms. A number of papers were produced during the time. *Financial Reforms in Modern China: A Frontbencher's Perspective* is a collection of 22 papers that represents my major points about the reforms.

The financial reforms in China were essentially incremental. In the reform of RMB exchange rate, the monetary authority has stuck to the principles of activeness, controllability, and incrementalism. Incrementalism was not emphasized apparently in other reforms, but it has been seen throughout the process. During the reforms, some of the financial markets were created within a very short period of time. In January 1994, the interbank foreign exchange market was established to unify exchange rates, and in June 1997 the interbank bond market was established, both accomplished within a single attempt. But the development of the overall financial market and the liberalization of market were mostly incremental.

As seen from the practice of reforms, the authority managed the pace of reforms subject to the internal and external circumstances, not necessarily slowly or rapidly. The reforms occasionally went back and forth in the face of significant events such as global financial crisis. To external observers, the principle of incrementalism may sometimes slow down the pace of reforms against expectation. But if we look at China's financial reforms from a horizon of 5, 10, or even 20 years, a clear path and evident outcomes can be identified. China's economy has grown rapidly, which means that from the perspective of growth, the reforms are successful. The reasons of the success of incremental reforms, in my point of view, can be summarized in four respects:

First, the dividends of reforms will be released gradually in incremental reforms. Reforms are positive institutional changes that are essentially the irreversible release of institutional dividends that would facilitate economic growth. If every step of reforms is able to activate the economy to the maximum subject to the constraint of the learning capability and circumstances, then the irreversible institutional dividends can be viewed as a kind of resources that should be released gradually rather than immediately so that the economic growth is able to retain the momentum. The economic achievement of China in the last 30 years is the result of economy of scale and the institutional transition from planned economy to market-based economy. In the future, as the demographic dividends is going to die out and the country is facing the Lewis Point, the benefits of scale will be replaced by the benefits brought by reforms as the pillar of China's economic growth. Therefore the incremental reform should speed up at the time.

Second, incremental reforms help reduce systemic risks. As we have seen from the history of financial reforms in emerging markets, when an economy was undergoing comprehensive and progressive financial reforms, systematic risks were likely to emerge under significant shocks of the internal or external circumstances. Uncertainty is growing as the global financial markets are changing at a faster pace. The authority can handle the pace of reforms better in incremental reforms; it may push forward reforms in favorable circumstance and it may slow it down otherwise. Taking note of the financial circumstance during reforms would help the authority of manage systematic risks and reduce the risk of total failure.

Third, different issues can be better coordinated in incremental reforms. There is no predefined ordering of the reforms of interest rates, exchange rates and the liberalization of capital account. The authority should be focused upon some of the reforms prudentially. But the reforms are logically interconnected. According to the extended version of impossible triangle, if the policy targets of these reforms add up to 2, the set of solutions might not necessarily be corner solutions such as [1,1,0]. It is more likely to be [0.5,0.5,1]. Therefore, different financial reforms should be coordinated. They might not be progressing simultaneously, but instead one by one. When a single reform has been going well, a solid foundation can be laid for another reform. For example, the interest rate differentials results in capital flow. But investors are really caring about the differentials adjusted by the exchange rate risks. Exchange rate reform is able to bring the rate to the equilibrium level and also strengthen the two-way elasticity of rate movements to press down the room of risk-free arbitrage. Thus large-scale capital flow and the subsequent disruptive impact on interest rate can be avoided. A better foundation for interest rate reform can be laid.

Fourth, incremental reforms can be paced according to the learning capacity of an economy. For the reforms to proceed, we not only need well-designed institution but also the understanding by microlevel players and repeated practice. If the participants in the system cannot fully understand the institution, then any institutional design will be rendered ineffective. Microlevel players would need time to adjust to a new institution and the more complex it is the longer it takes. Incremental reforms usually take a long time of preparation. The time was not only spent on institutional engineering and policy evaluation but also the spread of knowledge. The authority, enterprises and individuals are all learning. The better they understand the whole system, the more positive impact can be generated in every step of reforms.

The book is the collection of my points of view, as well as a summary of my thoughts about China's financial reforms. It is divided into four chapters according to the specific market it discusses.

Chapter 1 Money Market proposes that emerging markets cannot simply borrow from the experience of developed countries, which put the emphasis on interbank lending market. Based on China's circumstance, we should mainly develop the bond repo market that takes high-grade bonds as collaterals, compatible with market-based and well-developed monetary policies. The money market should have multiple levels. The interbank market whose major players are deposit-taking financial institutions should be separated from the market whose players include nondeposit taking institutions because it is essentially a credit market. There should be two interest rates in the two markets. The target of central bank monetary policy should be the real interbank interest rate that only reflects the liquidity of the banking sector.

Chapter 2 Bond Market studies the government-led innovation of institutions that features the interbank bond market established by People's Bank of China. There are several reasons for the success of such innovation. The central bank is not an innovator totally exogenous to the market. The progressive innovation has broken down the institutional trap, and the incremental reform latter has reduced the cost of institutional change. The central bank is also equipped with the necessary expertise. The chapter proposes to set up bond funds, bring corporate bonds to the OTC market, establish the management system targeting the outstanding amount of treasury bonds, and develop more derivatives of bonds. Most of the suggested practices have been realized so far.

Chapter 3 Foreign Exchange Market includes the comparative analysis of foreign exchange interventions in other countries, and the discussion of the RMB exchange rate reform and the choice of market institution. It proposes that the interbank exchange market should take the form of OTC exchange. This chapter also addresses topics such as capital flows and how central banks deal with it, RMB internationalization, and currency swap among central banks. In August 2007, the author predicted that the subprime crisis in the US would evolve into a global financial crisis; in May 2011, he stated that the European debt crisis would further deteriorate.

Chapter 4 Stock Market studies the liquidity freeze in the face of IPO in China's stock market, pointing out that it is due to the three factors of the IPO procedure in China, namely the lower IPO price, the purchase quota determined by the amount of money freeze and the verification method of fund freeze. The lower IPO price is crucial. It also discusses the relations between the stock market and macro-economy. In 2000, I have first proposed that there was bubble in the China's stock market and analyzed how it might hurt the economy and its cause in the economic policies. I have also proposed to open the market up to private capital. Since the sectors associated with consumption credit, real estate for example, have expanded and make interest rate a more effective instrument, the central bank should prefer price-oriented monetary policy instruments.

As I was doing the research of China's financial reforms, my supervisors and colleagues in the People's Bank of China, my teachers and classmates as well as many scholars have provided me with many valuable suggestions and inspiration. I have to give my special thanks to Zhou Xiaochuan, Shang Fulin, Hu Xiaolian, Yi Gang, Wujinglian, Li Yang, Lawrence J. lau, Ronald I. Mckinnon, Zhang Xiaohui. I wish to thank Zhang Yanchun who contributed to "Does the Expansion of Consumer Credit Sector Affect the Effectiveness of Monetary Policy" of chapter 4. For permission on using in this book, I would like to thank the *Capital Market* and *Caijing Magazine* for parts of chapter 2, and *Chinese Securities Journal, Listed Company,* and *Caijing Magazine* for parts of chapter 4.

CHAPTER 1

Money Market

China's Financial System Reform and Money Market Development[1]

A money market generally refers to a market for short-term financing of less than one year and consists of interbank lending market, repo, short-term bond market, market of jumbo certificates of deposits, commercial paper market, and other submarkets. Money market, an important venue for financial institutions to adjust positions and the platform on which the central bank conducts monetary policy, plays an important role in the healthy development of the economy and the normal operation of the financial system. In 1998, amid the continued spread of financial crisis in Asia and persistent fluctuations of the international financial market, the stable operation of China's money market played a positive role in managing financial risks and safeguarding the smooth implementation of monetary policy and fiscal policy.

I. Basic Information on Money Market Development

China's money market emerged in 1984 as the interbank market was formed; in 1994, the bond repo market was established. In 1992, the authority cleared up the "unregulated lending" on the market, and later in 1995, it further regulated the bond repo market. In January 1996, the People's Bank of China (PBC) coordinated a group of large-scale banks to build up the nationwide interbank market under the direct management of the PBC head office. The market members made use of the electronic network provided by China Foreign Exchange Trade System as the trade infrastructure, forming the so-called primary network, while leaving the lending activities of nonmember financial institutions to local financing centers. Since the PBC needed to collect financing data from financial institutions and publicize a comprehensive interbank lending rate, the financing centers of all provinces must report the statistics to the head office of the PBC through another set of computer network, which is called the "secondary network."

Since 1996, despite the establishment of a unified money market, there were no substantive changes to the lending market and bond market. Banks were barely aware of the importance of risk control and far less market-oriented than expected. Although the interbank transaction volume was large, the huge risk was unseen and the bond trading volume was shrinking. In June 1997, the PBC set up the interbank bond market to vigorously develop the entire bond market and strictly control risks of the interbank lending. In early 1998, in the face of the Asian financial crisis and emerging domestic financial risks, the PBC decisively stopped the lending activities of financing centers and spared no efforts to recover overdue loans. Under the policy guidance of the PBC, commercial banks gradually enhanced their risk control system and became more market-oriented, conducting transactions in the interbank lending market with greater prudence so as to manage risks effectively. The commercial banks came to realize that they could manage credit risks and make considerable profits through the bond market. The state-owned commercial banks took advantage of their high credit ratings to raise funds in the interbank market so as to lower financing costs and improve financial conditions; some small- and medium-sized commercial banks also traded actively in the bond market. The interbank market proved to be of high credibility and could help banks to adjust their reserves. The bond market also proved to be of low credit risk and high profitability. The interest rates in these two markets were widely taken as benchmark reference.

In 1998, despite the spread and growing momentum of Asian financial crisis and fluctuations of the international financial market, the money market of China performed soundly, with financial risks under control, and played an active role in ensuring the smooth implementation of monetary policy and fiscal policy. In 1998, commercial banks raised RMB384.3 billion through interbank lending and bond repos, among which RMB103.1 billion through interbank lending, RMB102.1 billion through commercial banks bond repos, RMB3 billion through bond transactions, as well as RMB171.9 billion through bond repos and RMB4.2 billion through spot bond transactions with the PBC. Meanwhile, the build-up of money market further accelerated, and a sophisticated market regulatory system has emerged; a growing number of new types of financial institutions have entered the market; the number of trading subjects has been increasing substantially, and market trading vehicles are being diversified. The bond issuance market has made ground-breaking progress, and the interbank lending market and bond secondary market have become increasingly standardized and active, while the market regulatory system has been improved constantly. The central bank also commenced its bond trading. A money market in line with the requirements of socialist market economy has taken shape.

1. The number of participants in the money market has increased substantially.

All the financial institutions in China can participate in interbank financing and bond trading according to relevant provisions of the PBC, and the participants of the money market have so far included all the financial institutions with required qualifications. Of which, the national interbank lending market is the interfinancial institution liquidity trading platform managed by the PBC. As of late 1998, the membership base of the national interbank lending market has increased to 176, nearly double that of early 1998, which was only 61. It included 15 commercial banks, 66 authorized branches of the commercial banks, 76 urban commercial banks, 9 foreign-funded banks with RMB business, and 10 insurance companies. Among them, there are state-owned commercial banks and joint-stock commercial banks as well as their authorized branches, a vast majority of urban commercial banks, foreign-funded banks engaged in RMB business, and insurance companies. In early 1998, commercial banks adopted unified fund management systems, in which fund surplus and deficits of bank branches were coordinated through intrabank fund allocation under the supervision of headquarters. Therefore, the major participants of the money market have switched to bank corporate legal persons instead of authorized branches. Other financial institutions with qualifications of interbank lending and bond trading business may carry out money market business according to the relevant provisions of the PBC; for example, a large number of rural credit cooperatives were enabled to purchase bonds issued by policy banks with commercial banks and insurance companies being their market agents, which has significantly expanded the scope of money market participants. The total deposits and total assets of the participants have accounted for over 90 percent of the financial system; therefore, the money market players have basically included the entire financial system in terms of the number, total asset ratio, and categories of the participants.

2. The interbank lending market gets on the right track and fulfills its basic functions.

In 1998, the PBC prioritized the standardized and stable development of interbank market over a blind pursuant of growing trading volume. Under the spreading and intensifying financial crisis in Asia and sustained fluctuations in the international financial market, the PBC, on the one hand, tried to contain the credit risks in the interbank lending market to the largest extent possible, and on the other hand, attempted to transform the market from a speculative, profit-making venue to a platform upon which commercial banks could adjust their short-term positions. In 1998, banks have generally improved their internal fund allocation system centered around the headquarters and established a stringent system to manage external credit risks and internal authorization procedure. Subsequently, market participants were remarkably more self-disciplined under the effective management of the PBC, transactions in the interbank lending market were basically conducted for commercial bank to adjust reserves. In 1998, the trading volume of the interbank lending market climbed to RMB98.9 billion; state-owned commercial banks accounted for 67 percent of the total lending volume and became the major market players. Although the trading volume of interbank lending dropped a bit compared with the previous year, the nature of interbank lending has changed substantively and the credit risk has been greatly reduced, and the interbank lending rate is widely seen as a good benchmark rate. The interbank lending has played a more important role in China's financial system (see Figure 1.1.).

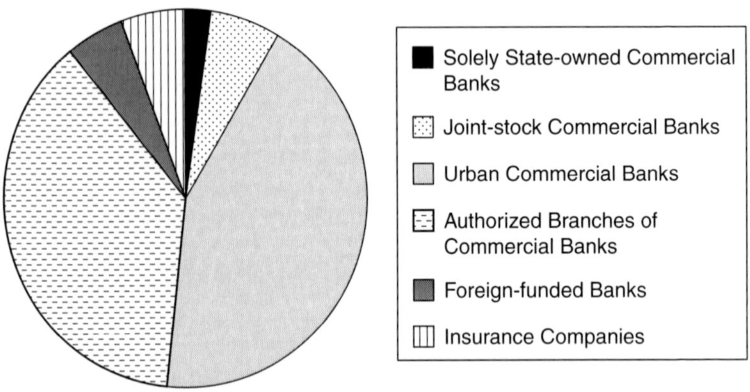

Figure 1.1 Member structure in the national interbank lending market.

Source: China Foreign Exchange Trading System (www.Chinamoney.com.cn).

3. The interbank bond market develops rapidly.

In 1998, the interbank bond market underwent rapid development, with doubled bond outstanding and active secondary market trading, making the interbank market the major platform for bond trading in China. The bond outstanding increased sharply from RMB420.4 billion at the beginning of the year to RMB957.1 billion, up more than one-fold, and over 15 times of that in Shenzhen Stock Exchange and Shanghai Stock Exchange.

Since July, the trading volume rose month by month, and the trading volume reached RMB22.6 billion in December; the annual bond repo transactions reached RMB101 billion and the spot bond transactions reached RMB5 billion. For bond repo transactions, the ratio of short-term bond repo rose significantly, and the bond repos with maturities up to seven days accounted for 37 percent and became the major trading category in the bond repo market; the transactions of joint-stock commercial banks and urban commercial banks were active, accounting for 93.4 percent of the total trading volume; funds mainly flowed from state-owned commercial banks and urban commercial banks in certain developed areas to joint-stock commercial banks; in respect of bond repos, treasury bond accounted for 78.18 percent of the total volume and was the major collateral. The bond repo, with zero default rate upon maturity, has become a major vehicle of financing for commercial banks, which also helped commercial banks load on more quality bond assets and optimize asset structure, and rendered the banks more market-oriented. Some small commercial banks addressed the payment problem in a timely manner and effectively guarded against risks through bond repo financing (see Figure 1.2).

4. Bond issuance process becomes more market-oriented.

Before 1998, the policy banks of China usually raised funds through a centrally planned allocation system, under which the PBC allocated the bond purchase quota to commercial banks. With the reform of the financial

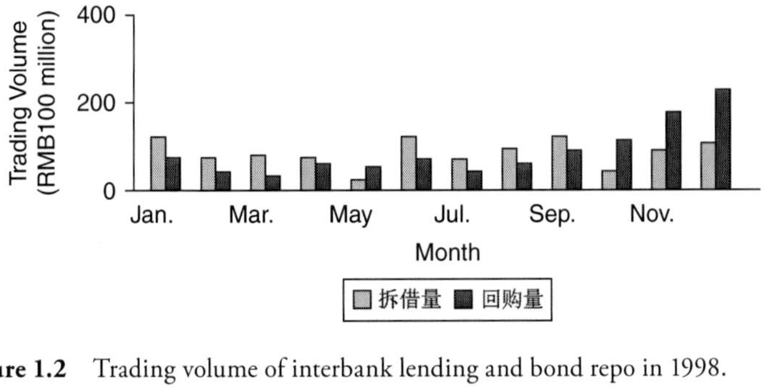

Figure 1.2 Trading volume of interbank lending and bond repo in 1998.

Source: China Foreign Exchange Trading System (www.Chinamoney.com.cn).

system and marketization of banks, the weaknesses of the planned allocation system became prominent. In November 1998, the PBC formulated the *Interim Provisions on the Administration of Issuance on the Financial Bond Market by Policy Banks* and other relevant provisions, organized the China Development Bank and the Export-Import Bank of China to issue financial bonds by means of bidding through the bond issuance system of the PBC; the China Development Bank has issued bonds five times and raised RMB35 billion; the Export-Import Bank has issued bonds twice and raised RMB6 billion of funds. The maturities of bonds range from three months, one year, two years to three years. Bonds were issued via lowest interest rate bidding or with discounts to commercial banks, commercial insurance companies, and urban and rural credit cooperatives. The issuance of policy financial bonds has changed from the planned allocation to the market-oriented mode, which was in line with the direction of establishing a market-oriented financial system, and has reduced the issuance cost, brought more buyers, and enhanced the liquidity of policy financial bonds. At the same time, market-oriented bond issuance also brought more players to the secondary bond market, facilitating the transformation of monetary policy and laying the ground for further development of the money market.

5. Interbank market has become an important platform for financial institutions to manage liquidity.

According to the existing policy, all types of financial institutions in China can conduct short-term financing business in the interbank market, whose core is the national interbank lending market. In 1998, the interbank market gradually assumed the major function of adjusting the short-term positions of commercial banks. Subsequently, commercial banks raised RMB205.2 billion in the national interbank lending market by means of interbank lending and bond repos. The market has basically met the needs of commercial banks for short-term financing.

In 1998, banks generally improved the internal fund allocation system and established stringent external credit management and internal authorization systems. In view of a high degree of self-discipline exercised by the participants in the market, the ratio of short-term transactions in the national interbank lending market went up in 1998. Among which, the ratio of interbank lending with maturities up to one month was 65.6 percent, up by 8.6 percentage points over 1997, which reflected that the position adjustment function of the interbank lending market was gradually reinforced.

6. The money market rates become important indicators for monetary policy implementation due to their growing sensitivity to the liquidity of financial institutions and the central bank policy.

The money market rates include interbank lending rate and bond repo rate, which essentially reflect the fund supply and demand in money market and liquidity of financial institutions. Under the condition that the total liquidity of financial institutions remains unchanged, the distribution of liquidity and commercial banks's changing judgment about the economy, policies, and other factors will also influence the demand and supply of liquidity, which in turn affect the money market rates. As a result, compared with total liquidity, the money market rates can reflect the willingness of commercial banks to create money in a more comprehensive and responsive manner. There are large differences in the credit ratings of China's financial institutions; therefore, the lending interest rates for financial institutions differ greatly. The lending interest rates for small banks usually fluctuate in a wide range, while the interest rates for major banks are more stable, hence making it more responsive to liquidity situation and therefore an effective indicator for the central bank. Since the bond repo rate does not involve any credit risk factor, and it is able to better reflect the liquidity position of financial institutions; the repo rate is also an important indicator. In 1998, the development of the interbank lending market and the interbank bond market got on the right track. The interest rates for interbank lending, bond repo, and bond issuance have become more responsive to the liquidity position of financial institutions and had greater cross-rate interactions; as a result, a coordinated money market rate system has taken shape.

In 1998, the money market rate showed a general downward trend, with the exception of a rise at the beginning of the year. The interbank lending rate was 8.4 percent early in the year and rose to 10.8 percent before the Spring Festival because of large withdrawal of cash and tightened positions of commercial banks. The PBC supplied base money timely through central bank lending, and the lending rate dropped to 8.64 percent in February 1998. After the central bank lowered the interest rate on March 25, 1998, the lending rate remained stable at about 7 percent. Since June 1998, the PBC interfered with the money market rate through monetary policy tools, such as open market operations, and managed to lower the interest rates for deposits and loans twice and reduced the deposit reserve ratio once again; the money market rate edged down in response to the central bank policies and the changes in the liquidity of financial institutions. The 30-day interbank lending rate of major banks at late December 1998 was around 4.26 percent, a drop of 4 percentage points compared with the figure early in the year; the seven-day bond repo rate was 4.04 percent, down about 4.7 percentage points compared with the beginning of 1998. During the three-day span in which the PBC lowered the interest rate, the interbank lending rate and the bond repo rate both responded immediately by drastic

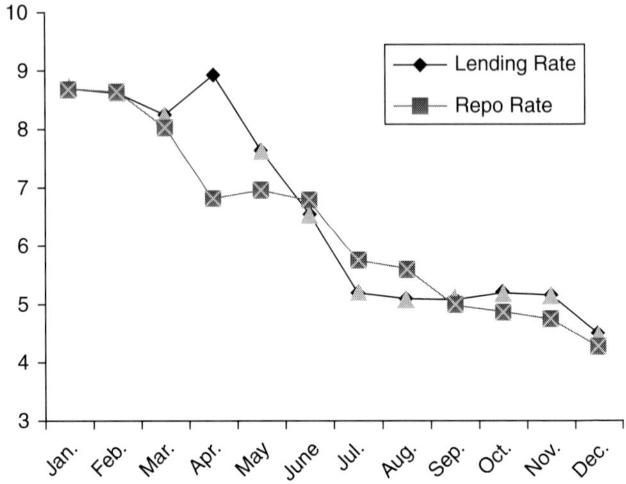

Figure 1.3 Money market interest rate in 1998 (%).

Source: China Foreign Exchange Trading System (www.Chinamoney.com.cn).

decline. The lending rate and bond repo rate of major banks accurately and timely reflect the liquidity of the financial system, and the changes in the money market rate have provided a reference for the monetary policy and become an important indicator for the central bank (see Figure 1.3).

7. The central bank makes direct entry into the money market.

The PBC resumed bond open market operations on May 26, 1998. In order to achieve the objectives of monetary policy, the central bank conducted bond repo and spot bond trading, regulated liquidity demand and supply, influenced the interest rate, improved bond liquidity, and activated the money market. The PBC began to operate in the bond market in May and the trading volume reached RMB176.1 billion at the end of the year.

II. Problems Facing the Development of the Money Market

As the financial system reform proceeds, the development of the money market are faced with certain problems:

1. The organization and regulatory framework of the money market have yet to be improved.

The members of the secondary trading network include urban credit cooperatives, rural credit cooperatives, authorized branches of commercial banks, insurance companies, trust and investment companies, securities companies, leasing companies, financial companies, and other small- and medium-sized financial institutions below the provincial level. The financing centers actually serve the function of coordinating fund flows between large and small financial institutions. After October 1997, financing centers went into liquidation and exited from the money market, which rendered it necessary to establish a new organizational framework for money market operations. The current organization of the money market is still in lack of certain functional institutions, and the responsibility and function of each component is not yet formalized, hence many of them are having difficulty performing their respective functions. The responsibilities of intermediary service organization and custodian institutions are blurred, hindering the full play of their functions. At present, banks in the money market have not yet had any self-disciplinary organization, and the self-regulatory system is far from complete.

2. It is difficult to match bid and ask in the market due to the lack of intermediary organization.

Due to the vast territory of China and enormous differences in the scale of financial institutions, it is necessary to establish intermediary organizations for market trading. The functions of such intermediary organization include: (1) provide information service for financial institutions; (2) organize small and medium local financial institutions to finance among each other so that they can meet their funding demand locally; and (3) coordinate short-term financing between large banks and small- and medium-sized financial institutions. Currently, the lack of such trading intermediary organization gives rise to two problems: first, the flow of market information is not smooth, and it is difficult for financial institutions to obtain information about the liquidity supply and demand of other institutions; second, due to credit problem, it is difficult to conclude transactions between small and large financial institutions and between small and medium institutions.

3. The lack of credit instruments obstructs the flow of funds and the small and medium financial institutions can hardly meet their financing needs.

The great number of small and medium financial institutions and the lack of exchange of fund supply and demand information between financial institutions, make it difficult to conclude transactions due to credit problem. With the enhanced financial regulation, financial institutions have increased risk awareness, and the ratio of bond collateral required in short-term financing is gradually rising. As a result, the development of interbank bond market is of vital importance to the uninterrupted flow of funds. Nevertheless, the existing bond market contains the following problems: first of all, the targets of bond issuance are focused too much on state-owned commercial banks; small and medium institutions are in need of bond assets, but in the current bond issuance system, small institutions can hardly acquire bond assets that could meet their demands; second, the nonmarket factors, among other reasons, of the bond issuance procedure have led to poor secondary market liquidity; third, the methods of bond custody and fund settlement are somewhat outdated given a growing number of financial institutions participating in the bond market. All these have become important issues that restrict further market development.

4. The interbank market credit shrinks.

Because of the underdeveloped credit system and the influence of some financial events in the year, the level of mutual trust among banks is declining, and regular interbank short-term financing has run into problems.

5. The procedure and structure of bond issuance still restrict the development of interbank bond market.

In 1998, policy banks issued bonds under market-based procedures; however, the volume of bonds issued by policy banks in a market-oriented manner was only RMB41 billion, 28 percent of the total bonds issued in 1998, which was fairly low, and moreover, all the treasury bonds in the year were issued in a centrally planned manner. At the moment, treasury bonds and policy financial bonds are mainly held by Industrial and Commercial Bank of China, Agricultural Bank of China, Bank of China, and China Construction Bank, while other banks only hold a small number of bonds, which cannot meet the demand for asset diversification. In 1998, the bonds issued by the Ministry of Finance mainly catered for Industrial and Commercial Bank of China, Agricultural Bank of China, Bank of China, and China Construction Bank, and the treasury bonds held by other banks were still of a limited volume.

6. The bond custody system has yet to be extended.

The existing bond custody system is under the management of China Central Depository & Clearing Co., Ltd. As China's financial institutions are massive in number and scatter across the nation, an all-inclusive electronic network connected to China Central Depository & Clearing Co., Ltd. can hardly be possible. With the further expansion of participants in the money market, the bond custody for new entrants, especially rural credit cooperatives and other small and medium financial institutions, has become an important issue in the next step of market development. With reinforced financial development, nonfinancial institutions and individuals have an increasingly urgent demand for paper-free bond custody. The establishment of a unified, safe, and efficient custody system has become a vital prerequisite for the setting up of the money market.

III. Measures Adopted by the People's Bank of China

Since 1998, for the purposes of promoting the growth of national economy and implementing indirect monetary policy, the PBC has adopted a series of measures to improve money market regulations, continued to expand the participant pool of money market, introduced more market trading vehicles, vigorously developed the primary bond market, and actively used indirect monetary policy tools in the money market, in an all-in effort to facilitate the development of money market.

1. In the light of the needs of money market development and the actual situation of financial institutions, the PBC continued to bring in more participants in the money market and reinforced the market in breadth and depth.

Three important measures were taken in 1998. As a result, the number of money market participants increased substantially and the national interbank lending market developed rapidly in terms of organization types, the number of members, and so forth.

In 1998, in order to assist commercial banks to strengthen internal fund management, commercial banks were approved, based on their respective situation, to authorize branches to participate in the national interbank lending market for the purposes of carrying out credit lending, bond repo, and cash bond trading business; in May 1998, as an important move in implementing step-by-step financial opening-up, the PBC approved foreign-funded banks wtih RMB business to enter the national interbank lending market; in October 1998, insurance companies were approved to join the national interbank lending market to conduct bond trading. In 1998, 35 urban commercial banks, 9 foreign-funded banks, 70 authorized branches of commercial banks, and 10 insurance companies gained entry into the national interbank lending market. By the end of 1998, the members of the national interbank lending market have grown to 176, an increase of 115 compared with the beginning of the year. New entrants include state-owned commercial banks, joint-stock commercial banks and their authorized branches, a majority of urban commercial banks, foreign-funded banks engaged in RMB business, and insurance companies; the total deposits and total assets of members accounted for over 90 percent of the financial system. The members represented the backbone of the national financial system in aspects of assets, reputation, variety, and influence and played a core role in the money market (see Table 1.1).

2. The PBC vigorously promoted the development of bond market and played an essential role in improving asset structure and guarding against

Table 1.1 Membership composition of the national interbank lending market

Types of members	*Number*	*Ratio (%)*
Solely state-owned commercial banks	4	2.3
Joint-stock commercial banks	11	6.3
Authorized branches of commercial banks	66	37.5
Urban commercial banks	76	43.2
Foreign-funded banks	9	5
Insurance companies	10	5.7
Total	176	

Source: China Foreign Exchange Trading System (www.Chinamoney.com.cn).

risks of banks, transforming the means of regulation and transmission mechanism of monetary policy, and implementing proactive fiscal policy.

The development of the interbank bond market was encouraged from three aspects in 1998: first, bond issuance procedures were liberalized. In 1998, the PBC formulated the *Interim Provisions on the Administration of Issuance on the Financial Bond Market by Policy Banks* and other relevant provisions, streamlined "Bond Issuance System of the PBC" and put forward specific measures for issuance of bonds via bidding. The PBC also pushed China Development Bank to issue five rounds of bonds, RMB35 billion in total via bidding through the system, and pushed the Export and Import Bank to issue two rounds of bonds, RMB6 billion in total. The maturities of bonds ranged from three months to three years. The issuance methods included base rate auction and discount issuance, and the issuance targets extended from state-owned commercial banks to banks, commercial insurance companies, and rural credit cooperatives. In the process of bond issuance, members of underwriting group were encouraged to actively coordinate quota distribution and establish business relationships with small and medium financial institutions and gradually carry out financing agency business. Eventually, 112 rural credit cooperatives associations purchased bonds of RMB5.408 billion, which provided instruments for small financial institutions to manage risks and improve their asset structure.

Second, financial institutions were coordinated for bond purchase. In 1998, the PBC organized the members of the national interbank lending market and rural credit cooperatives to purchase treasury bonds totaling 421.3 billion and policy financial bonds of RMB147 billion, which greatly supported the implementation of proactive fiscal policy and policy-oriented banking business, and led to a 10 percent rise of the ratio of bond assets of commercial banks to total assets at the end of 1998; the bonds traded in the interbank market amounted to RMB1010.3 billion, an increase of RMB 590 billion compared with the beginning of the year, among which book-entry treasury bonds accounted for 84 percent of the national aggregates. The increase of bond assets of financial institutions facilitated the gradual adjustment of their asset structure and risk management, laid the foundation necessary for the implementation of indirect monetary policy of the central bank, and lowered the bond issuance costs of the Ministry of Finance and policy banks.

Third, the bond circulation market was invigorated. In October 1998, the monthly trading volume of bond repos reached RMB10 billion for the first time and increased to RMB22.6 billion in December. The liquidity of bonds increased. Banks were able to better handle their short-term positions, and the bond issuers were able to lower their fund-raising cost.

Based on internationally recognized indicators for bond market evaluation, including the amount of issued bonds, bond issuance rate, outstanding bonds in the market, formation mechanism, and the importance of market interest rate, together with the risk management mechanism, the interbank bond market has become a major constituent of the bond market in China.

3. The PBC has increased trading instruments in the market and provided safe and effective management methods for financial institutions.

Money market instruments with high credit rating provided commercial banks with safe assets and reinforced their balance sheets and liquidity management. Together with the reform of the deposit reserve system, the PBC, and the Ministry of Finance jointly issued RMB270 billion special treasury bonds to state-owned commercial banks and RMB45 billion dedicated treasury bonds to other commercial banks and urban commercial banks, and the Ministry of Finance also issued RMB100 billion construction treasury bonds to state-owned commercial banks in order to implement the proactive fiscal policy, all of which have increased the amount of bonds held by commercial banks and optimized the asset structure of commercial banks. The dedicated treasury bonds and construction treasury bonds as approved by the PBC can be traded and listed in the national interbank lending market, which increased quality trading instruments in the bond circulation market. Policy banks have fairly high credit ratings due to the capital and liquidity support by the Chinese government. Under the condition that the amount of treasury bonds issued by the Ministry of Finance cannot satisfy the huge demand of commercial banks, growing policy financial bonds would be an ideal alternative. The PBC has coordinated policy banks to issue bonds under market-based procedures, adding more trading vehicles to the market.

The PBC then approved the spot bond trading and repo of policy financial bonds issued under market-based procedures in the interbank bond market, which greatly enriched the trading instruments of the market. As of the end of 1998, the bonds outstanding in the market increased from RMB420.4 billion early in the year to RMB975.1 billion, including treasury bonds of RMB497.7 billion, financial bonds of RMB442.6 billion, and central bank bills of RMB11.8 billion.

4. The PBC improved market trading rules, enhanced market operation efficiency, and guarded against risks.

In early 1998, the PBC laid out a principle for bond trading, which dictates that bond transactions, contracts, and settlement orders must be matched to effectively mitigate settlement risks. In May 1998, to solve the problem of overdiversification of financial bonds and subsequent difficulties for banks to trade standardized products, the PBC consolidated the policy financial bonds issued in 1996, 1997, and 1998 on an annual basis. In October 1998, for the purpose of lowering risks by means of bond repo and facilitating long-term fund allocation, the PBC extended the maximum maturity of interbank bond repo to one year. In November 1998, the PBC, in the *Rules for the Settlement of Interbank Bond Trading*, changed the original bond settlement model from T+1 to T+1 and T+0 at the discretion of the two trading parties, which made the position adjustment of commercial banks easier; after the reform, T+0 is preferred by banks to T+1.

5. In order to ensure the standardized operation of the money market, the PBC improved the regulation system for the money market, exercised stringent rules, and safeguarded the standardized and safe operation of the money market.

Since 1998, the PBC has approved a series of provisions, including the Rules for Interbank Bond Trading, the Rules for the Settlement of Interbank Bond Trading, the Interim Provisions on the Administration of Issuance on the Financial Bond Market by Policy Banks, in order to control the entry into the money market. The PBC started to regulate the maximum lending balance of trading members in the interbank lending market. Also the overdue reporting system that could be activated automatically in the computer system has been in place. With regard to the bond market, the bonds used by trading members in repos and spot bond transactions must be real bonds in full amount with full ownership. Short trade of bonds as well as bond leasing, bond lending, and securities financing were strictly prohibited. Financial institutions in violation of provisions were punished. PBC also required that the market exit mechanism must be rigorous, and the banks not meeting the requirements as trading members of the national interbank lending market must be disqualified. The PBC exercised rigid management of the qualifications for entry into the national interbank lending market, regularly approved and announced the maximum lending balance of members, conducted real-time monitoring, and timely adjusted the quotas according to lending compliance and other circumstances. The overdue reporting system has been implemented to strengthen the self-discipline and mutual supervision. The market exit mechanism disqualified nonconforming banks. With regard to the interbank bond market, the PBC rigorouly regulated financial institutions and strictly prohibited short selling of bonds; financial institutions in breach of provisions were punished. These provisions were the natural extension of those in 1997 and provided a legal basis for the money market.

6. The PBC reinforced open market operations and promoted the development of money market.

The open market operations refer to the trading activities in which the central bank buys or sells bonds in the money market, serving the main purpose of managing the money supply. The open market operations, moreover, are vital to the build-up of the money market. In 1998, the PBC resumed the open market operations of bonds and adjusted the base money by means of bond repo and spot bond transactions. Cumulatively RMB176.1 billion was lent out and net base money of RMB70.1 billion was injected. Through the adjustment of the liquidity of financial institutions, the PBC improved the liquidity of bond market and promoted active trading of interbank bond repos; the fund supply and demand in money market were balanced; the money market rate was regulated, and the development of the money market was reinforced.

7. The PBC regulated money market rate with the use of monetary policy tools to influence the macroeconomic situation and established the indirect monetary policy transmission mechanism.

The money market rates mainly include interbank lending rate and bond repo rate, which both reflect the liquidity status of financial institutions. Since June 1996, the PBC has lifted the restriction on the money market rates and hence made them fully market-oriented. In 1998, the central bank, on the one hand, injected more liquidity into financial institutions by appropriate monetary policy and indirectly led to the downward movement of the money market rates; on the other hand, besides the adjustment of interest rates for deposits, loans, and reserve rates for three times, the PBC also flexibly regulated the money market rates and sent monetary policy signals through open market operations and various monetary policy tools. Banks were able to adjust their balance sheets by means of trading in the money market. In this way, the monetary policy objectives were realized. Under the regulation of the central bank, the money market rate showed a gradual downward trend and dropped more than the deposit and lending rates, offering strong support to economic growth.

IV. Positive Effects of the Measures of the People's Bank of China

In general, under the furtherance of a complete set of measures of the PBC and active operation of financial institutions, the money market of China performed soundly and developed rapidly in 1998, and the market framework was gradually laid out. Commercial banks made fund allocation through interbank lending and bond repo to timely adjust positions, guarantee payment, and manage financial risks. The growth of bond holding of financial institutions and the active state of money market trading played a vital role for indirect monetary policy to take effect. The PBC coordinated financial institutions to make purchase of a large quantity of treasury bonds and bonds issued by policy banks in support of the proactive fiscal policy and policy banking business, and eased the fiscal burden. The smooth flow of fund in the money market enhanced the lending capability of banks, raised the efficiency of commercial banks in fund management, optimized the fund allocation in the financial institution system, and improved the functions and impacts of the base money of the central bank. Commercial banks started to find the money market a priority option to manage their short-term positions and have become more market-oriented. Some banks were very active in the interbank lending and bond market. At the end of 1998, the book-entry bonds made up of 11 percent of the total assets of commercial banks, a rise of 5.7 percentage points compared with 5.3 percent at the beginning of the year. The commercial banks not only improved asset structure and risk management but also achieved more flexibility.

1. The PBC developed the money market by adhering to the "standardized" principle and guarded against financial risks.

The trading parties of the money market are mostly commercial banks, whose liabilities are primarily deposits; therefore, the security of money market trading is of critical importance to the interests of depositors and the soundness of the financial system. Since the establishment of the national interbank lending market, the PBC has prioritized market standardization. It has gradually formulated and promulgated a series of provisions, exercised full supervision on market access, daily regulation on market exit, and formed a set of effective regulatory measures. Under stringent and standardized management, the risk awareness of trading members is strengthened noticeably. Even faced with sprawling foreign financial risks and the acute problems with China's domestic financial institutions, the money market of China has effectively managed financial risks. In general, there is no overdue in the interbank lending market, repayment ratio upon maturity in the bond repo market is 100 percent, and the market has been insulated from risks in the global money market.

2. The PBC has brought more trading members to the market, provided financing channels for more financial institutions and reinforced the transmission of monetary policy.

Commercial banks increase the funding channels through which authorized branches could finance in the market in addition to internal allocation of positions, which is beneficial to improving the efficiency of fund use, improving fund management, and better supporting national economic growth. This helps foreign-funded banks to make reasonable positioning and conduct liquidity management and helps the central bank to obtain the accurate trading information of such banks and carry out real-time monitoring of their money market business.

It also provides insurance companies with safe, efficient, and new channels in fund use. Insurance companies can buy various bonds listed and traded in the national interbank lending market, and adjust asset structure through bond trading. The huge volume of bonds traded in the national interbank market makes it easier for insurance companies to trade bonds. The entry of insurance companies diversifies the financial institutions in the market and contributes to the active state of bond trading in the national interbank money market.

To expand the trading membership of the money market, we are to provide more reasonable financing channels to financial institutions; meanwhile, we have to rigidly regulate the market with reference to the nature and functions of different segments of the money market, and expansion solely for the purpose of expansion must be avoided. The interbank lending market is a platform where commercial banks make reserve adjustment in the form of overnight credit lending; in view of the low creditability of nonbanking financial institutions and small demand for real interbank lending, we should keep strict control on the entry of nonbanking financial institutions. At present, the insurance companies approved by the PBC to enter the interbank bond market are only allowed to carry out spot bond trading.

3. The unimpeded fund flow in the money market strengthens the lending capability of banks and improves the efficiency of monetary policy transmission. In 1998, total lending and borrowing through the money market amounted to RMB168.1 billion. Funds flowed in the national money market from banks with loose position to banks with tight position or opting for expansion, which improved the efficiency of commercial banks in managing funds and increased the size of bank loans.

4. The money market has become the major preferred method for commercial banks to adjust short-term positions and has facilitated the marketization of commercial banks. Commercial banks would take the money market as the primary platform for borrowing and lending according to their respective funding positions.

5. The money market rate that reflects changes in the positions of financial institutions and monetary policy of the central bank gradually becomes an important target of the PBC's monetary policy as well as a main economic indicator and lays a good foundation for interest rate liberalization.

6. The development of the money market gives support to the implementation of fiscal policy and development of policy-based finance. Both the increase of trading members of the money market and the thriving bond market trading greatly improve the liquidity of treasury bonds and policy financial bonds. It lowers the issuance cost of bonds, reduces financial burden, increases the government debt level, increases the volume of financing through bonds issuance by policy banks, and supports the implementation of proactive fiscal policy and development of policy-based finance.

V. A Few Thoughts on the Development of Money Market

In 1999, Chinese government would continue to implement appropriate monetary policy and proactive fiscal policy, and the money market needs to serve a more dominant role in transmitting the monetary policy and thereby supporting the implementation of the fiscal policy. As the domestic and foreign financial risks are still pressing, it is very challenging to manage financial risks in the money market. In view of the situation and under the general guidance, we will, on the basis of the principle of containing financial risks, adhere to the direction of standardized development and continue to promote the development of money market from now on and strive to ensure the unobstructed fund flow of financial institutions, managing financial risks, and safeguarding the implementation of monetary policy and fiscal policy.

The general idea is to place the focus on bond issuance. We shall promote the agency business of financial institutions through increasing the volume of bonds held by financial institutions, establish the financing channel that links up big banks and small and medium financial institutions, and meet the financing demands of small and medium financial institutions; maintain robust trading between members of the national interbank lending market with the help of money market makers, short-term credit companies, and brokers; gradually solve the financing issues of nonbank financial institutions; meanwhile, attention should be directed to the improvement of the regulation system for the money market. We should ensure the uninterrupted fund flow of financial institutions, guard against financial risks, and guarantee the smooth implementation of monetary policy and fiscal policy through the aforementioned measures. In the long run, a multilayered money market would be established, centered on the central bank and major money market players; members of the national interbank lending market constitute the core of the money market and play a backbone role; other small and medium financial institutions would mainly raise fund through the agents of the aforesaid banks by means of bonds.

1. Formulate development plan for the money market and accelerate the establishment of multilayered money market system commensurate with the socialist market economy in light of the circumstances of China.

In light of the fact that China has a vast territory and daunting number of financial institutions, we should draw on overseas experience, formulate the development plan for the money market, and accelerate the establishment of the money market system commensurate with the socialist market economy. In the design of new money market structure, the following principles must be adhered to: first, it must be conducive to the timely and effective financing of financial institutions; second, it must have well-established risk prevention mechanism; and third, it must be convenient for the regulation and monetary policy operation of the central bank. The build-up of the money market and the establishment of the new monetary policy transmission mechanism should be promoted collectively. Under the new regulation mechanism, one of the primary means adopted by the central bank is operation in the open market that adjusts base money and transmits monetary policies through the 28 primary dealers to other financial institutions. In this regard, primary dealers should establish fund flow relationships with other financial institutions, including urban commercial banks, credit cooperatives, trust companies, finance companies, securities companies, securities funds, insurance funds, and other institutions to carry out trading, repo, and lending of bonds. The central bank has gradually switched to the money market to manage the total liquidity of the financial system.

2. Continue to reinforce market regulation, establish self-disciplinary organization for banks, exercise tight regulation, and create a safe and standardized market environment.

In 1999, the administrative provisions on interbank lending will be formulated, the relevant administrative provisions on bond repo and cash bond trading will be revised, the measures for the administration of market information service agencies and custodian institutions will be formulated, implementation protocols of various market provisions will be completed, and trading members will be organized to sign the master agreement for interbank lending and bond repo. A self-regulatory organization for banks will be established to strengthen the self-regulation of banks. The regulation will be stringent, and any institutions in violation of the relevant rules of the PBC will be resolutely investigated and punished so as to maintain the market order and create a safe and standardized market environment. In addition, the self-disciplinary system of interbank market members must be raised and the members of the national interbank lending market must be gathered to sign the Master Agreement for Interbank Bond Repo. The master agreement is a self-disciplinary document signed by members of their own accord and carries legal effect after signature, which will improve the degree of self-discipline exercised by members. Commercial banks should be encouraged to establish a system for internal authorization and external credit risk management.

3. Continue to make planned expansion of the market membership base.

When the relevant methods and regulatory measures are in place, a greater variety of financial institutions will be absorbed into the money market step by step according to the overall development strategy under the principle of security and standardization in a planned manner, and the depth of the market will continue to be strengthened.

4. Explore various money market trading modes according to the characteristics of different market segments, while keeping up the efforts in the existing trading modes.

Currently, China's money market has adopted the electronic network trading. The trading members negotiate through the computer network provided by the National Interbank Funding Center. From the experience of international money market, foreign exchange markets mainly adopt the method of electronic brokerage, while the interbank lending and bond markets primarily adopt the method of direct trading between trading parties or through brokers, according to the characteristics of trading varieties and market demands. With regard to the interbank lending market and bond repo market, we can actively explore various trading modes based on the characteristics of trading varieties while continuing with the existing e-network trading modes. After formulating the relevant administrative measures, intermediary institutions providing different trading modes will be formed. Under the principle of "mutual agreement, credibility, fairness and closest agent," financial institutions are encouraged to perform as the agents for small and medium financial institutions. In agency business, small and medium financial institutions are to be encouraged to increase bond holding in order to manage the biparty risks. The asset structure of small and medium financial institutions must be adjusted, and tradable bond assets proportion must be increased. At the same time, we should develop negotiable instruments, financial bonds, corporate bonds, and other credit instruments.

5. Explore the way to establish new trading intermediaries.

Countries with developed money markets usually have various types of trading agencies. At present, intermediary and brokerage agencies are less than enough in the money market so that market trading is not sufficiently active and smooth. In order to link up the supply and demand of the bond market, we should consider establishing short-term credit companies in the form of independent legal entity of nonbanking financial institutions and as joint-ventures set up by commercial banks and enterprise groups and under the direct supervision of the head office of the PBC. Its main business is proprietary bond repos and purchase and sale of spot bonds; however, it should not engage in other forms of investment, custody, or loan businesses. In some developed regions, we would consider establishing brokerage firms to engage in money market brokerage to the exclusion of proprietary trading.

6. Enhance money market information service, improve service quality, and lower market operation cost.

The money market adopts the trading method of negotiation among traders; therefore full and timely information is crucial to banks. We must further strengthen the administration over market information service institutions, urge them to enhance the money market information service, raise service quality and lower market operation costs. We are also to motivate the marketization of treasury bond and policy financial bond issuance.

In the future, China Development Bank and Export-Import Bank shall primarily make bond issuance in a market-oriented manner. On coordinating policy banks for bond issuance, the Ministry of Finance is to be consulted to motivate the marketization of treasury bond issuance to financial institutions. As for bidding rules, the measures for the administration of underwriters and their qualification standards should be established and the membership base of the underwriting group should be expanded properly. At the same time, small and medium financial institutions are encouraged to purchase more bonds. In the process of issuance coordination, the launch of agency business of financial institutions must be promoted. Amendments must be made to the measures for issuance of policy financial bonds, issuance procedures must be subject to regulation, and all aspects in relation to bond issuance must be under strict management. In the issuance of financial bonds, pilot financial institutions should explore multiple issuance methods of financial bonds. A rating system for financial bonds must be established and financial bonds with a high credit rating must be allowed to be traded and listed in the money market. The issuance of negotiable certificates of deposit by Chinese-funded and foreign-funded banks could be explored. The development of the primary and secondary markets for negotiable instruments must be promoted.

8. Widen the financing channels of nonbanking financial institutions.

In 1999, trust companies, securities companies, financial companies, and leasing companies are going through large-scale restructuring and reorganization. On this basis, nonbanking financial institutions are calling for new methods and sources of financing. The demands of nonbanking financial institutions for financing are pressing, and the major problem nowadays lies in the initial public offering system, in which new shares are issued at low price earnings ratio that gives rise to extremely high risk-free returns. If the existing initial public offering system remains unchanged, expanding the financing channels of nonbanking financial institutions will make the IPO process far more unfair than before and lead to a great surge and fluctuation in money market rate and adversely influence the normal operation of banks and operation of monetary policy. Upon proper resolution of the problems, the financing channels of securities companies and other nonbanking financial institutions will gradually be opened.

9. Consider the establishment of bond custodian clearing system and fund settlement system

The development of the money market and open market operation require efficient and secure bond custody and fund settlement system. Currently, we need a bond custodian clearing system of a unified framework, and we need to study the relations between bond settlement and fund settlement systems to contain risks in all aspects.

10. Step up efforts in open market operations.

In 1999, we would continue to intensify the money market interference of the PBC, increase open market operations, and improve the liquidity of bonds in the interbank bond market.

Direction for the Development of China's Money Market[2]

In 1998, the Asian financial crisis was spreading and aggravating, and continued to cause fluctuations in the international financial market. Against this backdrop of external adversity, China's money market maintained stable performance and played an active role in guarding against financial risks and ensuring the smooth implementation of monetary policy and fiscal policy. At the same time, after several years of rectification and adjustment, remarkable progress was made in the establishment of China's money market and significant breakthroughs were achieved in the bond market and other aspects in 1998. At present, in the face of complicated domestic and foreign financial conditions, the money market should ensure safe operations and grasp the opportunities of substantial regulation of the financial industry to build up the general framework of China's money market and lay a solid foundation for the standardized development of money market and smooth operation of the financial system.

I. Choice of the Structure of Chinese Financial System and Direction for the Development of China's Money Market

The financial system structure, that is, the balance sheet structure, credit structure, and bond holdings of financial institutions, determines the development direction of the money market. The specialty of the financial system structure of China has profound influence on the direction for establishing the China's money market.

Based on the scale and capital strength, the existing financial institutions in China can be divided into three groups: the first group consists of state-owned commercial banks, large-scale joint-stock banks, and urban commercial banks; the second group consists of banks other than those in the first group and large-scale cooperative financial institutions (urban and rural credit cooperatives) and nonbanking financial institutions; the third group includes other urban and rural credit cooperatives and nonbanking financial institutions. The last two groups are usually referred to as "small and medium financial institutions."

In countries with developed market economy, large banks mainly engage in loan and money market business, while small and medium financial institutions (including small and medium banks) absorb deposits and transfer funds to large banks. In China, for historical reasons, shortly after small and medium financial institutions were established, the big four state-owned commercial banks, including Industrial and Commercial Bank of China, Agricultural Bank of China, Bank of China, and China Construction Bank, had extensive branches nationwide, and small and medium financial institutions could hardly compete with large banks for deposits. However, due to the growing loan demand of enterprises and the problems with internal management, small and medium financial institutions have borrowed more intensively than large banks; the asset and liability structure of some small and medium financial institutions were unreasonable. Large banks usually have ample liquidity, while small and medium financial institutions are confronted with liquidity shortage.

The particularity of the financial system structure of China has remarkable influences on the development of China's money market:

(1) Large banks are generally having sufficient liquidity. With the fund support from the central bank, they do not have much demand for interbank financing; (2) small and medium financial institutions face long-term funding shortage and require fund from large banks; (3) from the beginning of the development stage, small and medium financial institutions failed to establish a relatively stable financing relationship with commercial banks and a lot of small and medium financial institutions are present in the money market as independent entity.

The functions of the money market are mainly manifested in three aspects: the interbank money market should facilitate the flexible and timely position adjustments of financial institutions; the retail money market should be able to meet the demand of the nonfinancial public for financial assets; and the interbank money market and retail money market must effectively transmit the monetary policy of the central bank. The peculiarity of the financial system of China has given rise to a special requirement for the money market that is, to satisfy the demand of small and medium financial institutions for independent borrowing of long-term funds.

Nevertheless, small and medium financial institutions have encountered three difficulties. First, they are faced with relatively higher credit risks. Although small and medium financial institutions ask for long-term fund, they lack sufficient creditability and great credit risks are involved. As a result we need an institution for risk undertaking or a mechanism for risk absorption; second, they are faced with information asymmetry. Since small and medium financial institutions are not represented by the agents of large banks, in order to coordinate fund supply and demand information between small and medium financial institutions and large banks and among small and medium financial institutions, the market needs broker institutions throughout the prefectures and cities of the country. Third, large banks and small and medium financial institutions have great differences in fund supply and demand, which made trading between them difficult. For example, the trading volume of large banks is usually of several billions RMB, while that of small and medium financial institutions mostly amounts to tens of millions of RMB and sometimes even several millions of RMB. Because of transaction cost, large banks are not willing to trade with small and medium financial institutions.

In 1995, the PBC restructured local financial markets and transformed them into financing centers to solve the problems above. In China, there were 43 financing centers in provinces, autonomous regions, and municipalities directly under the central government and cities under independent planning and 260 offices in prefecture-level cities, which basically cover the whole country. The functions of financing centers were to organize and manage the lending activities of local financial institutions, provide information services and carry out proprietary financing business; usually funds are lent from large banks to small and medium financial institutions. The financing centers facilitated fund flow from large banks to small and medium financial institutions by undertaking credit risks and breaking large financing demand into smaller batches or vice versa. This money market layout has played a very important role in the rapid expansion of financial institutions in China and supported national economic growth.

However, as institutions under the PBC, the financing centers nevertheless carry out commercial business and undertake interbank lending risks on the contrary to the position of the PBC as the central bank. In addition, the risks of lending to cover the long-term funding gap of small and medium financial institutions are unaffordable for most institutions. Due to the gradual exposure of risks of financing centers, the PBC withdrew financing centers in September 1997. The exit of financing centers from the money market eliminates institutions and mechanisms that undertake credit risks of small and medium financial institutions. The electronic trading system established in 1996 facilitated information exchange among large banks, but cannot yet solve problems such as credit risk, information asymmetry and unbalanced position between large banks and small and medium financial institutions.

For a long time, we have been aware of the financing problems of small and medium financial institutions, but are prone to simplification in solutions, overlooking the differences between large and small financial institutions, and hoping to establish a "unified" money market by mingling large and small financial institutions together. The long-term funding gap of small and medium financial institutions is expected to be addressed by fund allocation from large banks to small and medium financial institutions. This solution, however, came at the cost of relaxing management, which gave rise to the issue of "unregulated lending."

It has been proved that the operation of money market must follow the basic rule of market economy. Commercial banks, as enterprises engaging in money operation, are accountable to shareholders and depositors and have no rights or obligations to be held responsible for the operation of other banks. If commercial banks want to guarantee the security of funds, they must prevent funds from flowing to financial institutions without sufficient assets or credit. Providing relief to banks with bad asset quality for the security of the banking system is the responsibility of the central bank, the "lender of last resort." This is exactly why the central bank is in place. The money market can only channel fund flow from banks with loose position to banks with credit or quality assets and should not offer a direct solution to the issue of long-term funding gap of small and medium financial institutions arising from the financial system structure of China.

The long-term funding shortage of small and medium financial institutions cannot be solved in the short run, whether by means of money market or central bank relief. In this regard, I think it is necessary to reconsider the financial system structure of our country. The main characteristics of the financial system structure formed due to historical reasons are that both small and large financial institutions operate independently with completely identical scope of banking business and compete in all aspects without emphasis; large banks and small banks establish branches everywhere, fighting for deposit and loan clients, resulting in serious waste of resources. To learn from the experience of developed countries, small and medium financial institutions should be encouraged to put emphasis on deposit business and cut down loan business, while large banks should make full use of their credit advantages to focus on loaning and borrow fund from small and medium financial institutions at a cost much lower than establishing savings offices. In this case, the security and efficiency of the financial system will both be improved significantly and the problem with fund flow in the money market will be solved accordingly.

II. Direction for the Development of China's Money Market

From the analysis above, we can see that the direction for the development of China's money market is to gradually push forward the structural reform of the financial system through the development of the money market, thereby establishing an orderly financing structure, and eventually realizing a sophisticated money market system.

At present, the need to develop China's money market in various aspects are very pressing: the financing issue of small and medium financial institutions becomes increasingly prominent after financing centers cease their business; financial institutions have scarce mutual trust with each other, and truly credible financial institutions can hardly borrow fund. In order to implement indirect monetary policy, the central bank needs a secure and efficient money market to transmit and realize policy objectives; enterprises and individuals need convenient channels for investment into high quality bonds; nonbanking financial institutions, especially securities companies, have acute demand for expanding financing channels.

From the actual situation of the financial system structure of China and the experience of developed countries in the money market, China should develop a multilayered money market. On the basis of the monetary policy needs of the central bank and the practical circumstances of financial institutions, the money market is subsequently divided into four layers: the first layer consists of some large banks, which are the primary dealers and money market makers for open market operations of the central bank. They make public offers for interbank lending and bond trading on a daily basis and come up with market prices, which is the core of the money market; the second layer is the "National Interbank Market" managed by the PBC, with members of some 100 financial institutions at a certain scale, with good asset quality and reputation, and sound business management and internal control mechanism They form the main body of the money market; the third layer comprises other financial institutions (mainly small and medium financial institutions), which will establish relatively stable financing relationship with financial institutions of the first two layers. The three layers constitute the wholesale money market. The fourth layer is the retail money market, that is, nonfinancial public carrying out over-the-counter transactions with financial institutions.

Large banks at the first layer can directly conduct bond transactions with the central bank as primary dealers in open market operations of the central bank. They are also money market makers and are engaged in bilateral interbank lending and bond trading; the central bank may select several banks as quoting banks of the money market and announce "China Interbank Lending Rate" and "China Interbank Bond Repo Rate" through calculating the bilateral rates for lending or repo quoted daily. Large banks play a crucial role in forming the money market quotes: (1) provide price information to other financial institutions in order for other financial institutions to have reference price standards when carrying out money market transactions, which facilitates fund supply and demand in the money market; (2) enjoy advantages in managing their own fund supply and demand; (3) provide a stable, market-oriented benchmark interest rate as pricing basis for loans, forward settlement and sale of foreign exchange, and other financial transactions to align with the international financial market; (4) the interest rate can serve as an important basis for formulating monetary policy by the central bank; (5) the interest rate exerts strong impacts on the society, and the control of such interest rate by the central bank will directly affect the judgment of enterprises and residents and directly influence consumption demand and investment demand.

The financial institutions at the second layer have a certain level of credit and strength and finance by means of interbank lending and bond trading. Financial institutions finance by means of bond repo, which can effectively reduce credit risks, but the procedures for bond repo are rather complicated and affect the efficiency of fund management; in addition, bond repo is only a type of asset transformation which cannot expand the balance sheet; the bonds held by financial institutions are limited and demand for provisional large position cannot be met through bond repo. As a result, financial institutions cannot fully avoid the credit problem. Although financial institutions undertake credit risks themselves, a comprehensive information disclosure mechanism should be established to allow financial institutions to know who is creditworthy, so that players of good credit record can borrow in the market, and players with low credit record can be eliminated. Subsequently, interbank credit can be restored. Financial institutions are not to give up lending due to the lack of information of the credit of other financial institutions, and strong financial institutions would not fail to borrow money. The experience of developed countries and practice of China show that interbank lending market participants are mainly comprised of credible and robust financial institutions, which can timely adjust short-term position through effective credit lending and information exchange. Currently, the "Interbank Lending Market," as a financial institution organization, established and managed by the head office of the PBC, has a stringent mechanism for access, exit and routine regulation, and efficient mechanism for information dissemination; as these mechanisms gradually take effect, the national interbank market will become a "safety zone for interbank lending," and interbank lending will become an important financing mode among membership financial institutions. When funds cease to flow from banks with abundant funds to financial institutions without either credit or quality assets, it is exactly a sign of the maturity of the money market and reveals that the money market includes a mechanism for risk discovery and avoidance. Only when the money market mechanism is in place, the market can be insulated from the adverse effect of central planning, and financial institutions can be guided toward better credit and assets quality and enter a healthy cycle. The most important function played by a developed and efficient money market is to allow financial institutions with credit or quality assets to sustain rather than allow the low-quality institutions to thrive.

Small and medium financial institutions at the third layer carry out financing business with financial institutions at the first and second layers by means of bonds trade and establish business relations. When small and medium financial institutions are short of funds, they may raise money from commercial banks with interbank fund or bond as collateral; in case of loose positions, they may purchase bonds or lend money to commercial banks with bonds of the other party as collateral. Small and medium financial institutions may enhance understanding and gradually establish credit relationship based on the establishment of business relationship and bond trading with financial institutions at the first two layers.

With respect to the issue of establishing the financing network of financial institutions, the traditional idea emphasized the establishment of financing intermediary or trading system and building up of financing connection among financial institutions through an intermediary or trading system. However, since small and medium financial institutions and commercial banks have little understanding of the credit position and operating status of each other, coupled with the substantial differences in the trading volumes of large and small institutions, mutual financing can hardly be achieved. It would be costly to establish new intermediaries or trading systems everywhere, together with the disparity in information, credit and strength, the problem cannot be solved even with the financing network at place. Commercial banks have their own deposits, loans and financing business, as well as branches across the country; if small and medium financial institutions and commercial banks are able to build up financing relationship by means of bonds trade to solve financing problem, it would be cost-effective and efficient, and the actual funding problem of small and medium financial institutions can be addressed. Small and medium financial institutions of China are in great number, but suffer from information block, professionals shortage and insufficient credibility. For them, to select a large bank to establish a relatively stable financing relationship will not only save costs but also meet their demand. At present, a group of commercial banks with capital strength and good reputation are qualified to carry out the business. Commercial banks that engage in financing business with small and medium financial institutions not only satisfies their own fund needs but also assists small and medium financial institutions in satisfying their fund demand. The launch of this business allows commercial banks to make profits through fund operation and expand business network and improve reputation.

The financial positions of small and medium financial institutions can be divided into three types: first, they are in long-term loose financial status and in lack of channels for fund use, such as urban and rural credit cooperatives in certain developed areas; second, their fund demand and supply are fundamentally balanced but are subject to obvious seasonal fluctuations, as in the case of many rural credit cooperatives; third, there is a long-term funding gap. The first two types of institutions can buy quality bonds with surplus fund and quickly get cash through repo or sale of bonds when funds are required, thereby managing the profitability, security, and liquidity of the fund. In relation to the third type of institutions, we can provide them with a channel for purchasing bonds and encourage them to adjust asset structure while improving financial situation, increase the amount of bonds held, enter into a healthy cycle, and develop toward depositary institution.

The formation of bond trading network will gradually change the financial system structure of China and facilitate the rationalization of work division of financial institutions.

The money market fails to solve the problem of fund flow from large banks to small and medium financial institutions without credit or quality assets, but it can solve the problem of fund flow from financial institutions in loose financial status to those with credit or quality assets; some small and medium financial institutions with credit or assets can borrow money while small and medium financial institutions with funding can also efficiently lend money.

Nonfinancial public (corporates and households) at the fourth layer conduct money market transactions through financial institution counters and the trading instrument are primarily bonds. To date, there are several financial instruments traded in the retail money market of China, including treasury bonds and corporate bonds traded by residents through securities companies and other nonbanking financial institutions and certificate treasury bonds traded by residents at bank counters. The bond trading at exchanges are for profit making and with a high entry threshold and complicated procedure, therefore both residents and securities companies hesitated to trade; in fact the network of bond trading at exchanges only has very limited coverage. The target for certificate treasury bond issuance is individual resident, and the balance at the end of 1998 was RMB411.7 billion. Some commercial banks are selected to be the custodian of certificate treasury bond, while a unified custody system is not yet built up; consequently commercial banks cannot trade certificate treasury bonds with each other. The price for certificate treasury bonds cannot be available without a unified market. Therefore, certificate treasury bonds are only traded by a single means, that is, residents sell certificate treasury bonds to banks at a fixed price, resulting in a small market for certificate treasury bonds.

To develop a trading network that connects numerous nonbank entities and individuals, above all, there should be appropriate trading modes; trading through exchanges is expensive and therefore OTC trading is the major choice of the retail money market. Second, financial institutions are required to have a nationwide network. The branches of securities companies and other nonbanking financial institutions in China are mainly present in large- and medium-sized cities, and due to their limited capital strength, it is difficult for them to satisfy all the requirements for trading of financial assets of the public. Yet commercial banks in China have strong capital strength and extensive business network; therefore they are able to provide convenient and speedy services for the general public. Third, we should have an efficient and safe custodian settlement system. The trading instruments for the retail money market should all be paperfree to facilitate trading and settlement. Currently, there is a mature primary bond custody institution, China Central Depository & Clearing Co. Ltd.; however, the business scope of primary custody must be restricted and cannot solve the bond custody problems of all institutions and individuals. The payment and settlement system of China's central bank is separated from bond custody institutions; therefore, bond custody merely relying on the central bond custody institution would fail to cover the whole society and is incommensurate with the needs of numerous individual investors.

Commercial banks have made attempts with regard to the secondary bond custody system in custody of certificate treasury bonds; at present, the crux is to formulate a system in which custodians are prohibited from using bonds of clients without authorization and permission. It would improve regulations and guarantee the security of bonds and other financial assets of nonfinancial public.

The four layers mentioned above are not mutually exclusive, in that any two financial institutions can trade with each other, and the said constituents organically formed the whole money market. In order to build up a layered money market, we must establish interinstitution network to link up large banks, small and medium financial institutions, and the general public as well as resolve the credit risk problem of small and medium financial institutions in financing through further development of the bond market so as to gradually establish interbank credibility and change the monetary policy transmission mechanism to make a better market with bonds as the primary gripper.

III. Suggestions for the Upcoming Work on Money Market

In 1998, a series of measures adopted by the PBC to promote the development of the money market have achieved remarkable outcomes, such as increasing the number and types of interbank market members as planned; vigorously promoting the development of the interbank bond market, organizing the marketization of issuance of treasury bonds and policy financial bonds, and maintaining the dynamics of the bond circulation market; improving the regulation system; enhancing trading and settlement rules; controlling money market rate through monetary policy instruments; etc. Currently, the bond assets of commercial banks of China account for about 10 percent of the total assets, and interbank traded bond outstanding have reached RMB1 trillion. It is suggested that efforts should be made in the following aspects for development of the money market.

(I) Keep up the Marketization of Treasury Bonds and Policy Financial Bonds Issuance

Promote the marketization of treasury bond issuance to financial institutions; formulate administrative measures and qualification standards for underwriters, bring more members to the underwriting team, and actively explore new bond issuance methods to encourage bond holding by small and medium financial institutions; encourage the launch of agency business by financial institutions; strictly manage all aspects in bond issuance, remove grey areas in the regulation system, and prevent insider trading.

(II) Establish Market Maker System and Improve the Mechanism for Determining Money Market Rates

Shortlist some large-scale commercial banks with sound internal control mechanism as money market makers to collect bid and ask information and set market price. Meanwhile, calculate and announce interbank interest rate, provide more appropriate indicators for monetary policy, exert greater influence on money market rate, and encourage commercial banks to participate in the money market.

(III) Regulate Interbank Market and Gradually Restore Interbank Credibility

The interbank market is an interbank organization consisting of strong and credible commercial banks and other financial institutions. By gradually promoting credit lending in the interbank market, strengthening the self-discipline and regulation in the interbank market, establishing and perfecting the transmission mechanism for the information about fund supply and demand, and by improving the mechanism of entry and exit and the punishing measures on defaults, the interbank market has become the major short-term position financing method between financial institutions.. Afterwards, interbank credibility is restored through the financing relationship between these financial institutions and small and medium institutions.

(IV) Establish Unified Bond Custody System

Devise a unified treasury bond custody system and study the connection between the bond settlement system and the fund settlement system so as to contain risks. Eventually all financial institutions, enterprises, and individuals can hold certificate bonds and handle bond settlement in a secure, convenient, and efficient manner. The establishment of the unified bond custody system includes two aspects: first, the purchase of certificate bond by individuals, and second, the connection between China Central Depository & Clearing Co., Ltd. and Shanghai and Shenzhen Stock Exchanges. In view of the money market in developed countries, OTC bond trading is the mainstream. For example, in the United States, the bond trading volume of exchanges accounts for less than 5 percent of the total treasury bond trading volume. In June 1997, the PBC required commercial banks to withdraw from exchanges to establish an interbank bond market. Following the alignment of the development pattern of Chinese bond market with international practice, the relative scale and trading volume of the exchange bond market are greatly reduced, so that the connection between the two custody systems is no more a crucial issue. The principal issue is to establish a sophisticated secondary bond custody system.

(V) Rationalize the Financing of Securities Companies

According to the existing administrative provisions, securities companies may engage in overnight interbank lending and conduct bond trading at stock exchanges as nonbanking financial institutions. Recently, it is warmly appealed for relaxing the restrictions on the term of interbank lending involving securities companies and allowing securities companies and banks to engage in bond trading. I contend that the financing of securities companies should be included in standardized and reasonable channels since they do have their own financing demand.

Securities companies, as financial institutions that operate securities business, are different from banks engaging in the operation of money business. The major funding gap comes from underwriting of stocks and bonds, allotment of shares, and organization of enterprise restructuring. This type of fund demand is of a nature completely different from the short-term position adjustment demand of banks arising from deposit payment and fund settlement, which is also different from the demand of nonfinancial enterprises. As a result, solving the financing problem of securities companies by means of interbank lending will give rise to the following undesirable consequences: (1) it is difficult for banks to control risks of fund lending to securities companies. Banks have a set of stringent administrative measures and accountability systems for loan customers so that they can supervise the use of loans and control risks; while for interbank lending, the lender has no right to enquire the purpose of borrowed fund of the other party and to supervise fund use, and no constraints can be imposed on the borrower. As a result, banks can hardly control the risks in fund lending to securities companies. (2) Interbank lending mainly addresses the short-term financing demand of banks and involves overnight lending and other short-term lending. It is, however, not possible to meet the demand of securities companies. If interbank lending period is extended in order to solve the funding problem of securities companies, risks will unavoidably increase due to the lack of constraint imposed by management system similar to that for loans. Hence, the financing demand of securities companies should be included and solved within the institutional framework of enterprise loans and it is undesirable to allow securities companies to join the interbank lending market. At the same time, bond purchase in the interbank money market and bond trading with banks by securities companies are in line with their business nature. As such, in terms of bond trading, it is appropriate for securities companies to enter the interbank money market as financial institutions, but in respect of short-term financing, it is inappropriate for them to access the interbank money market as financial institutions.

At the moment, the problems with the initial public offering system also complicate the financing issues of securities companies. Under the current initial public offering system, new shares are issued at low price earnings ratio as planned. Under this policy, purchasing new shares brings about extremely high risk-free return. In the existing business classification, trust companies, securities companies, financial companies, and leasing companies are among nonbanking financial institutions and may purchase IPO stocks to reap high returns. If the nonbanking financial institutions are allowed to borrow from commercial banks to purchase new shares, it will severely distort fund flow in the interbank money market. When new shares are issued, flow of funds to the nonbanking financial institutions will render the IPO procedure unfair and give rise to substantial increase and wide fluctuations in money market rate, which affects the normal operation of commercial banks and the operation of the monetary policy of the central bank. In this regard, prior to the fundamental reform of the initial public offering system, it is inappropriate to allow securities companies and other said nonbanking financial institutions to conduct interbank money market trading with banks, nor is it desirable to permit securities companies to borrow money from commercial banks.

(VI) Step up Efforts in Open Market Operations

I suggest the PBC reinforcing money market operations, increasing the frequency of open market operations, refining bidding methods of open market operations, and improving the liquidity of bonds in the interbank bond market. From international experience, open market operations have served as a driving force for the development of the bond market. If open market operations take the form of bond repo, the development of derivative products of bonds and the bond repo market will be fostered; if open market operations take the form of secondary trading, the development of the secondary bond market will be enhanced. Under the present situation where spot bond trading is scarce, the open market operations should take the form of spot bond trading so as to facilitate the market development and provide an important reference price to the retail bond market and satisfy the needs of the central bank for rapid growth of base money.

The Supervision, Control, and Management of China's Interbank Lending Market[3]

I. Basic Situation of China's Interbank Lending Market

The development of China's interbank lending market started in 1984 and had experienced the crackdown of "wild lending" in 1992, the revocation of intermediary agency for interbank lending established by commercial banks, the establishment of financing centers led by the PBC local offices in 1993, the establishment by the PBC headquarters of a national unified lending market among financial institutions in January 1996, and the liberalization of interbank interest rate in June that year. Ever since then, a unified and standard interbank lending market has taken shape. In the national interbank lending market, there is interbank lending conducted by financial institutions through the trading system of the National Interbank Funding Center (the "primary network") and via local financing centers (the "secondary network").

Although a unified interbank market has taken shape, the position and function of the lending market has not undergone any substantive changes, and commercial banks are still unaware of financial risks and fail to see that financing centers and the electronic trading system cannot handle the growing risks. Besides, the lending volume is tremendous but with huge potential risks, and bond market trading is shrinking. In early 1998, amid the outbreak of the Asian financial crisis and the emergence of domestic financial risks, the PBC decisively stopped the proprietary lending of financing centers, spared no effort in clearing and recovering the overdue lending to banks and other financial institutions by the financing centers, and at the same time strictly controlled the risks in interbank lending market. Under the guidance of the PBC, commercial banks' risk awareness and commercial awareness have gradually been enhanced; they pay more attention to the credibility of trade counterparties and have effectively reduced the overall risks in interbank lending market.

In recent years, the PBC has adhered to the principle of rationalized development. Even under the circumstances of the deterioration of the Asian financial crisis and continuous turbulence in international financial market, China's interbank lending market has reduced the credit risks to the utmost extent and, at the same time, has realized the fundamental shift from a profit-seeking financing market to a lending market that aims to adjust short-term positions of commercial banks. All the banks have generally improved the internal capital allocation system and established a strict internal and external credit authorization system, with self-discipline of the transaction participants significantly improved. The nature of interbank lending has been changed substantively, and the credit risk is greatly reduced, while the reference value of the interbank interest rate is rising obviously, and the role played by interbank lending is reinforced remarkably.

In 1999, the trading volume in China's interbank lending market has increased substantially with the annual turnover being RMB391.2 billion, among which the national interbank lending market accounted for RMB329.2 billion; non-members of the national interbank lending market accounted for RMB62 billion. Annual lending volume has increased by RMB292.3 billion, three times more than that of RMB98.9 billion in 1998, and close to the volume in 1996 and 1997, which were RMB587.1 billion and RMB414.9 billion, respectively. It should be noted that the participants of the lending market in 1996 and 1997 were mainly the financing centers that functioned as intermediary institutions, while the lending volume of financial institutions as true providers of capital were much smaller than the data showed. In the regulated lending market, the trading participants are all of the legal entities of financial institutions and their authorized branches, so the lending volume fully reflected the amount of transactions. From the perspective of lending volume of financial institutions, the trading volume of 1999 in lending market exceeded RMB177.9 billion in 1996 and RMB277.3 billion in 1997, hitting a record high since the establishment of national interbank market in 1996.

China's interbank lending market has the following features:

(I) Interbank Lending Market Is Divided into Two Levels

All financial institutions in China may conduct interbank lending in accordance with the relevant provisions of the PBC. China's interbank lending market is divided into two levels according to the size and credibility of financial institutions. The first level is the national interbank lending market administered by the head office of the PBC, which is essentially a lending platform among financial institutions, and its market members are usually of large size and considerable strength. The second level is comprised of the financial institutions, which are not members of the national interbank lending market, and they have to file for record with the branches of the PBC before conducting interbank lending. In September 1997, PBC began to clean up and close financing centers, marking a beginning of rationalized development. Since 1998, the PBC has taken decisive measures to substantially enlarge the membership base of national interbank lending market. In early 1998, with an aim to facilitate the internal capital management of commercial banks, the PBC approved the commercial banks to authorize their branches to enter into the national interbank lending market and engage in credit lending, bond repo, and spot bond trading within the scope authorized by the head office of the PBC. In May 1998, as an important measure to gradually open up the financial sector, the PBC approved foreign banks with RMB businesses to enter into the national interbank lending market for interbank lending, bond repo, and spot bond trading. In October 1998, the PBC approved insurance companies to enter into the national interbank lending market to trade bonds. In February 1999, the PBC approved some rural credit cooperatives associations to enter into the national interbank lending market to engage in interbank lending, bond repo, and spot bond trading. In August 1999, the PBC approved securities companies to enter into the national interbank lending market to engage in lending, bond purchase, bond repo, and spot bond trading.

By the end of 1999, members of national interbank lending market have increased to 243, three times more than that in early 1999, which was only 61. The national interbank market participants include state-owned commercial banks, joint-stock commercial banks and their authorized branches, urban commercial banks, foreign banks with RMB business, insurance companies, rural credit cooperatives associations, securities investment fund, and securities companies. The total deposits and total assets of these financial institutions accounted for more than 90 percent of the financial system, so whether in terms of their quantity, total assets, types, or in terms of the position in the China's financial system, the members of the national interbank market have played an influential role in China's money market.

Financial institutions that are not members of the national interbank lending market may conduct interbank lending with any financial institutions with lending qualification, and this tremendously facilitates position adjustment and liquidity management. Whether or not they are members of interbank lending market does not affect their interbank lending businesses, with the only difference being that they need to file for record before each trade.

(II) Interbank Lending Interest Rate Has Become an Important Indicator for Social Economic Situation and the Central Bank's Monetary Policy

Under the condition that the total liquidity of financial institutions remains unchanged, the distribution of liquidity and the changes of commercial banks in their judgment about the macroeconomy, policies and other factors will also influence the demand and supply of liquidity by individual institution and generate impact on the interest rate of the interbank lending market. As a result, when compared with the total liquidity, the interest rate of the interbank lending market can reflect the willingness of commercial banks to create money in a more comprehensive and responsive manner.

There are large differences in the credit standing of China's financial institutions at present; therefore, the lending interest rates of financial institutions differ greatly, and the lending interest rate of small banks will fluctuate vehemently, while the lending interest rate of major banks remains stable, from which the liquidity situation can be reflected more accurately and timely. The interest rate becomes an observation indicator of the central bank.

(III) Interbank Lending Has Become a Preferred Method for Capital Management of Commercial Banks, Whose Market-Orientation Were Reinforced

With the development of the interbank lending market, commercial banks will first borrow money from the interbank lending market when they are in need. In the case of loose capital, they would also lend out fund through interbank market. This has changed the traditional practice of depending on the PBC for short-term financing; instead they operate in interbank lending market. Some banks that trade actively in the interbank market have formed extensive and stable trading networks, which can help them timely to meet the financing need.

Market-oriented operation of commercial banks needs to take profitability, liquidity, and security into account, and keeping an appropriate level of liquidity became crucial. The development and constant improvement of interbank lending market have provided the necessary and favorable external conditions for liquidity management and commercialized operation of commercial banks. Reversely, the commercialized operation of banks drive them to pay more attention to the interbank lending market, which has also facilitated the development of the interbank lending market.

II. The Starting Point and Principles for the PBC to Supervise and Regulate Interbank Lending Market

(I) The Starting Point for the PBC to Regulate Interbank Lending Market

Interbank lending market is the principal place for financial institutions to reach for short-term financing. Unlike bond repo and other financing methods, interbank lending is a direct exchange of money and credit without any guarantee, so interbank lending is a special way and the highest form of financing among financial institutions, mainly among commercial banks. This special nature of interbank lending has given birth to the distinguished feature of high efficiency but also potential credit risk. Therefore, the starting point for the central bank to regulate interbank lending market is to control the overall risks in the interbank lending market, that is to minimize the risks in interbank lending market while at the same time ensure the efficiency of interbank lending. During the 16-year development of China's interbank lending market since 1984, due to ongoing reforms of financial system and undervaluation of the importance of credibility, several risk events in China's interbank lending market have adversely affected the healthy development of the interbank lending market. Past experience shows that the central bank must put interbank lending market under strict supervision with tight risk control, which is the overall starting point for the supervision and control of interbank lending market.

(II) The Basic Principles for the PBC in Regulating the Interbank Lending Market

The central bank regulates the interbank lending market according to the principles of strict entry, self-management of risks, market fairness, and order and hierarchy.

1. The principle of strict entry

Interbank lending market is the market only for financial institutions to trade short-term liquidity. The capital flows between enterprises and financial institutions, however, are a debtor-creditor relationship. It is fundamentally different from short-term financing in that the loan-makers need to examine the borrower's credibility and put the use of loans to strict supervision, and the borrowers are restricted by relevant laws; however, the management of interbank lending is not so strict as that of loans, although there is certain requirements with regard to the credit of the borrowing party. The use of fund is not strictly supervised. Such difference is originated from the high credit rating of interbank lending entities, thus the qualifications for interbank lending shall be high. In the United States, only commercial banks with reserve account in the Federal Reserve Bank can participate in the federal funds market (i.e., interbank lending market). The main participants in China's interbank lending market now include all financial institutions. With strengthened regulation of interbank lending market, the scope will be gradually limited to deposit-taking financial institutions.

2. Principle of self-management of risks

A financial institution has to evaluate the credit of the counterparty before determining whether to engage in interbank lending. The credit risks in lending market could only be assumed by the market participants themselves. Although the PBC is responsible for the market management and overall risk control, it takes no risk in any transaction. Reviewing the development of lending market, we can find that the risk awareness of China's financial institutions is gradually reinforced, and they are more careful to choose the right counterparty. The risk-aware circumstance also incentivizes market players to pay more attention to their own credibility. Therefore, the security of the overall market is improved.

3. Principle of market fairness

Fairness means that the same market rules are applied to all market participants. Each financial institution engaged in interbank lending has to comply with the market rules and regulations stipulated by the PBC, be credible, and maintain market fairness. All financial institutions, from large commercial banks to small rural credit cooperatives, have to scrupulously keep their credit and follow homogeneous market standard.

4. Principle of order and hierarchy

Interbank lending market is hierarchical, because financial institutions are different in credibility and strength. It is easy for large banks to borrow money from small financial institutions, while it is hard for small financial institutions to borrow money from large banks. This is in line with the basic rules of market economy. Due to the hierarchical nature of interbank lending market, capital flows follow certain rules. The small and medium financial institutions usually take deposits and provide liquidity in the market, while big banks usually borrow from other financial institutions at a cost lower than deposit rates. At the same time as big banks have high credit and large fund surplus, mutual lending is also frequent.

III. The History of Supervision and Control over Interbank Lending Market by the PBC

In 1986, the PBC published the *Provisions on Improving the Measures for the Administration of Credit Fund* and *Several Provisions Concerning the Administration of Credit Fund* in 1987. The PBC clarified that (i) lending market transactions are administrated and managed by the PBC, and interbank lending can be conducted in the same city or in different places; (ii) interbank lending is limited to financial institutions, and any financial institutions as an independent legal body can participate, while nonfinancial institutions and individuals shall not directly participate in the interbank lending market in any form; (iii) the principle of voluntary lending and emphasis on credibility; and (iv) the time frame for any lending of funds shall not exceed four months, and shall be used mainly to tackle temporary or seasonal liquidity drain. These stipulations constitute the basic framework for the management of China's interbank lending market, the main principles of which still serve as an important starting point for the management of interbank lending market.

In 1990, the *Trial Measures for the Administration of Interbank Lending* released by the PBC has provided for the first time comprehensive and systemic regulations for the management of China's interbank lending market, which specifically ascertains that the nature of interbank lending is short-term fund financing between the banks and nonbanking financial institutions. It ensures the establishment of a market organization for interbank lending, explicitly stipulates the source and primary use of funds raised, stipulates the maximum ratio of liquidity financed from interbank market, the regulation system and time frame, and explicitly requires that interbank lending interest rates and service charges shall be settled through account transfer, and no cash shall be paid and accepted.

With regard to the turmoil on the lending market in the second half of 1992, the PBC issued the *Notice on Further Strengthening the Administration of Interbank Lending* in February 1993, and the *Notice on Further Rectifying and Standardizing the Order of Interbank Lending Market* in June, which have played a positive role in maintaining market order and regulating lending activities.

In February 1994, the PBC issued *the Interim Measures for the Administration of Credit Fund*, which has extended the concept of interbank lending market to the money market for the first time, and provided more detailed and reasonable stipulations on the time period and the maximum balance of lending funds.

In the second half of 1995, the issuance of the *Notice on the Withdrawal of Intermediary Agency of Commercial Banks in Conducting Interbank Lending* by the PBC marked a beginning in establishing national interbank lending market, which was formally established in 1996. In May, the PBC issued the *Notice on the Abolition of the Administration of Upper Limit for the Interest Rate of Interbank Lending* and decided to liberalize interbank lending interest rates since June 1. Interest rates from then on shall be determined at the discretion of the trading parties.

In 1997, overdue lending in financing centers around the country became a prominent issue; in the second half of that year, the PBC began to terminate the business of financing centers, clear up overdue lending, and abolish the financing centers based on regulations such as the *Notice on Relevant Issues Concerning the Clearing Up of Lending Funds by Financing Centers* and the *Notice on Speeding Up the Work of Clearing Up of Overdue Funds of Financing Centers*.

In 1999, the *Notice on Several Issues Concerning the Financing of Rural Credit Cooperatives* and the *Notice Concerning the Administration of Financing in Rural Credit Cooperatives and Other Financial Institutions* issued by the PBC specifically provide that all financial institutions can engage in interbank lending, and commercial banks and rural credit cooperatives associations are encouraged to act as financing agency. In August, the *Provisions on the Administration of Securities Companies Entering into the Interbank Lending Market* promulgated by the PBC stipulates that securities companies may, upon the recommendation of the China Securities Regulatory Commission, apply to the PBC for entry into the national interbank lending market to conduct interbank lending and other financing services. These regulations, together with a series of documents promulgated by the PBC in recent years, have constituted the basis for the supervision and control of interbank lending market.

IV. The Supervision and Control of Interbank Lending Market by the PBC

(I) The Management of Lending Activities in Financial Institutions

1. The term management of interbank lending

The purpose for the administration of the PBC over the term of financial institutions' interbank lending is to prevent term mismatch and to control the risks of credit. Since 1984, China's interbank lending market has experienced several major risk events, and the main reason is the investment of short-term funds from financial institutions to the real estate sector and other projects that have longer return period. The term for assets and liabilities do not match, so the funds cannot be flexibly used, and the liquidity of assets is low, which have caused default and the accumulation of credit risks. In view of this, the PBC has taken more stringent regulatory measures with regard to the lending term of financial institutions in the *Law of the People's Republic of China on Commercial Banks*, the *Measures for Punishment of Illegal Financial Acts,* and other laws. Article 46 of the *Law of the People's Republic of China on Commercial Banks* stipulates that "interbank lending shall be in line with the term provided by the PBC, and the maximum term shall not exceed 4 months." Article 17 of the *Measures for Punishment of Illegal Financial Acts* stipulates that "financial institutions engaged in lending activities shall not conduct the following act, (a) holding the fund raised for longer than the maximum term as stipulated."

The key point for the PBC to control the lending period of financial institutions is to control the term structure of the borrowing party, and by stipulating that the term for lending shall not exceed the maximum term for borrowing by the counter party, it thereby controls the term structure of both parties.

The PBC has classified maximum lending terms of financial institutions. Currently the maximum lending term of financial institutions are as follows: the maximum term for financing between commercial banks and rural credit cooperatives is four months; the maximum term for financing between state-owned commercial banks and authorized branches of joint-stock commercial banks shall be determined by their head offices but shall not exceed four months; the maximum term for financing between foreign banks shall not exceed four months, and foreign banks may engage in RMB interbank borrowing, but such RMB borrowing cannot fall into the scope of interbank lending; the maximum term for financing among trust investment companies, financial companies, and leasing companies is seven days; the maximum term for financing among securities companies of the national interbank market is seven days, while the maximum term for financing among securities companies outside the national interbank market is one day; the branches of securities companies shall not conduct such lending; and the insurance companies can only lend funds instead of borrowing funds.

To ensure that the funds financed in the market are not used for long-term investment and to prevent financial institutions from evading the term control, the PBC stipulates that financial institutions shall not in any apparent or disguised manner extend the term upon expiration, and the financial institutions borrowing funds shall, upon expiration, return all the principal and interests. In addition, any act of avoiding the term control will be punished by the PBC in accordance with relevant regulations.

2. The quota management of interbank lending

The PBC conducts quota management of lending by financial institutions for the purpose of preventing risks incurred by financial institutions' lending beyond their capacity. The lesson is learned from the unregulated lending before 1993.

The PBC carries out a differentiated quota management system for different financial institutions and also a graded management system for members and nonmembers of national interbank market. The quota for the members in national interbank market will be ratified by the head office of the PBC, while the quota for nonmembers in national interbank market will be monitored and examined by the branches and subbranches of the PBC.

The provisions regarding the lending ratios for different financial institutions are that the maximum balance for the borrowing funds by commercial banks shall not exceed 4 percent of the balance of deposits, and the maximum balance for lending by commercial banks shall not exceed 8 percent of the balance of deposits; the maximum balance for the lending by state-owned commercial banks and the authorized branches of joint-stock commercial banks shall be determined by the their head offices, but the balance of the total lending of commercial banks as a legal person shall not exceed the abovementioned ratio; the maximum balance for lending by trust investment companies, financial companies, leasing companies shall not exceed 100 percent of the paid-in capital; the maximum balance for lending by securities companies shall not exceed 80 percent of the paid-in capital; the maximum balance for lending by insurance companies shall not exceed 80 percent of the paid-in capital; and the maximum balance for lending by foreign banks shall not exceed 150 percent of their working capital in RMB.

The lending quota stipulated by the head office of the PBC on member financial institutions in national interbank market is verified every six months based on deposits outstanding of commercial banks and relevant information from nonbanking financial institutions. In case of major changes, financial institutions may apply to the Monetary Policy Department of the PBC head office for adjustment of lending quota.

3. The filing of interbank lending records

The purpose for the PBC to require the filing of interbank lending record by financial institutions is to acquire information about the overall situation of the lending market in a timely manner, monitor credit risks of financial institutions, and promptly respond to unexpected incidents. The data filed by financial institutions can serve as a reference in central bank's decision-making process and is closely connected with market supervision, which is an essential part of market management. In recent years, due to the violent fluctuation of international financial market, in Asian financial crisis and other financial turbulences, the speculative forces all started from the interbank currency lending market in the host country. The crisis usually spread through the foreign exchange market, to the lending market and then the capital market. Therefore, the central banks of all countries have to keep close attention to transactions in financial market. Since the very beginning of the establishment of interbank market, China has set up a sound management system and implemented a comprehensive management for record filing.

The management for record filing in China's interbank lending market has gone through several stages. Before 1996, the financial institutions were required to conduct lending through financing centers, and then financing centers conducted such lending transactions by means of intermediary authentication or proprietary trading, assuming the de-facto function of record filing. In 1996 after the establishment of the National Interbank Funding Center, the interbank lending transactions among members in national interbank lending market were mainly controlled by the electronic trading system of the Funding Center, which actually took charge of record filing. Those financial institutions not using electronic trading system had to conduct lending through the authentication of financing centers. From September 1997, the financing centers terminated proprietary trading and cleared up overdue lending before they were totally abolished. The PBC head office stipulates that the branches and subbranches of PBC can designate their financing centers or the department of money and credit to conduct record filing. In early 1999, the PBC issued a document (Yin Huo Zheng [1999] No. 64), which stipulated that interbank lending among rural credit cooperatives and other financial institutions that are not members of national interbank market had to be filed for record with the departments of money and credit of the branches or subbranches of the PBC where it is located. The PBC branches, after collecting relevant data of financial institutions within the region, shall report to the Monetary Policy Department of the PBC head office before the tenth day of each month. Based on the record filing, the PBC knows the capital flows and interest rate of the interbank lending market and obtains useful information for the implementation of monetary policy. In addition, the management of record filing, as an integral part of risk management, reinforces term management and quota management to pinpoint risks in lending market, track and control lending risks, avoid small risks from triggering chain reactions, prevent the occurrence of systemic risks, and ensure a smooth operation of the financial system.

In actual operation, there are five critical points with regard to the management of record filing in interbank lending.

1. Record filing on both sides

It is stipulated that the lending parties shall file with local branches and subbranches of the PBC for the purpose of helping the PBC branches to know the lending situation of financial institutions in their jurisdictions, control the local lending risk, and better realize term and quota management. The local branches and subbranches shall separately do statistical analysis and report to the PBC at a higher level. Recording filings on both sides can avoid incomplete collection of statistics incurred from ambiguity and also provide convenience for the branches and subbranches of the PBC to keep abreast of the funds of financial institutions and capital inflow and outflow within the jurisdiction. The head office and branches of the PBC can be clear about geographical distribution of funds and capital flows with the complete record of data, which is helpful for the formulation and implementation of monetary policy and credit policy.

2. Prefiling

Financial institutions shall file for record before engaging in transactions. The PBC will examine the filing based on the qualification of the subject, and its term and quota. If the three requirements are met, the filing will be approved. The branches and subbranches of the PBC are not responsible for examination and approval of the interest rate of the lending and other nonregulatory factors. The specific time for prefiling is to be determined by the branches and subbranches of the PBC.

3. The form of veto

The branches and subbranches of the PBC may, according to the actual situations, formulate relevant measures to clarify the record filing form. The record filing shall take the form of veto, that is, if the record filed by financial institutions is not rejected by the PBC within a certain period of time, it will be deemed as an acknowledgement by the PBC of the compliance of the lending transaction. The branches and subbranches of the PBC do not have to approve the lending transaction one level by another.

4. All rural credit cooperatives are required to file for record.

So far, the PBC head office has approved 19 rural credit cooperatives associations to join the national interbank lending market, and rural credit cooperatives can also use the trading system of the lending center in accordance with the principle of fair compensation. To ensure comprehensive supervision over the system of rural credit cooperatives, and keep the branches and subbranches of the PBC abreast of the situation of rural credit cooperatives within their jurisdiction, the head office requires the rural credit cooperatives to file for record before lending, whether or not the trading system is used.

5. The branches and subbranches of the PBC shall report the statistical data filed for record to the head office in a timely manner to ensure the integrity of national statistical data.

(II) The Management of National Interbank Market

The national interbank market is an interfinancial-institutional organization established and managed by the head office of the PBC. The members of the national interbank market are state-owned commercial banks, joint-stock commercial banks and their authorized branches, urban commercial banks, foreign banks with RMB businesses, urban and rural credit cooperatives, insurance companies, and securities companies.

V. The Evaluation and Analysis of the Management of Current Lending Market

There are three critical points for risk management in the interbank market. First, the central bank strengthens supervision, engages in real-time market monitoring, and controls market risks by means such as setting the maximum balance for the adjustment of credit lending. Second, a credit rating system should be established based on the organizational structure of the market so as to fully strengthen the information exchange, construct a mutually binding system among financial institutions, and push financial institutions with bad credit out of the market. However we need to keep in mind that the banks have to bear all the credit risk, because the services provided by the market are to ensure the full flow of information, and the supervision of the central bank is to solve aberrant problems and control risks within a certain boundary but do not directly solve the risk problems in lending. Third, small banks or banks not well acquainted in the market should be allowed to conduct financing through bond repo and spot bond transaction, because under the bond custodian system, there is no credit risk problem for bond transaction and settlement. The capital surplus and deficiency of financial institutions can be solved through bond transaction, and the parties involved may gradually become acquainted with each other's credibility and establish credit relations, which is beneficial for credit lending.

At present, it is rather difficult to realize the trading demands of large banks, which also shows that internal fund management needs to be further improved. Under the current situation, commercial banks can always authorize their branches with large fund capacity to enter the market conditionally, breaking down large trading demands into many smaller trading demands to make deals possible. The *Notice on Commercial Banks' Authorization of Their Branches to Join the National Interbank Lending Market* issued by the PBC in 1998 provides that commercial banks may authorize their branches to join the national interbank lending market for interbank lending authorized by their head offices. By the end of 1999, there were 90 branches authorized by the commercial banks in the national interbank lending market. Because the issuance mode for new shares have large influence on the positions of commercial banks, and there are strong demand for fund transfer in Shenzhen and Shanghai branches of state-owned commercial banks, the branches authorized by commercial banks may operate in the national interbank lending market, so as to facilitate capital management and meet short-term position demand. The trading volume of lending in Bank of China Shenzhen Branch, Industrial and Commercial Bank of China Shenzhen Branch and Shanghai Branch, and China Construction Bank Shenzhen Branch are all very large. The annual volume of financed by the branches authorized by commercial banks amounted to RMB103.553 billion, 31.46 percent of the total lending volume.

Commercial banks require speedy realization of transactions. Although the current market has reflected the financing demand of commercial banks, the number of transactions is small, causing inconvenience to the commercial banks. In order to solve this problem, we may consider allowing some institutions to serve as market makers to make bilateral quotes in the market and absorb the borrowing and lending funds, similar to the regional money center banks in the United States. The proprietary trading of financing centers mainly includes fund adjustment within and without provinces, instead of being a market maker. Market makers should be big banks, while money brokerage companies may be established to assume this responsibility. However, they are required to be subject to stringent examination and real-time monitoring to guarantee that there is no deviation from their functions.

In summary, in order to evaluate interbank market from the perspective of overall environment of financial operation, the key point is to see whether the lending market has a sound price realization mechanism, what functions the lending market has performed, and what roles the lending market has played in the operation of the financial system and the implementation of national macroeconomic policies. Simple comparison of the transaction volume, the transaction participants' number, and the abundance of the transaction varieties is by no means the appropriate indicator for the success of the lending market.

Lending market shall become the primary and principal means for commercial banks to manage funding position. First of all, commercial banks should trade with each other. After sufficient flow of base money, if there is still over- or underliquidity, as reflected by the interest rates, the central bank shall formulate and implement monetary policy accordingly. The setting-up of interbank market not only enables the central bank to have appropriate reference for total liquidity but also stabilizes commercial banks and is conductive to the transmission of monetary policy. The aim of the supervision and control of the central bank over the lending market is to bring the abovementioned functions into full play and prevent the general risks in the market, which has almost been achieved judging from the practice of supervision and control of the central bank over interbank lending market in recent years.

The Current Situation and Reflections on China's Paper Market[4]

I. The Current Situation of China's Commercial Paper Market

Paper market, as an important component of the money market, refers to the commercial paper market in China, in which banker's acceptance and commercial acceptance are traded.

(I) Development History

China's paper market started in late 1970s when the PBC began to approve some enterprises to issue commercial acceptance in 1979. In 1982, the PBC introduced "three papers and one card" (bill of exchange, promissory note, cheque, and credit card) to promote the development of bill acceptance and discount businesses of commercial banks. In 1986, the promulgation of the *Interim Measures for Rediscount* by the PBC represented the launch of the rediscount business for the first time. In 1994, with regard to loan arrears and cash flow problems of some enterprises in key industries and the obstructed allocation and sale of agricultural by-products, the PBC in conjunction with relevant government departments proposed to promote commercial bills in "five industries and four varieties" and set aside for the first time a rediscount special fund of RMB10 billion, starting to use rediscount as a monetary policy tool. In 1995, the official promulgation and implementation of the *Negotiable Instruments Law of the People's Republic of China* laid the legal foundation for the development of the paper market. In 1998, the PBC carried out the reform of discount rate and rediscount rate formation, transforming rediscount rate into an independent index for interest rate, on which the discount rate was determined by commercial banks at their own discretion; the paper market was further developed.

(II) Overview of the Market

As of 2010, the balance of the accepted commercial bills is RMB5.6 trillion; the amount incurred is RMB12.1 trillion, representing 35 times and 32 times of those in 1998, respectively; the discount balance is RMB1.5 trillion, and the amount incurred is RMB26 trillion, 27 times and 108 times of those in 1998; and the rediscount balance is RMB77.2 billion, and the amount incurred is RMB 168.5 billion, 2 times and 1.6 times of those in 1998.

The development of the paper market has displayed the following characteristics:

1. The acceptance and discount balances continued to grow, while the rediscount has fluctuated.

As seen from Table 1.2, acceptance and discount have basically seen a trend of gradual growth, with discount balance down only in 2007 and 2010, while the rediscount business has been fluctuating, experiencing a sharp decline in 2002 and 2004–2008 but substantial increase in 2010, despite the significant gap to the 2000 high. The rediscount shrinkage appears first because the liquidity of financial institutions was relatively abundant, and second because the rediscount rate, higher than other market rates, did not have price advantage, which explains why commercial

Table 1.2 Development of paper market from 1998 to 2010 (Unit: RMB 100 million)

Year	*Acceptance*		*Discount*		*Rediscount*	
	Balance	*Incurred*	*Balance*	*Incurred*	*Balance*	*Incurred*
1998	1,595	3,841	547	2,400	331	1,001
1999	1,873	5,076	552	2,499	502	1,160
2000	3,676	7,445	1,536	6,447	1,256	2,667
2001	5,111	11,973	2,814	14,322	655	2,798
2002	7,347	16,139	5,752	23,173	68	246
2003	12,776	27,797	9,171	46,395	766	1,058
2004	14,840	34,176	11,521	47,058	33	225
2005	19,574	44,481	16,149	67,509	2	25
2006	22,075	54,263	17,232	84,918	18	40
2007	24,362	58,676	12,818	101,116	57	138
2008	31,888	70,802	19,279	135,087	23	110
2009	41,267	102,654	23,850	231,558	181	249
2010	56,075	121,613	14,810	260,219	772	1,685

Source: People's Bank of China (www.pbc.gov.cn).

banks would rather choose to profit from rate arbitrage from rediscount and repo business.

2. The trading volume increased slowly compared with other markets.

As seen from Table 1.3, the trading volume in the paper market (the sum of acceptance and discount amount incurred), when compared with that in lending and repo markets, has increased more slowly, dropping from 76 percent of the total liquidity of all three markets in 1998 to less than 30 percent since 2007, while the trading volume in the repo market (the sum of pledge and outright transactions) has increased from 12 percent to 57 percent with a large number of investors and advanced trading infrastructure.

3. Banker's acceptance has absolute advantage.

Since the paper market is mainly backed by bank credit, the market is overwhelmingly dominated by banker's acceptance. Taking 2010 as an example, the amount incurred in acceptance and discount of the year by banks accounted for 98 percent and 93 percent of the total market value,

Table 1.3 Trading volume in submarkets of money market from 1998 to 2010 unit %

Year	*Paper*	*Lending*	*Repo*
1998	76	12	12
1999	51	22	27
2000	38	18	43
2001	35	11	54
2002	26	8	66
2003	34	11	54
2004	43	8	50
2005	39	5	56
2006	33	5	62
2007	22	15	63
2008	22	16	62
2009	27	16	57
2010	25	18	57

Source: People's Bank of China (www.pbc.gov.cn) and China Foreign Exchange Trading System (www.Chinamoney.com.cn)

respectively. As rediscount is subject to the structural guidance of the central bank, the amount of bank notes incurred made up a lower portion at 83 percent. At the same time, the volume of discount, mainly conducted by banks, is restricted by the volume of loans, where a decrease in new loans will accordingly decrease the balance of discounted bills; thus bill financing is in fact the provision of loans by banks to enterprises.

4. There are still regional differences despite the marketization of direct discount rate and transfer discount rate.

The paper business is affected by factors such as control over the scale of credit loans and fund availability; the changes of interest rate generally commensurate with the changes of other market-oriented interest rates, and become more sensitive to the changes of the scale of credit loans. In addition, there are still regional differences in prices due to the absence of a unified market, from September 2009 to December 2010, the weighted average interest rates of direct discount and transfer discount in Guangdong were 3.97 percent and 2.87 percent, respectively, while in Shanghai 3.78 percent and 3.21 percent, respectively.

II. Problems of the Paper Market

(I) Great dependence on Bank Credit and Slow Development of Corporate Credit

The development of financial markets in the United Kingdom, the United States, and other developed countries follows an echelon development pattern in the sequence of money market, bond market, and capital market, whereby enterprises could first obtain financing by issuing short-term debt instruments in the money market to expand business and improve business performance, thus establishing a good market reputation, and then obtain financing by issuing long-term debt instruments in the bond market and equity instruments in the capital market. The establishment of credit system of enterprises is the basis for the development of the money market from commercial credit to bank credit and national credit, and ultimately the establishment of social credit necessary for the development of the capital market.

With the original intention of establishing China's paper market to solve the problem of enterprises' loans in arrears, clearing up debt chain, and making up for the lack of credit of enterprises, the introduction of bank credit can ensure banker's acceptance and discount-backed bills to be used as effective instrument for payment and financing, which enterprises are willing to use, and the low rediscount rate set by the central bank allows commercial banks to profit from the difference between rediscount rate and discount rate, which enables commercial banks to be willing to engage in acceptance and discounting business. Under the situation of "heavy dependence of enterprises on commercial banks, and heavy dependence of commercial banks on the central bank," there is no incentive for enterprises to improve their credit to make the bills they issued and accepted a more accessible payment instrument and low-cost finance instrument. Therefore commercial credit instruments become more dominated by banks, and enterprise credit has been developing relatively slowly as acceptance and discount businesses are dependent on banks.

(II) Commercial Paper Mainly Serve the Function of Financing, But Regulations Focus More on Restricting Its Payment Function

Although commercial paper serve the functions of payment and financing, the *Negotiable Instruments Law*, the *Measures on Payment and Settlement* and other relevant laws and regulations focus on the regulation of the payment function, which emphasized that notes should be backed by genuine transactions, stressing the format requirements of negotiable instruments, so that financial institutions have spent a lot of human resources in checking whether the negotiable instruments have met the requirements for payment. In fact, the financing function of negotiable instruments can promote the development of the modern paper market, but in China the debtor qualification check has not received due attention, with a lack of rating and information disclosure; except for the bank, it is difficult for other market participants to understand the status of enterprises, which might hinder the cultivation and promotion of business credit and renders the market dependent on bank credit, resulting in relatively small ratio of commercial acceptance bills.

(III) Pure Financing Instruments Are Lacking, and the Emphasis on Trading Background Will Nonetheless Provoke Rule Violation of All Kinds, Resulting in the Risks of Repetitive Granting of Credit

Negotiable instruments with financing function can be traded and circulated as investment product to facilitate the allocation of resources and to undertake the function of transmitting monetary policy. The trading instruments in the paper markets of the United Kingdom, the United States and other developed countries include banker's acceptance, negotiable bank certificates of deposit, treasury bills, commercial paper, and other short-term debt certificates, and the leading trading instruments have all experienced the evolution from banker's acceptance to commercial paper, that is, from negotiable instruments with both payment and financing functions to negotiable instruments with pure financing function. Currently, the markets for banker's acceptance have been shrinking gradually in countries such as the United Kingdom, United States, and Japan, and the mortgage accepted by the rediscount window of the Bank of England does not include banker's acceptance; 30 percent of the total amount of their commercial paper markets are Euro commercial paper. The Fed ceased to purchase banker's acceptance since 1977, and commercial paper, as an important trading instrument in the US money market, can be divided into commercial paper of financial institutions, commercial paper of nonfinancial institutions, and asset-backed commercial paper of different credit ratings. By the end of 2010, the size of the commercial paper market has reached USD1.04 trillion, with an average daily trading volume of USD84.3 billion. It is an inevitable result for the development of commercial paper, as a flexible financing mode with low cost[5] and beneficial for the issuing enterprise, to establish a good market reputation to outperform that of banker's acceptance.

China's Negotiable Instruments Law and *Measures for Payment and Settlement* specify three types of negotiable instruments, namely bills of exchange, promissory notes, and cheques, among which bills of exchange include bank bills and commercial bills, promissory notes are confined to bank promissory notes. Except for commercial bills, bank bills, promissory notes, and cheques do not serve the function of financing, while commercial bills must be issued on genuine transactions, which is first a payment instrument in nature before serving as a financing instrument, and there is no pure financing negotiable instrument. In the context where only commercial bills can be used for financing, and among commercial acceptance bills it is easier for the financing of banker's acceptance, in order to obtain financing, enterprises in lack of real trade-based businesses usually issue banker's acceptance by illegal means, such as forging contracts and old-for-new, and obtain fund through bank discount, resulting in repetition of bank credit and the risk of undue expansion of bank credit.

(IV) Small Number of Participants, with Risk Concentration in the Banking System

The participants in the paper markets of the United Kingdom, the United States, and other developed countries are composed of individuals, enterprises, governments at all levels, and commercial business organizations, forming a multilevel market system of a large scale. However, in China, the negotiable instruments after being discounted will only be circulated in the banking system with a high degree of homogeneity, excluding investors such as securities, insurance, fund, and enterprises, concentrating risks on the banking system. However, starting from 2007, nonbank institutions have made sizable investments[6] in negotiable instruments with funding from wealth management products, which indicates the need of nonbank institutions to expand investment channels through the paper market.

(V) It Is Hard to Make Electronic Bills Popular Only with Banks' Efforts, and the Lack of Electronic Platform Will Make the Paper Market as a Monetary Policy Instrument Less Effective

In China, bill acceptance and discount are dependent on banks, and electronic bills can only be actively promoted by banks as well. In the business flow of electronic bills, the advantages of banks are reflected more in the process of bill discount and rediscount, while electronic issuance of commercial bills, as the carrier of interenterprise credit, cannot be done without the motivation in the aspects of legal, institutional, and infrastructure development, as well as active participation of enterprises. Due to the lack of government and corporate support, most negotiable instruments are still paper-based, and an efficient and unified electronic platform fails to gain widespread popularity; together with the fact that regional differences are always present and the absence of a nationwide unified market, the central bank's supervision of the paper market and price transmission through the paper was hindered.

III. Reflections on the Development of the Paper Market

(I) The Key to Paper Market Development Lies in a Fundamental Reform

The experience in the development of onshore and offshore paper markets shows that the basic function of the modern paper market is to provide short-term financing for enterprises. In China, the commercial paper has been assigned the dual function of payment and financing and is more prone to the payment function, resulting in the weakening of the financing function. Nevertheless, the payment function of negotiable instruments, compared with that of currency, is quite weak, which makes it more difficult to play any role especially in the absence of strong government support. Bills accepted by enterprises themselves in China account for less than 2 percent, indicating that the payment function of bills is minimal. However, the relevant rules of bills such as the *Negotiable Instruments Law* all emphasized the payment function of bills, which means that commercial bills that must be based on a genuine trading background not only fail to meet the financing need of enterprises but also trigger various irregular operations driven by the financing need of enterprises. Currently, the key to the development of the paper market lies in a fundamental reform, specifying the financing element of negotiable instruments and designing the relevant mechanisms directed at bringing its financing function into play. The term "promissory notes" in the *Negotiable Instruments Law* refers to bank promissory notes only, excluding commercial promissory notes with financing function, while issuance, custody, trading, clearing and other institutional arrangements are crucial to financing bills, they could hardly be included in the *Negotiable Instruments Law*. In light of this, we can consider revising the *Negotiable Instruments Law*, or explore the feasibility of formulating special rules for financing bills prior to the revision of the *Negotiable Instruments Law*.

(II) The Foundation for the Development of the Paper Market Is Commercial Credit

The development of financial markets in the United Kingdom, the United States, and other developed countries is in the sequence of a money market for maritime trading services, a bond market for government war services, and finally a capital market for publicly listed companies. Such an echelon development pattern is in line with the basic features of the financial market. Among the three features of "safety, liquidity, and profitability," investors are more concerned about the safety and liquidity of financial products, therefore the bills of commercial credit corresponding with the three-month voyage period, and the goods on board appeared first; then national bonds supported by government credit emerged, followed by high-risk stocks with emphasis on profitability. The development of China's financial market is, however, in the opposite order, with capital market being developed first, followed by the bond market, and finally the money market. The development in the money market is lagging behind, and commercial credit has never been fully established, especially for the paper market. The percentage of commercial papers purely based on commercial credit (i.e., accepted by enterprises themselves) is less than 2 percent; the function of most bills is simply for discounting at banks, and the paper market has been heavily dependent on bank credit. As a result, the development of the paper market is subject to bank credit loan offering, the fluctuations of which directly affect the stability of the market, and the function of bills in supporting the financing of enterprises especially SMEs is impaired. A paper market tool with relatively short term, small amount, little price fluctuation and controllable risks are more appropriate to be developed as the basic platform for the development of business credit. In this case, the commercial paper market development should focus on commercial credit so as to guide enterprises to obtain financing with their own business credit.

(III) The Paper Market Must Develop on an Electronic Platform

International experience shows that e-market is an important prerequisite for promoting paper market development, an example being the participants of Euroclear who deposit the physical form of securities in a warehouse of secondary trustees who will then transfer the securities information into electronic information and save it in Euroclear's system for settlement. This is the case with most commercial bills with image being captured and placed in a fixed form in a depository trust company (DTC) for electronic settlement. Currently, the electronic commercial bills develop slowly in China, so paper-based commercial bills are still dominant in the paper market. In order to accelerate the development of the electronic commercial bill system in China, we must promote the centralized deposit and settlement of electronic information of paper-based commercial bills by drawing on the experience of imaging, depositing in the form of bookkeeping and settling commercial bills in developed economies. Through the concurrent operations of the two mechanisms, they can supplement each other for joint development and lay a solid foundation for electronic bills.

CHAPTER 2

Bond Market

Success of Government-Led Institutional Innovation—Analysis of the Institutional Change of China's Bond Market[1]

The national interbank bond market founded by the PBC in June 1997 is a key and characteristic component of the current bond market of China. Therefore, thorough understanding of China's bond market cannot be acquired without observation of the whole institutional change process of China's bond market. We may make a case study of the establishment of China's interbank bond market to discuss the topic. This requires answers to several questions: first, why was China's bond market first built upon the exchange market; second, what caused the institutional change from the former exchange-based market to the interbank market, and why did the central bank promote an over-the-counter (OTC) bond market; and third, what drives the rapid and steady development of China's interbank bond market? So to speak, China's bond market, in its set-up and development, becomes a genuine embodiment of the characteristics of China's market-oriented reforms. In particular, China's interbank bond market turns into a successful case of a government-built market, which is rare in the history of China's economic restructuring. It is worth analyzing its differences from the institutional innovation and reforms in other economic fields and exploring what have made it successful. However, to understand the limitation of such a development pattern is also required.

I. Formation of China's Bond Market

Based on the specific nature of financial instruments, there are generally two mechanisms for deal-making in practice, namely the order-driven mechanism and the price-driven mechanism. Order-driven mechanism means that after investors place orders, those orders will automatically become effective and be matched through Out Cry or computer matching. Price-driven mechanism means that an investor provides a quotation, while other investors decide whether to trade or not based on such quotation. This difference in trade mechanism results in two general categories of trading, that is, exchange-based trading and OTC trading. Investors may adopt the order-driven mechanism when trading in stock exchanges and follow the price-driven mechanism when trading over the counter through market makers and brokers.

Bonds and stocks differ considerably. First, their pricing mechanisms are very different. Largely affected by interest rate, bonds are financial instruments with fixed yields, stable cash flow, single source of information, and standardized pricing mechanism; while stocks are financial instruments with nonfixed yields, multiple sources of information, many price-affecting factors, and a relatively complex pricing mechanism. Second, the trading entities differ; a large number of individual investors trade in the stock market, and only a modest number of institutional investors trade at the bond market. Third, the intermediary institutions are different. Stocks are traded through securities dealers, while a substantial proportion of bonds are also traded through banks. Fourth, the trading volumes are distinct. Stock market attracts more individual investors with relatively small volume in a single transaction, while in the bond market large-volume transactions are widely seen. Fifth, they are different in liquidity requirements. Since the main trading parties in the bond market are institutional investors, such as commercial banks, the bond market imposes relatively high requirements for liquidity.

The precondition for conclusion of financial transactions is that buyers and sellers expect different prices for the same financial instrument; in other words, the estimations of price between buyers and sellers are different. The biggest difference between bonds and stocks is that investors usually have diverse estimations of stock price, as they are affected by various factors, making it more efficient to adopt order-driven mechanism and match trading. That is why exchange trading prevails at the stock market. Whereas bond prices are mainly affected by interest rates, on which the general public usually have a convergent point on their price estimations. Therefore, expectations of bond price are likely to be identical, making it difficult to conclude trading through order-driven mechanism. If order-driven mechanism is adopted, bond market turnover may fall sharply because institutional investors may place large-volume orders that can hardly be met by an opposite order at the same price in a short time. The investor would need to break down orders into smaller ones at various prices, which will cause a drastic fluctuation in the price and thus freeze the liquidity of bonds. Therefore, if bonds are traded in exchanges, it may bring along such problems of low liquidity and price fluctuations, thus keeping institutional investors away.

For individual investors, the calculation of bond yield and maturity portfolio is complicated, with a relatively high knowledge acquisition cost. In developed countries, individuals invest in bonds mainly through money market funds or bond funds that operate in the OTC market. Personal direct investment in bonds usually targets stable cash earnings. Most individual investors will hold their bonds to maturity or cash in bonds shortly before expiration. As a result, they will generally accept the quotation for bonds given by bank and sell them to the banks prior to maturity, which is more convenient for them than trading at bond market. Therefore, exchange trading is not a suitable choice for most individual investors. Some individual investors participate in the exchange bond market mainly to obtain the spread return on bonds. These investors account for a small percentage of the whole investor body. Based on the analysis above, we can come to the conclusion that the nature of bonds deciding the OTC mechanism is the most suitable choice.

As for bond markets of developed countries, the OTC bond market is the primary component and mainly adopts the price-driven bargaining mode. In the treasury bond markets of the United States and Japan, two of the largest treasury markets in the world, 99 percent of the trading volume is conducted in the OTC market through bargaining. In Germany, whose treasury bond market ranks third in the world, the OTC market embraces 85–91 percent of the treasury bond trading volume. In developed countries, bond market usually means OTC bond market, while exchange-based bond market is a supplement to OTC bond market and generally has a very small scale. In a sense, the exchange-based bond market may even be omitted. In Eastern Europe and other transitional economies, most of the bond trading are conducted over the counter, inter alia, 90 percent of Czech's bond trading is dealt by the OTC market, and the trading of Hungarian OTC electronic system accounts for 75 percent of the government bond market. In Poland, bond trading is conducted in the Warsaw Stock Exchange with relatively poor liquidity. Almost every market participant reached a common understanding that government bond trading by institutional investors shall not be conducted in stock exchanges and requires a new trading system (Earl and Kurz, 1997). The practices of bond markets in developed countries and transition economies prove that, for both institutional and individual investors, OTC bond market features measurable risk control, simplicity in trading, and readiness in conclusion of transactions. Therefore, OTC bond market shall also be an inevitable choice for China's bond market. However, China's bond market has gone through twists and turns in this respect.

(I) China's Bond Market before 1997

China resumed the issuance of treasury bonds in 1981. In 1988, the Ministry of Finance carried out pilot projects for treasury bond circulation and transfer in 61 cities all over China and opened trading over the bank counters, which marked that China's secondary treasury bond market took shape. In 1994, Shanghai Stock Exchange (SZSE) and Shenzhen Stock Exchange opened treasury bond trading, which led to the coexistence of OTC trading and exchange-based trading patterns. China's bond market originated from the OTC market rather than bank counters. Since the Ministry of Finance did not attempt to issue book-entry treasury bonds, the treasury bonds purchased and sold via bank counters were all bearer physical bonds, the custody and closing of which both required physical transportation; the risk and cost were relatively high. What's more, some of the treasury bond intermediary institutions privately carried out custody business, which led to overissue and short sale of treasury bonds by means of issuance of custody bills. In 1995, Ministry of Finance started to print the uniform treasury bond custody certificate to curb violations in T-bond custody. Even so, serious short sale and false repo problems occurred in Wuhan Securities Exchange Center, Tianjin Stock Exchange Center, and STAQ system, which were then ordered to close for correction by the government.

Bond issuers and regulatory departments put the blame on the OTC market for problems arising out of having no uniform bonds custody institutions or book-entry bonds and considered book-entry bonds to be unique in exchange trading. In August 1995, China suspended the OTC bond trading, leaving stock exchanges the only legitimate platform for bond trading. In 1996, Ministry of Finance started to issue large amounts of book-entry treasury bonds in Shanghai Stock Exchange and Shenzhen Stock Exchange and opened bond repo transactions. Since then, a relatively complete exchange-based bond market (see Table 2.1) has formed. The issuance and trading of bonds on China's bond market were centralized to stock exchanges, inter alia, Shanghai Stock Exchange was where most of the treasury bonds were traded. In 1995, Ministry of Finance carried out pilot projects to issue book-entry treasury bonds with an amount of only RMB11.7 billion and issued another RMB111.67 billion six times in stock exchanges in 1996, accounting for 52.5 percent of the treasury bonds issued that year. Meanwhile, the

Table 2.1 Treasury bond issue modes (1981–1996)

Year of issue	*Administrative allocation*	*Underwriting*	*Over-the-counter sales*	*Tendering*
1981–1990	Bearer			
1991		Bearer		
1992		Bearer		
1993	Bearer	Book-entry		
1994		Bearer	Certificate	
1995		Bearer	Certificate	Book-entry
1996				Book-entry & Bearer

Source: CHINA CENTRAL DEPOSITORY & CLEARING CO., LTD. (www.Chinabond.com.cn)

trading volume of the secondary market also expanded rapidly. The year 1996 saw an increase of nearly ten times in bonds trading in Shanghai Stock Exchange and Shenzhen Stock Exchange over the previous year; inter alia, bonds traded in Shanghai Stock Exchange accounted for over 95 percent of the total bonds traded in exchanges (see Table 2.2).

In the development of China's stock market, the exchange market overshadowed the OTC market. Under the influence of stock trading modes and due to problems occurred in OTC bond trading, both financial practitioners and theorists had reached the consensus that OTC trading had too much risks and the exchange mode would be the best choice. China's bond market should be built into a trading platform for treasury bonds based on centralized transactions and supplemented by decentralized OTC transactions. As planned by the bond issuers and securities regulatory authorities, China's bond market had for a time converged to the exchange mode.

(II) Reasons Why Exchange-Based Bond Market Becomes the Main Mode

As a form of bond market, the exchange-based bond market has its grounds. Despite that the OTC bond market dominates the bond market in developed countries; the exchange bond market still exists and some medium and small investors conduct some small-value bond trading in the exchanges. But in general the bond market of a country shall be based on OTC. This chapter will focus on the reasons why China's bond market has for a time

Table 2.2 Treasury bond trading of Shanghai stock exchange and Shenzhen stock exchange

Year	*Trading value (RMB 100 Million)*				*Trading volume (10,000 lots)*			
	Spot		*Repo*		*Spot*		*Repo*	
	SHSE	*SZSE*	*SHSE*	*SZSE*	*SHSE*	*SZSE*	*SHSE*	*SZSE*
1994	713.55	11.1	88.9	12.63	6,269.5	104	844.1	126.3
1995	764.44	28.2	1,171.59	76.92	6,005	275.51	11,716	2,748.67
1996	4,962.37	66.85	12,439.16	569.47	45,537	620.81	124,391.6	5,694.82
1997	3,458.41	114.35	11,912.16	963.91	31,518	1,097.2	119,121.6	9,639.06
1998	6,046.67	13.25	15,188.54	352.29	45,858	116.58	151,888	3,523

Source: Quarterly Statistical Report of the People's Bank of China, 1999.1, p. 34, the Statistics and Analysis Department of the People's Bank of China.

been exchange-based. It proves that such an exchange bond market system was in line with the interests of relevant market players given the conditions at the time.

1. The order-driven trading mode in exchange makes it possible for securities companies and insurance companies to profit from rate spread.

In China, in order to trade treasury bonds in stock exchanges, investors need to open an account in a securities company, which involves a complex procedure and a relatively high commission fee. As a result, individual investors making relatively small investment seldom participate in the exchange-based bond market. The trading entities in Shanghai Stock Exchange and Shenzhen Stock Exchange bond markets are mainly securities companies, insurance companies, and urban and rural credit cooperatives. The order-driven trading mechanism of the exchange-based bond market will bring about substantial fluctuation in price. For example, from January 4, 2000, to June 5, 2000, the average annualized volatility of the five treasury bonds (696, 896, 9704, 9,905, and 9,908) traded in the Shanghai Stock Exchange was 6.7493 percent, while the standard deviation of bond market in developed countries are generally around 1.8 percent. The substantial price fluctuation made it difficult for institutional investors to control risks and might lead to poor market liquidity, making it harder for treasury bonds to work as a substitute for currency. Moreover, it allows some institutional investors to manipulate the market price and profit from spreads. However, manipulation of bond price by means of matched orders and so forth are not deemed as illegal by the authority, as they are in the stock market, nor are relevant regulations and rules in place. Therefore, it is possible for major institutional investors in the exchange bond market, namely securities and insurance companies, to profit from spreads in the bond market by manipulative means as employed in the stock market. If a small number of institutional investors are able to manipulate the market price, then price volatility would actually be profitable.

2. Bond repo in the exchange market makes supply and demand sides of liquidity both benefit from policy arbitrage.

In exchange-based bond market, the securities companies are the major repo sellers, while the insurance companies and urban and rural credit cooperatives are the major repo buyers. The terms of bond repo transactions are mainly three-day and seven-day. The fund financed by securities companies will be invested in the secondary stock market and for the purchase of IPO stocks. Due to administrative regulations and "the absence of the general public," there has been an extremely high price spread between China's primary and secondary stock market, making the purchase of IPO shares risk-free and with a return much higher than interest rate and general profit margin in the market. It created a high return "swirl," which would attract capital from the whole society (Sun, 1998). However, the authority dictates that only securities companies and securities investment funds are eligible to purchase IPO shares. In this regard, securities companies and securities investment funds are able to get financing from other financial institutions and pocket the exclusive policy-arbitrage return. In the process, a small portion of profit will be distributed to the institutions that finance the purchase. Exchange-based bond market is the primary platform where financing for policy-arbitrage is completed. Securities companies and securities investment funds financed to purchase IPO shares pocket a high return even after the financing cost. However, though other financial institutions are not eligible to purchase IPO shares, they can still obtain a yield higher than that from bank deposits by lending to securities companies. Thus, the exchange-based bond market becomes a distribution center of policy-arbitrage return and benefits both the supply and demand sides of capital.

3. Securities regulatory authorities need an exchange-based bond market to support the stock market.

Securities regulatory authorities simultaneously administer the stock market and exchange-based bond market, with the main task being developing stock market to support the reform of state-owned enterprises. The bond repo market of the exchange provides sufficient funds for the primary market and secondary stock markets, which assists securities regulatory authorities to accomplish the policy goals for the stock market. Therefore, the exchange-based bond market has to a large extent been considered by securities regulatory authorities as a tool of supporting the development of stock market.

4. The market players at that time were relatively small, and the exchange mode has satisfied all the trading needs.

At that time, the large-scale trading entities in the market were securities companies and insurance companies, but the number was small and the sizes were not big in the absolute sense. Not many corporate or individual investors were seen in the exchange-based bond market, and their tradings were of a trivial size. Securities investment funds did not exist at that time. Since the No.45 Circular of the State Council in 1996 required commercial banks to sell out the treasury bonds they held, commercial banks largely stayed out of the bond market. Real institutional investors were absent from the exchange-based bond market, so were demands for large-volume transactions. The order-driven trading mode of the exchange could basically satisfy the needs of the trading parties at the time.

5. With small issuance amount, treasury bonds did not have urgent demand for an OTC market.

Due to restrictions on trading mode, exchange market is for small-volume bond trading, and its major shortcoming is that it allows no large-volume bond issuance and trading. As China adopted balanced fiscal policy at that time, treasury bonds issued then were of relatively small sizes. The shortcoming of exchange bond market was not fully revealed. Bond issuers and investors were satisfied with the exchange market.

Before 1997, China's bond market adopted the exchange-based mode similar to that of the stock market. The exchange-based bond market witnessed active trading and became an important platform for capital flows and bond transactions. As a success at that time, the market showed no signs of any institutional change before 1997.

(III) Problems Reside in the Exchange-Based Bond Market

The exchange-based bond market celebrated rapid development before 1997; however, many problems existed in China's bond market system with the exchange-based bond market as the mainstay:

1. China has no independent bond market, and no independent government bond market in particular. Government bonds and other bonds were issued, traded, cleared, settled, and registered on stock exchanges. However, the stocks and bonds shall be traded respectively in different places according to international practices. So the united bond and stock market put clearing and settlement of treasury bonds in risks (Earl and Kurz, 1997).

2. No minimum standards for bond settlement and custody were established. The international banking system has different standard in terms of settlement and custody of bonds from that of the international securities companies. As the global organization for management of banking operations, Bank for International Settlement has a more positive and prudent attitude than the International Organization of Securities Commissions toward the bond clearing and settlement system. China's bond market has followed the roadmap formulated by the international securities management for a long time and deviates further and further from the common practice and standards of the international banking system.

3. The clearing and settlement structure are highly decentralized. Exchanges and trading centers have their own registration and clearing companies, which are run under varied clearing and settlement rules, thus making transfer of ownership records quite inconvenient. Members of stock exchanges are mainly securities companies with lower credit standing than commercial banks. Their participation in clearing and settlement system will likely put clearing companies and exchanges under risks. What's more, stock exchanges and clearing companies in China are combined, which enables

stock exchanges to lift the requirements on bond custody and clearing to "vitalize" the market and thus bring greater risks to clearing companies.

4. Trading based on centralized price-matching model exposed the bond market to systemic risks. Exchange-based bond market adopts the centralized price-matching model, in which the market participants settle trades with the exchange as their counterparty. Once large-volume repo of any institution cannot be paid on time, and its bond collateral is insufficient to repay the principal and interest, the exchange will have to suffer the loss. In the OTC market, clearing is conducted between trading parties, and risks will be taken by participants themselves, and the entire market will be insulated from the risks. But in the exchange market, it is exchanges that bear the risks; however, exchanges have only limited capital, without any specific and sufficient financial guarantee to afford the risks. Once an exchange fails to repay other investors, it will trigger a chain reaction leading to systemic risks. If the loss resulted from risks in clearing is beyond the capital strength of the exchange, the exchange will face bankruptcy, imposing a threat of market close-down. In bond repo trading, Shanghai Stock Exchange and Shenzhen Stock Exchange both adopt the practice of "standard bond," in which trading parties all deposit their bonds into securities depository companies of the stock exchanges to as the pledge for their financing activities. Therefore, the amount financed should be commensurate to the value of bond collaterals. In order to contain risks for the exchange, the haircut rate for the bond collaterals shall be larger than the market rate. However, since securities companies and other institutions are to support the stock market by financing via bond repo, exchanges will make a compromise on the haircut in order to encourage stock trading. For example, No. 896 treasury bonds issued by Ministry of Finance in 1996 broke the buck on the day of listing, so did No. 9908 treasury bonds issued in 1999. Their prices fluctuated around the par value for a long time, but Shanghai Stock Exchange set the repo price at their par value. It means that when the counterparty was unable to make payment at maturity, the exchange would have to suffer part of the loss on selling the bonds. In fact, this put the exchange under the settlement risk.

5. Poor market liquidity. Liquidity refers to the ability of a financial asset to be readily converted into cash without any price loss. It covers four dimensions: width, as determined by the bid-ask spread for a given number of securities; depth, the quantity of securities that can be traded at given bid and ask prices; immediacy, referring to how quick a trade can be made; and resiliency, referring to how fast prices revert to former levels after they changed in response to trades of abnormally large volume. Liquidity is the major factor that affects the level of indirect trading cost, thus having a

decisive influence on investors. Exchange-based trading cannot satisfy institutional investors in all four respects. Prices of bonds will plunge when trading quantities soar and vice versa. As a result, institutional investors are unable to manage the trading cost, and it is difficult to provide an accurate evaluation of the future value of bonds, thus it greatly limits the bond trading of institutional investors.

6. The interest rate and price cannot be taken as benchmarks. The yield curve representing the interest rates and prices of bonds is expected to be the benchmark rate of the general financial market. However, prices in the exchange-based bond market fluctuate dramatically from time to time. As a result, the yield curve is inadequate to represent the long-term interest rate. Bond repo mainly serves to finance the stock market and is largely subject to influences exerted by issuance cycle in the primary market and fluctuations of prices in the secondary market; therefore, the interest rate volatility will grow and disqualify it as a benchmark.

II. Establishment of Interbank Bond Market

(I) The Internal Need to Establish an Interbank Bond Market

1. A relatively independent government bond market is needed to maintain economic and financial stability.

Government bond market and stock market differ in their level of risk and roles in the national economy. Investors of government bonds believe that government bond market is a relatively safe market with certainties and should be the "safe harbor" under explicit or implicit guarantee of the government. (Earl and Kurz, 1997) In addition, a safe bond market means sufficient liquidity, which can provide global investors with sufficient, sensitive, and accurate information and rich investment instruments. It is one of the decisive preconditions for the internationalization of a country's currency. In case of internal and external impacts, a stable bond market is very important to the economic and financial stability of a country. And the Asian financial crisis has much to do with the fact that Southeast Asian countries lacked sound bond markets. (Greenspan, 2000) The bond market is also of great significance to other financial markets. Government bonds will serve as the role model for issuers of other securities, and the yield curve based on the market will become the benchmark of all interest rates of the economy. Therefore, different from other financial markets, government bond market is under strong regulation and thorough intervention by the government. Both Ministry of Finance and the central bank represent the government, but Ministry of Finance is the debtor of government bonds, and it is inappropriate for the debtor to manage trading activities of creditors and the book-entry system of investors. Therefore, usually the central bank is the one that manages the government bond market. The central bank usually acts on behalf of the government to manage treasury and issue treasury bills and bonds. To minimize the fundraising cost for government, central bank should optimize the market structure for government bonds. Therefore, the government bond market is required to work as the cornerstone for the entire bond market. The bonds traded in the interbank bond market include treasury bonds, bonds of the central bank, and financial bonds of policy banks, all of which are government bonds and quasi-government bonds. With relatively high reputation and quality, they guarantee the safety of interbank bond market and lay a foundation for further development of the market.

2. Implementation of indirect monetary policy by the central bank needs a mature OTC bond market.

An important objective of China's financial reform is to establish a monetary policy regulatory system under the central bank, which requires innovation and transformation of monetary policy tools. And the actual conditions for establishment of monetary policy operations are also of great importance. Monetary policies of the central bank are delivered mainly in two ways: one being that the central bank adjusts the quantity and price of base money and then influences the total quantity and price of money via asset adjustment of commercial banks; the other being that the central bank influences price in the financial market and expectations of the public by means of intervening in the financial market (Sun, 2000). The financial market plays its role in two respects: first, when monetary policy is delivered, commercial banks will adjust their balance sheet through the financial market to accomodate the external impact that resulted from the change of base money; later, commercial banks will have to adjust credit assets due to the fact that the overall quantity of base money will be changed regardless of the accommodative trading in the financial market. Meanwhile, the pressure of commercial banks in terms of trading in financial market will be reflected on price of the base money market, which becomes the target and basis of judgment for the central bank's decision-making on monetary policy (Sun, 1996). In the second way monetary policy is delivered, the central bank's operation will be directly reflected in the financial market, changing expectations of the general public as well as their income and spending activities, so that the monetary policy objective will be realized. Therefore, financial market plays an important role in the monetary policy operations of the central bank. Financial market must meet the following conditions to serve as a vehicle of the monetary policy operations of the central bank: (i) financial instruments are of relatively low risk and may be held by the central bank;

(ii) the market width and depth shall be sufficient; (iii) the market has high liquidity; (iv) the central bank's monetary policy has a powerful regulatory and control impact on prices; (v) commercial banks proactively participate in trading; and (vi) the regulation and control of the central bank will not undermine the capability of financial market to allocate resources. Not all financial markets are appropriate vehicle of monetary policy. The indispensable precondition for market-oriented monetary policy operations is that the government bond market has met the said conditions and become the important channel for transmission of monetary policy. Therefore, government bond market has the direct bearing on the central bank's capacity to control monetary policy operations, which affects the overall stability of monetary system. Government bond market is crucial to monetary policy and stability.

3. To improve the velocity of money and enhance financial efficiency.

Under the current monetary system, money is created by banks. The nonbank public needs to pay a cost, that is, the interest spread between deposits and loans, to obtain money that can be used as a medium for the trading of goods and financial instruments. Financing activities allow the public short of money to obtain liquidity from economic entities with surplus money, which increases the velocity and efficiency of money, and therefore reduces the nonbank public's overall demand for money. Financial markets of developed countries are relatively well established, with a high velocity of money. Therefore, demands for money grow slowly and so do supplies. This reduces interest rate spread between deposits and loans of banks and decreases the aggregate cost for nonbank public to obtain money and therefore enhances efficiency of the economy. In developed countries, the scale of OTC bond market greatly exceeds that of the stock market, and plays an important role in accelerating the money flow. Therefore, China relies on development of OTC bond market for further financial transformation and restructuring of public's financial assets.

(II) "Institutional Trap" and the PBC to Lead the Institutional Innovation

From the perspective of institutional supply and demand, if the cost to establish a new institution is smaller than the gain, institutional innovation may be possible. The "primary action group" in institutional innovation can timely capture the opportunities to profit from the uncertainty of environment resulted from institutional change (North, 1991), but if all the parties are able to benefit from the entrenched institution, "primary action group" cannot rise and institutional change will be obstructed. If the parties that can benefit from the new institution are greatly scattered and lacking the power for collective action, plus objections from opposing forces, the institutional innovation would be unlikely. This status cannot be explained by accidental path dependence (North, 1994) or "non-neutrality of institution" and "rational ignorance" (Zhang, 1994). In this chapter, I call the institutional stalemate the "institutional trap."

Before 1997, the relevant parties of China's bond market included the securities regulatory authorities (China Securities Regulatory Commission), bond issuers (mainly Ministry of Finance), and investors (including securities companies, insurance companies, rural and urban credit cooperatives, enterprises, and residents). This chapter has discussed the fact that the existing exchange-based bond market system is short of participants with creativity and power of action. This can be partially attributed to the status of Ministry of Finance. Large-scale development of the treasury bond market needs the OTC bond market. From 1998, China started to implement proactive fiscal policies and greatly increase the issuance of treasury bonds, which proved the importance of such demand. We should see that Ministry of Finance is an entity with potential creativity and power of action, but there was insufficient pressure on treasury bond issuance before 1997. From the second half of 1996, the Ministry of Finance met the pressure as residents had growing demand for treasury bonds. It wouldn't have been a problem if the Ministry of Finance developed book-entry bond market for bank counters, but it chose to issue nontradable certificate treasury bonds that were relatively easy to put forward and neglected OTC bond market. Therefore, the existing exchange system failed to produce the action group for institutional innovation but was caught in the "institutional trap." The entities of institutional innovation can only come from outside of the established system.

Let's analyze the potential benefits of the institutional change. If the exchange market was transferred into OTC market, all the investors would benefit, but they do not have strong power of action. Therefore, the central bank, which has both the need for institutional innovation and the capability of innovation, assumed the role of institutional innovation leader.

In the development process of exchange-based bond market, the central bank did not intervene. After the establishment of interbank bond market on June 16, 1997, a series of changes upon the financial system and the banking system made the central bank the largest beneficiary of the institutional change.

First, in September 1997 interbank lending was bogged down due to the removal of financing centers by PBC, which cut off the original financing channel between commercial banks. The collapse of interbank credit resulted from Asian financial crisis and closure of Hainan Development

Bank also froze the interbank market for a while. After September 1997, the turnover in national interbank lending market dropped sharply. In 1998, the turnover was merely RMB98.9 billion, down 76.16 percent, compared with RMB414.9 billion in 1997. The shrinking interbank lending market caused by credit problems of banks was a problem for many emerging economies. In Turkey and other countries, only a few banks conducted interbank lending, for most of the others lack credit and cannot participate in interbank lending. In this case, bond repo market with bonds as collateral must be developed to solve the interbank financing problems. Moreover, without bond repo market being the financing channel of banks, banks must borrow from the central bank to boost liquidity. And the pressure on liquidity of all financial institutions will directly come to the central bank, which will be made to lose its initiative in regulation and control over banks' liquidity, thus weakening the effects of monetary policies. In addition, the increase of central bank lending to small- and medium-sized financial institutions will intensify the credit risk faced by the central bank. These all require the central bank to establish an interbank bond market.

Second, the absence of a mature OTC bond market restrains the establishment of indirect regulatory regime. In 1996, the PBC started open market operations of bonds. Due to the absence of OTC bond market and limited capacity of exchange-based bond market, the trading volume of the open market operations of the central bank in 1996 was less than RMB10 billion, and the central bank ceased the operations in early 1997. In order to develop open market operations and complete the transition from direct monetary policy regulation and control to indirect ones, the central bank needs to develop a OTC bond market.

Third, problems occurred in securities trading center and stock exchange-based bond market exposed commercial banks to serious risk when conducting bond trading in these venues. The central bank needs to build up a standardized bond market to provide a safe trading platform for commercial banks so as to prevent any financial risks. In a broad sense, the central bank is also the final undertaker of risks of other financial institutions; therefore, establishing an OTC bond market may reduce risks to the entire financial system.

(III) The Design and Development of Interbank Bond Market

Precisely when the PBC had the impetus to establish a new institution, accidental external shocks occurred and cooled down the overheating stock market. This further facilitated the establishment of interbank bond market. Before June 1997, members of stock exchange-based bond market, including commercial banks and other financial institutions, were able to conduct bond repo, purchase, and sale. As for flow of funds, securities companies and other nonbank financial institutions got financing from commercial banks via repo tradings. In the first half of 1997, stock prices of Shanghai Stock Exchange and Shenzhen Stock Exchange rose sharply. Behind the sizzling stock market were inflows of large amount of banking funds financed by exchange bond repo. In order to restrain the overheating stock market, in accordance with overall arrangement of the State Council, the PBC decided to withdraw all commercial banks from bond markets of SZSE and Shanghai Stock Exchange and establish an interbank bond market. The PBC regulated that all commercial banks may use the treasury bonds, central bank notes, and policy financial bonds deposited with the China Central Depository & Clearing Co., Ltd. for bond repo and spot bond trading. At the initial stage of the interbank bond market, there were only 16 members that are the head offices of commercial banks, and the bonds traded in this market will be quoted and traded through the trading system of the National Interbank Funding Center, and the bonds will be under centralized custody and settlement by the China Central Depository & Clearing Co. Ltd., while fund clearing will be made through the clearing system of the PBC.

The opportunity to establish an OTC bond market in China presented itself when the government took administrative measures to order commercial banks to withdraw from exchange bond market so as to cool the overheating of stock market, which was unexpected by the academia and the banking sector. Because the purpose of establishing the interbank bond market was to regulate and control stock market price, therefore the academia once thought its establishment was nonmarket-oriented. In fact, the opportunity leading to the institutional change has no direct correlation with the nature of the new system and its development. The external shock is meaningful in that it restrains the force in favor of the existing exchange bond market and counters the objection against institutional innovation.

In a historical view of institutional change of China, many of institutional changes emerged from external shocks. Where the cost of institutional change is relatively high, in particular if the established system is in "institutional trap," accidental external events always play an indispensable part in pushing forward successful institutional innovation for action groups that make that change happen. But a certain factor contributing directly to a new system cannot produce benefits out of the system, though it may reduce the cost of institutional change. Therefore, whether a new system can evolve by itself mainly depends on the capability of the new system to continuously satisfy the need of players and attract more support to survive. Accidental external conditions themselves are not the most important factors for the success of a new system.

The set-up of China's OTC bond market was kickstarted by the withdrawal of commercial banks from exchanges to cut off funds flowing into stock market. This opportunity reduced the resistance from the players of the exchange-based bond market and was conducive to institutional change. It has made China's OTC bond market into an interbank bond market and made the OTC bond market different from exchange bond market not only in trading patterns but also in the base of market participants. In early stage of market development, the difference between these two markets was reflected in the structure of market participants. For a while, the interbank bond market was based on banks that did not participate in the exchange-based bond market. As the only OTC bond market in China, interbank bond market cannot cover all bond investors of society. This largely restricted its functions. Thus, it became a long-term important task for the interbank bond market to make up its inherent defects by bringing in more market trading participants and gradually including all bond investors of the society.

The establishment of the interbank bond market changed the development course of China's bond market from exchange-based to OTC-based. As commercial banks started to substantially intervene in the bond market and become the dominant force, it facilitated the process of the development and changed the whole pattern of China's bond market. In this development process, the PBC formulated the uniform market rules after negotiation with market trading parties and issuers and took market-oriented measures to develop the market according to the experience of developed countries and their OTC bond market. Due to the change of economic trend in different periods and the change of macroeconomic systems and the demands of different parties also changing continuously, the interbank bond market presents different characteristics in different development stages.

1. In the Second Half of 1997—Financing Center Shut-down

In the second half of 1997, the PBC ceased propritary lending operations of the financing centers and started to solve overdue lending problems. As the dominant force withdrawing from money market, the financing centers fundamentally changed the mode of operation in the money market. Originally, commercial banks and other financial institutions mainly adjusted their short-term positions via interbank lending in the financing centers and actually deemed interbank lending with the financing centers to be a long-term investment. The shut-down of the financing centers reminded financial institutions of the harsh fact that market credit risks shall be assumed by themselves. As a result, their short-term financing were turned to bond repo. In order to find a way out for surplus fund, their demand for bonds greatly increased, which provided the necessary conditions for the development of the bond market. In rectifying and closing the financing centers, the PBC started to bring in more participants to the interbank bond market and approved 48 urban commercial banks to the market in the second half of 1997. These commercial banks, finding their way to financing via bond repo after the interbank lending channel originally provided by the financing centers was cut off, turned to the interbank bond market quickly. The interbank bond market in this period mainly satisfied the short-term financing demand of urban commercial banks.

2. In the First Half of 1998—The Reform of Monetary Policies and Fiscal Policies Put Forward Higher Requirements for Interbank Bond Market, Which Plays a Far More Significance Role

In the first half of 1998, the PBC undertook major reforms of the monetary policy regime, abolished the management of loan size, transformed the direct monetary policy to indirect monetary policy, and demanded commercial banks to strengthen assets and liabilities management. In this way, the demand of banks to purchase and trade bonds has grown. The series of measures taken for the monetary policy reform began with restructuring the internal operation mechanism of market players, namely commercial banks, and cultivating their business incentives to provide a market-oriented foundation for the interbank bond market.

In the early stages of interbank bond market, there were treasury bonds of RMB40.7 billion transferred for custody from stock exchanges and central bank notes of RMB11.8 billion issued by the central bank. Plus the policy financial bonds of RMB308.3 billion apportioned according to plans, the total amount of bonds in the market was only RMB350.8 billion. And those bonds were mainly held by the four state-owned commercial banks, with only a very small amount at the hands of joint-stock commercial banks and urban commercial banks. In the beginning of 1998, the PBC designed and published a reform scheme of the deposit reserve system to hedge against the risks of lowered reserve ratio. And the Ministry of Finance issued special treasury bonds valued at RMB42.3 billion to all joint-stock commercial banks and urban commercial banks, which commonly hold high-quality bonds for a short time. It increased the amount of bonds held by commercial banks and changed the unbalanced distribution of bonds. In April, the PBC approved the listing and trading of special treasury bonds in interbank bond market, which immediately became the major variety of bonds for repo for commercial banks.

In May 1998, the PBC resumed bond open market operations. China's bond open market operations started in 1996, and later stagnated due to the financial environment, market condition, and trading tools (Dai, 1999).

The development of interbank bond market laid a solid foundation for open market operations and facilitated its rapid development. According to monetary policy targets, the then open market operations were mainly based upon purchase of bonds and injection of base money via reverse repo, which provided direct support for liquidity of bond trading of commercial banks and immediately vitalized the interbank bond market trading. In this period, interbank bond market directly supported the central bank's monetary policy reform and open market operations, which enabled the central bank to benefit from the institutional change.

3. In the Second Half of 1998—Organize and Promote Market-oriented Issuance of Bonds by Policy Banks

In the past, policy banks mainly relied on financial bonds allocated by PBC for financing. In the beginning of 1998, the PBC put forward the reform of market-oriented issuance of bonds by policy banks. After preparation, in September, the State Development Bank had for the first time issued financial bonds via the bond issuance system of the PBC by means of public tender. Following the initiative of the State Development Bank, Export-Import Bank of China also started the market-oriented bond issuance. In 1998, the two banks issued bonds of RMB41 billion in total. The success of market-oriented issuance of bonds by policy banks drove the reform of market-oriented issuance of treasury bonds. As a result, in the second half of 1998, market factors were considered during the issuance of treasury bonds. Since the issuance interest rate was determined by the market, it provided good conditions for the circulation of bonds in the secondary market. Such "market-oriented" bonds improved the structure of bond varieties in the interbank bond market. Commercial banks continued to participate in bond issuance, which motivated the market to use and trade bonds. As commercial banks engaged in bond underwritings more frequently, more and more urban and rural credit cooperatives joined the interbank bond market, which brought the market to a broader and deeper level. In the second half of 1998, the Ministry of Finance issued construction treasury bonds of RMB100 billion on interbank bond market, dedicated treasury bonds of RMB270 billion, special treasury bonds of RMB42.3 billion, and other treasury bonds of RMB51.3 billion. In 1998, the Ministry of Finance issued treasury bonds totaling RMB463.6 billion, registering an unprecedented level. And the policy banks issued bonds with a value of RMB159 billion via planned apportion in the first half of 1998 and conducted market-oriented issuance of bonds with a value of RMB 42.3 billion in the second half, totaling RMB201.3 billion. By the end of 1998, the bonds outstanding in the interbank bond market valued RMB1,010.3 billion, a 200 percent increase compared with the end of 1997.

In the beginning of 1998, the PBC allowed branches of commercial banks, foreign-funded banks, and insurance companies to enter the market; in the meantime, PBC accelerated approvals of urban commercial banks for entry into the market, with altogether 116 financial institutions approved in the year. The number of market participants has increased dramatically. In October 1998, the formerly sluggish market trading was activated, with a large increase in turnover. By the end of 1998, the monthly turnover has exceededRMB 10 billion. Some commercial banks began proactive operations and became the dominant force in the market.

In 1998, the interbank bond market backed up the large number of treasury bonds issuedby the Ministry of Finance and the issuance of financial bonds by policy banks. Therefore, it obtained support from important bond issuers, becoming the major platform on which the Ministry of Finance issues treasury bonds and facilitates the transformation of policy banks to follow market principles in bond issuance. Development of the interbank bond market benefited the commercial banks that purchased bonds. Thus, the bond issuers and commercial banks became the dominant force in the new system, and the new system was further promoted.

4. In 1999—Deepening of Market-oriented Issuance of Bonds and Entry into the Market of Urban and Rural Credit Cooperatives, Securities Companies, and Securities Funds

In 1999, under the organization and promotion of the PBC, market-oriented issuance of treasury bonds and policy financial bonds became the mainstream of the market. Policy banks all adopted the tender model to issue bonds and the Ministry of Finance also for the first time issued treasury bonds in interbank bond market via tender at the lower-bound interest rate. Due to institutional advantages and advantages of market participants of the interbank bond market, interbank bond market became the primary platform for China's bond issuance. In 1999, the Ministry of Finance issued book-entry treasury bonds with a value of RMB275.6 billion in the interbank bond market, accounting for 89.3 percent of the total. The State Development Bank and the Export-Import Bank of China issued policy financial bonds with a value of RMB167 billion, all of which were issued in the interbank bond market. In 1999, bonds issued on interbank bond market accounted for 74 percent of the total amount of bonds issued in China. By the end of 1999, outstanding bond in interbank bond market valued RMB1,340.2 billion with negotiable bonds valued at RMB1,050 billion.

In the beginning of 1999, the PBC allowed urban and rural credit cooperatives to conduct bond trading freely in the interbank bond market. As a result, in 1999, 325 urban and rural credit cooperatives were approved to enter the market. This mobilized many of the participants that were full of energy and vigor in China's financial system. A large proportion of the financial institutions in China participates in and significantly broadens the interbank bond market. The PBC also adopted progressive measures to solve problems concerning access to interbank market by the nonbank financial institutions step by step. The PBC first approved insurance companies to enter the market in October 1998 and allowed insurance companies to transfer bonds in custody of stock exchange to the interbank bond market. In August 1999, the PBC issued Regulations on Administration on Entry into Interbank Bond Market by Fund Management Companies and Securities Companies. From September 1999 to October 2000, PBC approved 14 securities companies and all securities investment funds to enter the interbank bond market. By communication of the trading entities, interbank bond market representing China's wholesale bond market can be connected with stock exchange bond market where small- and medium-sized investors participated. This enabled the monetary policy to influence the entire capital market via money market. The soaring number of market participants and tools brought the market to a new level, prominently reflected on the trading volume. The turnover on the bond repo market in 1999 was enlarged dramatically, with total turnover valued at RMB396.6 billion, an increase of RMB294.5 billion compared to 1998.

The expansion of interbank bond market created demand and improved market liquidity of bonds and benefited the market participants. From 1998, China has been confronted with insufficient domestic demands, slowed economic development, and a decline of corporate profits. It was a time when commercial banks found it hard to find good clients that are thirsty for bank loans. Due to relatively higher yield and low credit risk, treasury bonds and financial bonds of policy banks were welcomed by banks. Especially for state-owned commercial banks and other large banks, holding high-quality bonds may improve their total return. Starting from 1999, the State Council and the PBC paid more attention to the profit indicators of commercial banks. Commercial banks increased their holding of treasury bonds and policy financial bonds, with the percentage of bond assets rising to 11 percent of their total assets. In addition to increasing returns of bonds, commercial banks took high-quality bonds as secondary reserves and reduced excessive reserves at hand to get financing via bond repo when liquidity is required. Since the yield of bonds is obviously higher than the reserve interest rate and less risky, commercial banks increased their revenues by investing in the interbank bond market. The market created stable revenue stream for the participants and hence boasted their loyalty, making the successful operation of the system possible. In 1999, how the participants may profit from the interbank bond market has basically been determined.

5. In 2000—Transformation of the Interbank Bond Market.

The year 2000 saw relatively remarkable changes in the market. The four major state-owned banks, namely the Industrial and Commercial Bank of China, Agricultural Bank of China, Bank of China, and China Construction Bank, were purchasing a growing number of bonds in the primary market, yet their total shares started to drop. The major reason behind this transformation was that the PBC had expanded the participant base of the market. As urban and rural credit cooperatives, securities companies and securities investment funds were joining the market, and the market structure had undergone substantial changes. Though large banks still played a dominant role, the influence of other financial institutions in the primary and secondary markets was reinforced. The mechanism to shape up interest rates and prices of interbank bond market was further improved. In 2000, the bond repo turnover of interbank bond market reached RMB1,578.1 billion, nearly a triple of that of 1999, and the spot bond turnover was RMB68.1 billion, an increase of 784 percent over 1999 over a high-growth tendency, which manifested the institutional advantages of OTC market.

In August 2000, the central bank commenced bilateral open market operations, that is, simultaneously injected and withdrew base money. The PBC has significantly improved its capacity for regulation and control over the liquidity of commercial banks and market interest rate. Since the central bank can always control liquidity of banks at an appropriate level, the supply and demand for capital in bond market was kept in balance. Besides, the problem of shrinking trading volume in both interbank lending market and bond market because of homodromous change of commercial banks' liquidity was eliminated. From August 2000, the trading volume of interbank bond market increased sharply with the highest daily turnover volume surging to RMB40 billion. The market has opened a new chapter with greater vigor.

After observing measures that the PBC had taken to promote the development of interbank bond market, we could discover three principal lines: first, we saw a growing number of market players and bond outstanding. Market players were expanded from the 16 head offices of commercial banks in 1997 to 606 financial institutions of all types by the end of August 2000, while the bond outstanding in the market increased from RMB350.8 billion by the end of 1997 to RMB1,713.1 billion by April 2001. Second, the market regulatory system has been improved. Thanks to existing laws and regulations for operations and administration, no major violations have been reported during spot bond and repo trading in the interbank bond market so far. Third, it guided the establishment of bond custody system. Bond custody system is the core of the bond market in terms of risk management. Bond trading system, book-entry system for central bonds, the PBC's bond issuance system and computer network system have been updated and upgraded, which strengthened the market's capacity in managing risks, enhanced efficiency in market operation, and laid the crucial technical foundation for future development of the bond market.

(IV) Gains of Relevant Market Players from the Establishment of Interbank Bond Market System

The birth of the interbank bond market has created a new environment and space for actions by market players such as the central bank, the Ministry of Finance, commercial banks, etc., all of which have reaped tangible returns via their operations in the interbank bond market and become more enthusiastic in promoting the development of the market. The central bank, as the market supervisor, regulated the market by unveiling laws and regulations and provided liquidity support via open market operations; the Ministry of Finance and policy banks have increased their bond issuance in the interbank bond market; commercial banks, using this market as the major platform for liquidity and asset management, have increased its transactions. Therefore, the interbank bond market has embarked on a fast track of development.

1. Central Bank Reformed Monetary Policy Operations System and Transmission Mechanism.

With a high reputation and stability, government bonds surely have become the primary tool for monetary policy operations of the central bank. Only the OTC bond market allows the central bank to realize huge amounts of bond trading while limiting its impact upon bond prices. Therefore the interbank bond market laid a foundation for open market operations. From 1998 to 2000, open market operations of the PBC have accumulated to RMB1,402.5 billion, becoming the major daily monetary policy tool of the central bank. It plays a role in regulating and controlling base money and guiding the market interest rate. It marks the smooth transformation from direct monetary policy framework represented by loan size management to indirect monetary policy framework represented by open market operations.

Development of the interbank bond market also laid a foundation for interest rate liberalization. The interest rate liberalization of China started from the money market. Since the establishment of interbank bond market in 1997, the bond repo interest rate has been completely determined by trading parties. In 1998, the issuance of policy bonds was also highly market oriented, as was the issuance of treasury bonds in 1999. In 2000, except for certificate treasury bonds, market-oriented principles have been adopted for bond issuance, and the PBC also possessed the capacity to regulate and control the interest rate of money market and bond market via open market operations and other monetary policy tools. This provided favorable conditions for the liberalization of the deposit and loan interest rates.

2. Ministry of Finance Implemented Proactive Fiscal Policy, and Policy Banks Expanded Their Sources of Fund.

The primary market of interbank bond market was built on the principle of market orientation. Active trading in secondary market provides a firm ground for banks to hold bonds. Therefore, the interbank bond market is able to accommodate a large amount of new bonds. From 1998 to the end of 2000, the Ministry of Finance issued bonds in the interbank bond market with a total value of RMB652.8 billion, and policy banks issued bonds with a total value of RMB372.5 billion. The bonds issued during this period totaled RMB1,025.3 billion. However, bonds still fell short of demand. After the PBC lowered the interest rate for the last time in June 1999, the bond issuance interest rate still stayed low for the next two years. The interbank bond market strongly supported the Ministry of Finance to implement proactive fiscal policies and expansion of business scale of policy banks.

3. Commercial Banks Improved Assets Structure with Accelerated Process of Reform in Commercialization.

In the past, the asset structure of China's commercial banks was relatively monotonous, with loan assets generally accounting for over 70 percent of the total assets. High proportion of loans was disadvantageous for liquidity management and revenue growth of commercial banks and also affected the commercial operation of state-owned banks. The development of interbank bond market provided room for state-owned banks and other commercial banks to hold large amount of bonds to timely adjust liquidity and decrease excess reserves. By the end of April 2001, bonds deposited in China Central Depository & Clearing Co., Ltd. valued RMB1,713.1 billion, inter alia, treasury bonds valued RMB937.1 billion, financial bonds of policy banks valued RMB744.7 billion, and other bonds valued RMB31.3 billion. In the meantime, the bond assets of commercial banks accounted for 17 percent of their total assets, while in 1997 it was only 5 percent. Commercial banks became more active in the interbank bond market. In addition, operation of commercial banks in bond market became a key growing source of profits and facilitated commercialization of banks.

III. Reasons for the Success of the Government-Led Institutional Change of China's Bond Market and Its Restrictions

China's reform is a typical government-driven institutional change. As the supplier of system, the government dominates the evolution of external rules; while social members also spontaneously engaged in institutional innovation in search of appropriate internal rules. In the history of China's reform of economic system, a prominent feature is that some successful innovations are initiated by the public and followed by the government. It shows that by means of laws and regulations the government will recognize spontaneous experiments conducted by nongovernment entities with demand of reforms. On the contrary, reforms initiated by the government will usually fail to work as they had been designed without due respect of the market. After observing development of stock market and other financial markets in history, we could find out that these markets are the outcome of long-term theoretical discussions, practice, and exploration by local governments and nongovernment organizations. The central government would then learn from the experience and step up to help build the market and promulgate relevant regulations.

As for the interbank bond market, it has something very different from other reforms in the economic system, making it a rare successful case of government-driven development of market. This process of institutional change is organized and driven by the PBC, as the government representative, and followed by banks and other market participants. In this process, the government always takes the leadership. The PBC is responsible for designing the market, formulating the scheme, publishing market rules, and leading institutional innovation, while market players have a weaker appetite for innovation. Nevertheless, interbank bond market makes a great success and the market-oriented operation has been continuously improved.

(I) Reasons Behind the Success of Institutional Change

The government-led institutional change has succeeded in China's bond market. It has five differences from reforms in other economic fields:

1. The PBC is an institutional innovation organizer rather than one that is completely exogenous to the market.

As the government representative promoting this institutional change, the PBC has a unusual relationship with the bond market. The PBC is more like a market participant in terms of monetary policy operation and therefore is close to the market. As the PBC formulates market rules, instead of giving purely administrative orders, it has full communication with market players. Different from reforms in other economic fields in which the government maximizes the overall social welfare, this institutional change allows the PBC to benefit from market development more easily and therefore enhances its determination and power of action. The Ministry of Finance as a government department mainly plays the role of bond issuer, also a market player in bond market, with the main purpose of issuing a certain number of bonds with lower issuance cost. All such factors ensure that although the government leads the development of interbank bond market, it is more involved in the market than simply playing an administrative role.

2. Radical Set-up and Progressive Development

Interbank bond market was established in the way stipulated by PBC on June 16, 1997, as the market framework was simultaneously formed. Different from many other reforms in the economic fields of China, it has been set up without going through any pilot projects. This radical process shortens the time for reform, which was conducive to overcoming resistance of the entrenched interest group and minimizing the cost of institutional change. In addition, the sufficient knowledge of the authorities in this respect also provides necessary conditions for this radical reform. Another advantage of the radical set-up is that demanders of a new institution emerge quickly. Through operation in interbank bond market, commercial banks have rapidly improved the financing capability to get financing, restructured assets, and obtained benefits of institutional innovation, making them the loyal supporters of the new system. After the set-up of the interbank bond market, the central bank adopted progressive development measures to orderly promote new rules to improve market framework step by step. Since it takes a long time for the market to take shape, the progressive development enables market players to accept new rules more easily. In addition, initial operations of some commercial banks set examples for other market players, allowing them to keep pace with each other in terms of commercial awareness and understanding of the system to reduce the cost in the process of institutional change.

3. The PBC has the required expertise.

Government is usually deemed as lacking of relevant knowledge of the nature of the market economy and the evolutionary process under the established conditions, therefore it will "explore with prudence" (Yang and Yang, 2000). However, in the process of the set-up and promotion of interbank bond market, the PBC learnt from the experience of developed countries about national OTC bond market operation and had relatively sufficient knowledge in this respect. All sectors of the society and market participants were familiar with the exchange-based model but without much knowledge about the OTC model. The launch of the system began mainly with new market rules made by the central bank, followed by some responsive commercial banks and were gradually accepted by the market later. This reduced the cost of the institutional change.

4. Interbank bond market was under collective, uniform, and orderly management from the very start.

China's stock market and other financial markets have been through a long process of reforms from chaos to order, experiencing significant risks, paying relatively high prices for reforms, and running into lots of obstacles. On the contrary, interbank bond market has been highly centralized and uniform since the very start. Bonds are under collective custody with China Central Depository & Clearing Co., Ltd, and uniform commercialized issuance of bonds is conducted through the bond issuance system of the PBC. Bond trading is bargained via quotes in electronic trading system of the interbank lending center, while bonds are registered and settled by the central bond book-entry system of China Central Depository & Clearing Co., Ltd. And all market participants operate in accordance with the market rules formulated by the central bank. Thanks to uniform market conditions and rules that manage risks and guarantee standardized and orderly market operation, not a single case of default has been reported since the set-up of the market. Different from other financial instruments and commodities, bonds are characterized with relatively high stability. Collective custody and orderly management build up the confidence of investors, while the uniform market rules enhance the efficiency of market operation.

5. Market players are not nongovernment entities, and institutional innovation can only be promoted by the central bank.

As far as participants of interbank bond market are concerned, such state-owned commercial banks such as the Industrial and Commercial Bank of China, Agricultural Bank of China, Bank of China, and China Construction Bank play the leading role, which cannot be classified into "nongovernment entities" as they haven't established the modern corporate governance structure. Therefore, they have no impetus for institutional change, and no market rules were generated. External forces were required to promote the establishment of the market. As the organizer and administrator of interbank bond market that is also responsible for regulating commercial banks, the central bank is the appropriate body to facilitate market development.

(II) Restrictions of Interbank Bond Market and Direction of Further Development

Seen from the institutional change process of China's bond market, government credit has always played the leading role during the whole course of the market-oriented reform. Market players are usually subject to strict limitation, while financial vehicles traded in the bond market are treasury bonds and financial bonds based on sovereign credit. On the one hand, all such factors have contributed to stable operation and development of the bond market since its birth; but on the other hand, they fundamentally restrained the development of interbank bond market. To develop China's bond market, we need to be well aware of three major defects of the current market that are mainly caused by reliance on government credit. We need to clarify the relationship between government credit and nongovernment credit and effectuate the transit from government-based credit to nongovernment credit. We need to do more in the following three aspects.

1. Cultivate real institutional investors.

In the early stage of China's OTC bond market, due to accidents and common demand of relevant players, the bond market was built in the form of an interbank market. What was good about the system is that it helped all players harvest returns promptly, making the establishment and rapid development of interbank bond market system possible. But when this new system fulfilled its initial purpose as designed, its development was also restricted. Currently, trading in interbank bond market is mainly bond repo, and the market mainly serves for interbank bond mortgage and lending. And such important functions as restructuring of residents' financial assets and bond price discovery have not been realized. Market players, namely commercial banks, have not built the modern corporate governance structure, so they are not institutional investors in the full sense. Institutional investors, represented by funds, are still not large enough in size. It is a long way to go for interbank bond market to fulfill its target to cover all OTC bond markets of the society. Therefore, it needs to continuously bring in more trading parties and cultivate the real institutional investors.

The advantages of OTC bond market lie in its dispersive structure and low cost. T-market players of the interbank bond market must therefore be extended to all financial institutions, nonfinancial enterprises, individual residents, and nonresidents to the extent that all legal persons and natural persons that wish to make bond investment may participate in the interbank bond market. In the mean time, for OTC bond market, the main purpose for commercial banks to hold bonds is to hold them as secondary reserves. They do not manifest strong desire to trade them for cash. Besides, as special institutions, banks have different judgment on interest rates and prices from the nonbank public. Therefore, banks are important investors of bond market, but investment funds and insurance companies play a far more important role. Currently, commercial banks in the interbank bond market are mainly state-owned commercial banks, which lack commercial motivation, so it is less likely for them to play the role of real institutional investors. State-owned securities companies and securities investment funds have similar problems with state-owned enterprises. Therefore, bond market funds shall be established so as to cultivate real institutional investors.

2. Develop corporate bonds.

Government bonds may provide a benchmark for the bond market; however, in order to vitalize the national economy, development of corporate bonds may bear greater significance than that of treasury bonds. The issuance of corporate bonds by enterprises is conducive to improving the liability structure of enterprises, expanding the sources of the funds of small- and medium-sized enterprises, establishing active financing channels, and building up nongovernment credit system. In the mean time, development of corporate bonds also provides more investment tools for investors of interbank bond market. An OTC bond market with sufficient width and depth must be provided with sufficient amount of bonds. Under the current treasury bond issuance system, treasury bond issuance mainly serves for fiscal policies and is linked with fiscal deficit. The quantity of treasury bonds issued is subject to efforts and time China employed to carry out proactive fiscal policies, and the amount of treasury bond outstanding is difficult to grow as fast as it was in the recent years. Policy banks issue bonds to expand their balance sheets, though the growth rate is somehow limited. The expansion of corporate bonds is of great significance for increasing bond varieties and quantities in the interbank bond market.

3. Design derivative financial instruments.

Prices of bonds are subject to the influence of interest rate, which is usually cyclical and has its own momentum. If the central bank continues to keep interest rates rising for a certain period, prices of bonds will definitely go down. For bond-holding investors rising rate inevitably means loss. Therefore, developing derivative financial instruments may provide hedging tools for investors, which is more important for institutional investors that make large amount of bond investment in a long run. To some extent, development of financial derivatives of bond makes an important precondition for greater development of institutional investors in the bond market and the growth of market trading volume.

Whether or not interbank bond market can realize further institutional innovation depends on the potential benefits and power of the PBC, the organizer of interbank bond market system, as well as potential benefits for market trading parties and bond issuers.

Currently, all players in the interbank bond market can benefit from institutional innovation: the central bank is deepening the reform of monetary policy. As for operations in open market, the sheer number is large enough, but if the PBC wants to improve the accuracy and improve the influence of operation, it needs to further expand the interbank bond market. The Ministry of Finance and policy banks need more investors to participate in the interbank bond market in order to reduce the cost of bond issuance. As for commercial banks, as they are currently marked with capital advantage in the interbank bond market, their strengths in networking have not been given full play. If more players are brought into the interbank bond market, commercial banks may provide intermediary services for enterprises and individuals when they participate in market trading. This will carve out new businesses and growth potential for commercial banks. As for enterprises and individuals, they are the potential beneficiaries of institutional innovation outside interbank bond market. Given the context of current low interest rate, the benefits of low-cost financing are more important than investment. Therefore, enterprises have relatively large potential benefits they are able to issue corporate bonds, which might reinforce institutional change. Since enterprise and individuals have limited knowledge about bonds, plus the trading cost and meager demands for bond trading, it requires bond market funds to develope. Driven by the demand of all relevant parties, further institutional innovation of interbank bond market can be expected.

The Bond Market Puzzle[2]

The objective of China's bond market development is to transform the interbank bond market into a uniform OTC bond market.

Since China's accession to the WTO, bond market, as the cornerstone of financial market of a country, has embarked on a journey to join the international bond market. Such a process is faster than other financial markets. In fact, China's bond market has in its development formed a double-market structure consisting of an exchange-based bond market and an OTC bond market based on the interbank bond market. The OTC bond market is the primary model of an international bond market, so it is an inevitable choice for China to adopt OTC bond market. China will eventually build the interbank bond market into a uniform OTC market.

In the early stage of China's OTC bond market, due to occasional external shocks and common demand of market players, the form of interbank bond market is adopted. The benefit of such system is that all players can profit from the institution promptly so that the interbank bond market system can be made possible within a short period of time. Despite the original objective of the new system being achieved, its further development is restricted, which is reflected in the following respects:

First, the interbank bond market is more like a money market than a bond market. Bond repo is the major form of trading made on the market. It serves for credit risk-free financing between banks, benefiting banks' operation, and implementation of monetary policy of the central bank. But bond repo is in nature mainly a type of money market transaction. In fact, spot bond trading is what defines the secondary market of bond, in which financial institutions adjust their balance sheets and price and interest rate are to be discovered. Repo trading is merely a derived product from bond trading. At present, repo trading in the interbank bond market overshadows that of bond trading, showing that the market is essentially a money market rather than a bond market.

Second, the participants of the interbank bond market are mainly financial institutions such as commercial banks, excluding most other investors. China's OTC bond market was formed in 1997 when commercial banks were ordered to withdraw from the exchange bond market so that fund flow to stock market would be cut off. This opportunity facilitated institutional change and enabled China's OTC bond market to take shape in the form of interbank market, in which participants were limited to commercial banks and a small portion of financial institutions, totaling a few hundred in number. Enterprises and individuals who want to purchase bonds could only purchase certificate treasury bond without much varieties or room for bargain. Residents' demand could not be satisfied. Moreover, commercial banks at that time were undertaking reform and still exploring to build the modern corporate governance structure, which means that they are not institutional investors in the real sense; as for institutional and individual investors, the interbank bond market is not yet accessible.

Interbank bond market relies more on government credit than nongovernment credit. From systematical progress of China's bond market, we can tell that in the course of the market-oriented reform, government credit has always been playing a leading role. Among all participating entities, state-owned commercial banks have taken the dominant position and most of the varieties traded in the market are treasury bonds and policy financial bonds based on sovereign credit. These factors have contributed to the stable operation and development of bond market since its establishment, but have also restrained the development of interbank bond market in a fundamental way. Therefore, to transform the interbank bond market into a uniform OTC bond market, we shall be aware of the problems brought by overdependence upon government credit and have it balanced against nongovernment credit to prepare for the next step of market reform.

The three problems above lead to two deficiencies in the current interbank bond market:

The first deficiency is poor liquidity in the market.

Liquidity of bond market is mainly reflected by the trading volume of spot bonds. Interbank bond market has relatively large quantity of bond repo, while outright bond trading is relatively small, resulting in poor liquidity in the market. Although bonds in the market approximate to RMB2 trillion, it is far from sufficient for financial institutions such as commercial banks to adjust their balance sheets through the market. Therefore, demand of bonds exceeds supply in both the primary and secondary markets, which are manifested from the reluctance of investors to sell out their bond holdings. As a result, investors have to pay more to purchase bonds.

The primary reason behind the poor liquidity in the interbank bond market is that the most important market players are banks, which are more likely to hold bond to maturity instead of engaging in proprietary trading. This is also one of the main reasons why Asian bond markets are commonly marked with poor liquidity. Banks shall be active players in the bond market. In bond markets of developed countries, a substantial amount of trades made by banks is to trade on behalf of clients, so that the advantages of large banks are given full play. At present, the participants of China's interbank bond market are only 600-plus financial institutions, without sufficient volatility and responsive price-forming mechanism, leading to inactive transactions in the market. In addition, the immature market maker system is one of the important reasons for the poor liquidity. Market maker system and OTC bond market are of the same nature. Without a mature market maker system, investors have to negotiate with a large number of potential counterparties before making a single deal, making it costly to trade and therefore the liquidity would fall. Furthermore, interbank bond market relies heavily upon government credit since state-owned banks make the majority of the market. As they are far from market-oriented, banks have little incentive to trade actively.

Poor liquidity in the market results in discontinuity in market prices. As a result, financial institutions cannot take market prices as the benchmark in bookkeeping profits and losses of holding bonds. Instead, they calculate P/L on the basis of the purchase price, so that financial institutions would suffer no loss as long as they hold bonds to maturity. This will definitely reduce the number of trades in the market and make market prices less indicative of supply and demand.

Liquidity problem of the interbank bond market, which is the result of monotonicity of trading parties, exists in exchange-based bond market as well. In practice, it is a problem for all China's bond markets. The rapid development of China's bond market in recent years was attributed largely to the falling interest rates, and most of tradable bonds are in the hand of banks and securities companies. These institutions usually share similar expectations of the move of interest rate. Therefore, once financial institutions anticipate a rebound of interest rate, they will try to sell off bonds and poor liquidity may haunt the secondary market bond.

The second major deficiency is that the yield curve of bond is not typical.

Since 1998, the trading volume of exchange bond market has kept declining. The bond trading volume of Shanghai Stock Exchange declined from RMB604.7 billion in 1998 to RMB365.7 billion in 2000, while the repo trading amount dropped from RMB1,518.9 billion in 1998 to RMB1,314.7 billion in 2000. In 2001, the Ministry of Finance increased the amount of bonds issued in Shanghai Stock Exchange to RMB96 billion for the whole year, and the bond outstanding has doubled. However, the trading volume of bond and repo stayed at the same level as in year of 2000, while the turnover plunged by around 50 percent. In the meantime, exchange bond market saw more severe price volatility than the interbank bond market. So for institutional investors, holding exchange bonds may lead to liquidity problems. Exchange-based bond market found it difficult to attract more and larger-sized institutional investors.

The exchange-based bond market shares the same trading system and trading venues with the stock market, so it is more closely connected with stocks. Such close connection is reflected on not only the fact that bond prices are prone to the volatility of stock price but also the trading parties in the stock market. Investors have to go via securities companies that have seats in stock exchanges for bond trading. As a result, trading parties in the exchange bond market are similar to stock investors, and in general residents without any stock investment will hardly participate in exchange-based bond trading through securities companies. Thus, trading parties in exchange-based bond market will be limited and exclude residents. (It shall also be noted that with the development of stock market and increase of branches of securities companies, investors participating in exchange-based bond market may increase with that of stock investors to a certain extent. Exchange-based bond market has certain potential to bring in more trading parties and trading instruments. As for market demands, it takes time for interbank bond market to be developed into a uniform OTC market. Certificate treasury bonds cannot be traded, so a proportion of investors of the whole society may still need the exchange-based bond market to satisfy their demand of bonds. As a developing country, China may keep the exchange-based bond market as a component of its bond market for a long period.)

Since the exchange-based bond market is closely connected to the stock market, the repo interest rate and bond price are under the strong influence of stock price and the yield curve doesn't contain independent information of the bond market. The interbank bond market is much less influenced by the stock market, but the interbank market consists of only a small portion of the total investor base, thus the repo rate and bond price in the market cannot represent the market expectation of enterprise and residents (see Figure 2.1).

Banks are a special type of institution, with deposit being their liabilities and required reserves being their assets. Banks shall take borrowing cost and yield of holding required reserves into consideration when estimating bond yields. While for residents, deposits are their assets, the return of which is taken into their consideration. Hence, estimates made by banks are different from those of the nonbank public. In developed countries, after the liberalization of interest rates, interest rates of deposits and loans are influenced by those of money market and bond market, and medium- and long-term interest rates of deposits and loans are determined by banks with reference to the yield of bonds. On the contrary, given incomplete liberalizaiton of interest rates in China, the yield of bonds in interbank bond market is determined by the interest rates of deposits and loans in banks to a great extent, thus it is less representative. Moreover, banks are sensitive to short-term interest rates and their estimates on medium- and long-term interest rates may be subject to fluctuation of short-term interest rates. In particular, given a insufficient number of instruments in bond market and

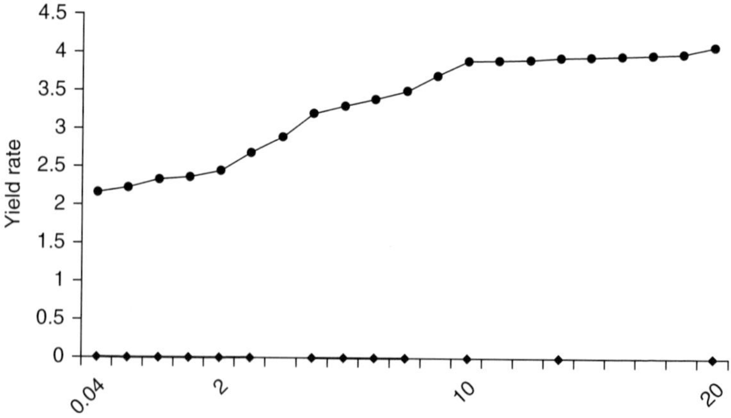

Figure 2.1 Yield curve of the interbank bond market (BENCHMARK NOV. 09, 2001) (%).

Source: Report on Analysis Concerning Macro- Economy, Finance and Bond Market of This Year, R&D Department of China CentralDepository & Clearing Co.Ltd.

immature market operation of commercial banks in China, banks tend to reflect expectation of short-term interest rates and pressure of excessive liquidity on the yield of long-term and ultra-long-term bonds, leading to a flat bond yield curve of China's interbank bond market, which is different from the steep ones of developed countries.

As a result, for the purpose of adapting to OTC bond market that covers the whole society, interbank bond market shall make changes in three aspects: the first is to change from the interbank market between financial institutions into an open market to include all investors; the second is to change from the market based on repo trading into a market based on spot bond trading; the third is to change from the market based on treasury bonds into a market of treasury bonds and corporate bonds based upon both government credit and nongovernment credit.

Terminology

Interbank Bond Market: China's Over-the-Counter Bond Market established by the People's Bank of China. Early members were commercial banks, and current members consist of all types of financial institutions, with such trading varieties as treasury bonds and financial bonds of policy banks.

Over-the-Counter Bond Market ("OTC Bond Market"): the bond market without regular trading floors. The trading is directly carried out between traders and entrusting clients via telephone or computer network, without going through stock exchanges, on the basis of price-driven mechanism.

Exchange-based Bond Market: the bond market, the trading in which is conducted through stock exchanges where investors close their deals under order-driven mechanism.

Bond repo Trading: the trading in which a seller of certain security consents to repurchase such security at an agreed price on an agreed date in the future.

Certificate treasury bonds: the registered treasury bonds issued by the Ministry of Finance and sold by commercial banks, which cannot be traded or transferred in the market.

Book-entry Treasury Bonds: the registered treasury bonds issued by the Ministry of Finance under the custody of the bond depository company, which can be traded and transferred in the market.

Bond Yield and Yield Curve: Bond yield, also known as yield to maturity (YTM), is the annual interest rate enabling the present value of future cash flow of bonds to be equal to its market value. Yield curve is the curve that is arranged in temporal sequence on the basis of the yields of bonds, usually treasury bonds, with different maturities at a given point in time.

Counter Trading System: the system where commercial banks trade bonds with investors at bank counters.

Benchmark Interest Rate: refers to the interest rate acting as the benchmark to other interest rates within the interest rate system; and usually, the short-term benchmark interest rate is the interbank lending and bond repo rates and the medium- and long-term benchmark interest rate is the medium- and long-term yields of treasury bonds.

Market Maker: institutions that are willing to, at a certain time, purchase a security at a price and sell out the same amount of the same security at another price, thus realizing the balance of market supply and demand as well as continuous trading.

Convertible Bond: the debt instruments with fixed interest rates, the holder of which is entitled to exchange the bonds and all the remaining interests with the issuer for common shares or other debt instruments of a certain quantity at a date and price as prior agreed.

T-bond Futures: the futures contracts based on the nominal mid- and long-term treasury bonds, in which the buyer and the seller agree to conduct reverse purchase and sale of treasury bonds at a particular date in the future, with transmission of guarantee funds by the two parties on a percentage basis.

Evolution of China's Bond Market[3]

China's bond market in a modern sense started from the resumption of the issuance of treasury bonds in 1981 and has made great achievements after twenty years' development, especially after 1997. In the current national bond market, the bond outstanding is valued at more than RMB2 trillion, and the average daily trading volume exceeds RMB20 billion; a great number of institutions and individuals flood into the bond market for profit. The bond market has left the stock market behind, whether in respect of quantity and trading volume of trading instruments or the types and quantity of investors. The imbalanced pattern of China's financial market, which placed much weight on the stock market but overlooked the bond market in the past, has experienced fundamental changes. However, given the national economic development and China's entry to WTO, China's bond market still has a long way to go. It is time to promote bond market development based on the foundation laid and bring the market into a new phase.

The bond market is marked with bulk transactions of institutional investors seeking fixed income from the market. Based on the practice of the bond market in developed countries and emerging economies, OTC bond trading is the mainstream model of the bond market, and it is widely preferred by general investors. The United States and Japan, the two treasury bond market giants in the world, have 99 percent of the trading in terms of value done in their OTC market, and nearly all federal government bonds, federal institutional bonds and most corporate bonds are traded in the OTC market. Currently, the US Securities and Exchange Commission is considering to end all the bond trading in the exchanges. In emerging economies in Eastern Europe and other places, bond trading is mainly conducted in the OTC market. China's bond market has gone through three stages: (i) immature OTC market as represented by the physical bond counter market, (ii) floor trading-dominated transaction as represented by Shanghai Stock Exchange, and (iii) mature OTC market as represented by the interbank bond market.

The Period of Physical Bond Counter Market (1988–1993)

Since China resumed treasury bond issues in 1981, the bond market hasn't been substantiated for as long as seven years, in which the treasury bonds was not traded in the bond market. The real start of bond market dated back to 1988 when the Ministry of Finance carried out pilot projects for treasury bond circulation and transfer in 61 cities. It marked the formal beginning of and China's secondary bond market.

In December 1990, the Shanghai Stock Exchange was established to provide custody for physical bonds, and then the physical bonds were changed into book-entry bonds for trading, so that floor trading and OTC trading coexisted. However, the trading volume at the Exchange had long been small before 1994. In the bond market at that time, no uniform custody institution was responsible for the physical bonds, and such physical bonds were managed by custody agencies separately. In this case, trading may only be conducted at the place where the custody agencies are located, and no cross-regional trading was possible.

The OTC trading of physical bonds are fundamentally different from the OTC bond market in a modern sense, because the market has no uniform electronic custody system.

Especially after 1994, it was common for institutions to overissue and short sell treasury bonds, which has posed a great risk to the market. The OTC treasury certificate market was shut down because the service agencies of regional government financial departments, trust companies and securities companies issued faked treasury certificates. Some regional treasury bond repo markets, as represented by the Wuhan Securities Trading Center, were haunted by the problems of false treasury bond. Moreover, many people financed their investment in the stock and real estate market through bond repo. Finally, the regional markets were closed in 1995.

Although the OTC paper bond market failed for many reasons, the lack of book-entry bonds is critical to its failure. The paper bonds can't be traded across different regions and therefore the custody system was highly decentralized and the paper bonds were difficult to verify. It is proved empirically that no matter what form of bond trading is adopted, book-entry bonds and centralized custody system are always necessary.

The Period Dominated by Exchange-Based Bond Market (1994–1996)

In 1994, the Ministry of Finance issued treasury bonds valued at RMB102.8 billion, doubling that of last year, which facilitated the active bond trading on the exchanges. More importantly, the exchanges began treasury bond futures trading that year, because bond trading in the exchange-based bond market had started to expand significantly. Active trading lasted until May 1995, and thereafter the treasury bond futures market was closed and the trading volume suddenly shrank.

At that time, the Ministry of Finance and the market regulatory departments attributed the problems to the OTC market and considered book-entry bond should be exclusively traded in the exchanges. In August 1995, the government officially called to stop all OTC bond markets, and the stock exchanges became the only legitimate bond market in China (see Table 2.1).

In 1995, the Ministry of Finance made an attempt to issue book-entry treasury bonds valued at RMB11.7 billion. But in 1996, it started to issue a large amount of treasury bonds in Shanghai Stock Exchange and Shenzhen Stock Exchange. In the same year, the two stock exchanges issued book-entry treasury bonds valued at RMB111.67 billion six times, accounting for 52.5 percent of the treasury bonds issues that year. Meanwhile, the trading volume in the secondary market had rapidly increased. The bond turnover of the two stock exchanges in 1996 recorded a growth nearly ten times of that in 1995, among which Shanghai Stock Exchange accounted for more than 95 percent of the total turnover. Besides, with the development of bond repo trading, an exchange-based bond market system had taken shape (see Table 2.3).

Table 2.3 Trading of treasury bonds in Shanghai stock exchange and Shenzhen stock exchange

SHSE	*1992*	*1993*	*1994*	*1995*	*1996*	*1997*	*1998*	*1999*	*2000*
Treasury bond	7.13	87.13	19,574.6	51,627.6	17,401.5	15,380.6	21,235.2	17,400.9	16,804.3
Cash bond	7.13	61.02	457.27	764.44	4962.38	3,468.4	6,046.7	5,276.77	3,657.05
Repo		0.42	63.15	1,171.6	12,439.2	11,912.2	15,188.5	12,124.1	13,147.2
Futures		25.72	19,054.2	49,691.6	0	0	0	0	
Corporate bonds	0.12	0.08	0.02	0.61	1.16	15.5	31.32	45.84	
Financial bond	0.52	0.04	0.01	0	0	0	0	0	
SZSE	1992	1993	1994	1995	1996	1997	1998	1999	2000
Treasury bond			336.67	7,732.38	636.35	1,078.25	365.55	790.5	2,086.88
Cash bond			11.1	10.76	66.87	114.35	13.25	24.09	500.43
Repo			12.63	76.92	569.48	963.91	352.3	766.41	1,586.45
Futures			312.94	7,644.7	0	0	0	0	
Corporate bonds		24.36	9.95	7	0.3	2.58	29.67	46.88	
Financial bond		0	0	0	0	0	0	0	

Source: China Securities and Futures Statistical Yearbook (1996–2000), www.csrc.gov.cn

The exchange-based market emerged and dominated because it was aligned with the interests of relevant market participants, which is reflected in the following respects:

Price volatility allowed institutional investors to harvest spread return. The exchange adopted the trading mechanism of order-matching, which caused a relatively large fluctuation of price. Since the number of institutional investors is relatively small, the order-matching mechanism failed to accommodate bulk trading. Any bulk transaction would have a huge impact upon the market price. The annual volatility of the bond price of Shanghai Stock Exchange in 2000 exceeded 6 percent, while those in developed countries are generally around 1.8 percent. The strong market volatility attracts too many speculators, which in turn intensifies market fluctuation. When a few bulk transactions were able to influence the market price significantly, speculations were widely seen.

The repo market allows all financial institutions to share the return of the stock market. There always exists a relatively large spread return between China's primary and secondary stock markets, and the return of purchasing IPO stocks is much higher than the average social profit ratio and with lower risk. Therefore it is attractive to all investors to profit from the spread. However, the policies require that only securities institutions may purchase IPO shares; therefore, investors reached a consensus that the securities companies would purchase IPO shares with financing from other financial institutions so that the returns are shared by all parties. The bond repo market became the platform on which the securities company got financed. Hence, that is exactly the reason why the exchange bond repo market will show a large volatility on stock market IPOs.

The liquidity maintained by the small- and medium-sized investors basically satisfy the demand of the market. Although there are some institutional investors including brokers in the exchange bond market, due to its small scale of assets and that the State Council requested commercial banks to sell to the general public all the treasury bonds they held in 1996, small- and medium-sized investors have become the major players on the exchange bond market. Due to their frequent and small amount of trading, an efficiently competitive price is formed, and this makes up the deficiency that the bond price is easily convergent and enables the exchange bond market to have a high liquidity and can basically satisfy the demand of the market.

There is no large demand for OTC market due to the small scale of treasury bonds. The treasury bond market scale is too small to reflect the lack of bulk transactions in the exchange-based bond market.

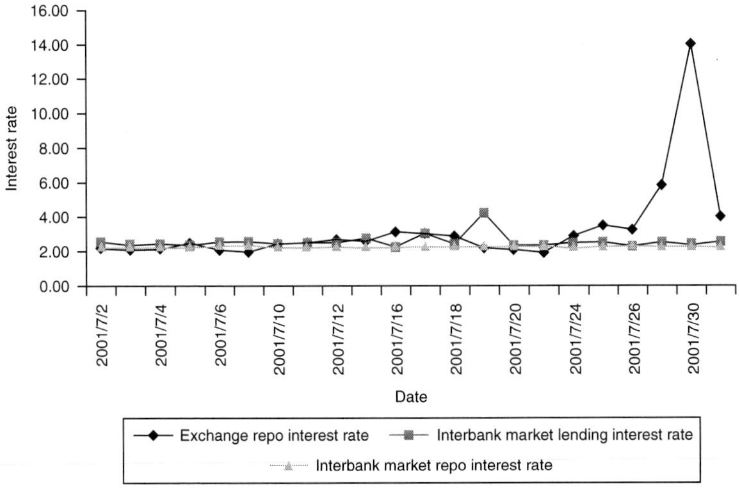

Figure 2.2 Comparison of seven days repo interest rate between exchange and interbank market (%).

Source: China Foreign Exchange Trading System.

To sum up, exchanges dominated China's bond market from 1994 to 1997. And we have to admit that the exchange bond market is a success under the specific historical conditions. However, the exchange bond market is defective inherently because of its small liquidity. Due to the fact that the exchange adopts the automatic order-matching system, it cannot naturally guarantee that the trading demands of the buyer and the seller can be matched at any time. Accordingly, purchase and sale of a large amount of securities at the exchange will cause large price fluctuation, which gives rise to the inability of institutional investors to manage the cost of trading and therefore it is difficult for them to make an accurate evaluation of the market. This limit excluded some of the institutional investors, and the yield curve so formed will be impossible to become the benchmark interest rate (see Figure 2.2).

Emergence of the Interbank OTC Trading Market (1997)

In 1997, driven by the financial system reform and occasional external shocks, China's OTC bond market emerged in the form of the interbank bond market, grasped a historical opportunity, and made rapid development.

The OTC bond market was established mainly based on three considerations: (i) the central bank needed to transition from the direct monetary policies to the indirect monetary policies. The lack of OTC bond market limited the establishment of the indirect monetary policy regime. The open market operations of the central bank has to rely on the OTC bond market of a large scale and good liquidity; in 1996, the PBC started to conduct open market operations for bonds, but due to the lack of support to China's OTC bond market, such operations were stagnated in early 1997. (ii) The government implemented proactive fiscal policies. Large-scale bond issuance needed an OTC bond market dominated by institutional investors. (iii) Commercial banks had to obtain interbank financing via the bond repo market and increase the percentage of bond assets to improve their asset structure.

In addition to the need to break down the old system, an opportunity to do so was also critical. In the first half of 1997, a large amount of bank funds flowed into the stock market, financed by the exchange-based bond repo, which caused the overheating of stock market. Under the arrangement of the State Council, the PBC ordered all commercial banks to withdraw from the bond markets of the Shanghai Stock Exchange and Shenzhen Stock Exchange and switch to the interbank bond market.

The PBC required that all commercial banks may only use the treasury bonds, central bank notes, and policy financial bonds under the custody of China Central Depository & Clearing Co., Ltd. for bond repo and spot bond trading. At the early stage of the interbank bond market, there were only 16 head offices of commercial banks as its members, but it was an important start to show that a large scale OTC bond market was emerging.

In accordance with the experience of developed countries, the unit trading cost in the OTC bond market is merely one-tenth of that of exchange, and this facilitates various investors to participate in the OTC bond market. China's OTC bond market, which appears in the form of the interbank bond market, has limited its membership base to banks from the very start, which makes the type and quantity of the trading parties in the OTC bond market fewer than those of the exchange-based bond market. Therefore, it cannot cover all bond investors of the society and greatly limits its functions.

However, it should be particularly pointed out that, with the emergence of the interbank bond market, China's bond market has broken into the interbank bond market and the exchange-based bond market; and worse than that, the two markets developed separately, and it was increasingly difficult to combine those two markets.

Start from Interbank Financing (1997–1998)

During this time, the interbank bond market helped solve the problem of interbank financing. In the second half of 1997, the PBC ceased the lending business of the financing centersand started to solve the overdue lending problems. At the same time, the PBC started to greatly expand the membership of the interbank bond market and facilitate commercial banks to shift to bond repo for financing.

In May 1998, the open market operations of the PBC continued, and injection of base money via bond purchase and reverse repo was made to provide liquidity support for commercial banks, which immediately vitalized the trading in the interbank bond market.

In 1998, the interbank bond market had not yet become the major place for issuance of treasury bonds, but showed gratifying momentum. The Ministry of Finance issued bonds valued at RMB463.6 billion in the interbank bond market, including RMB270 billion of special treasury bonds for state-owned bank capital supplement, RMB42.3 billion of dedicated treasury bonds to sterilize the liquidity brought by reserve ratio cut, RMB100 billion of construction treasury bonds, and RMB51.3 billion of treasury bonds. Certificate treasury bonds still dominated the market this year.

In September 1998, the China Development Bank conducted its first market-oriented issuance of financial bonds by means of public tender via the interbank bond issuance system, and thereafter the Export-Import Bank of China also commenced to issue bonds in a market-oriented manner. In 1998, these two banks issued bonds totally valued at RMB41 billion. By the end of 1998, the value of the bonds issued by the Ministry of Finance, and policy banks in the interbank bonk market reached RMB1,010.3 billion, doubling that of the last year (see Figure 2.3 and Table 2.4).

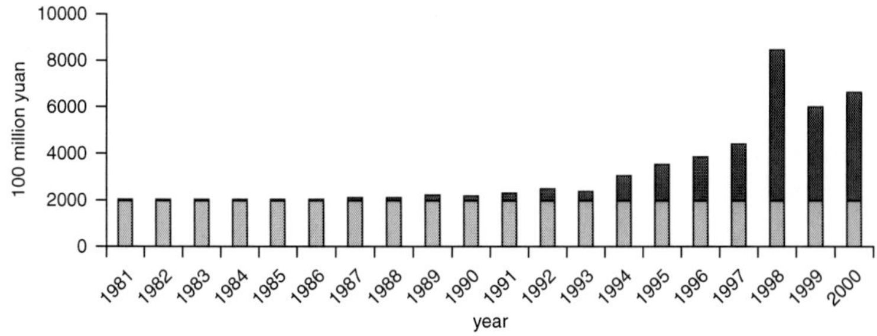

Figure 2.3 Issuance volume of China treasury bond (1981–2000).

Source: China Central Depository & Clearing Co., Ltd.

Table 2.4 Issuance and trading in the interbank bond market

Year	*Members*	*Business days*	*Treasury bond issuance*		*Policy financial bond issuance*		*Total trade*	
			Issue	*Quantity*	*Issue*	*Quantity*	*Number*	*Closing volume*
1997	31	128					276	476.66
1998	118	252	1	90	7	410	2,181	2,082.51
1999	428	258	11	2,100	19	1,670	7,198	7,805.58
2000	650	251	10	2,259.5	17	1,645	29,611	31,696.35

	Cash bond		*Initial payment of*		*Maturity of Repo*			
Year	*Number*	*Closing volume*	*Number*	*Closing volume*	*Number*	*Closing volume*	*Average interest rate (%)*	*Turnover rate (%)*
1997	10	8.7	165	298.51	101	178.15		13.59
1998	41	30.72	1105	1,009.55	1,035	1,042.24	5.69	14.19
1999	107	98.37	3587	3,949.08	3,504	3,758.13	3.07	39.57
2000	915	644.82	14,545	15,676.87	14,151	15,374.66	2.37	215.88

Source: China Central Depository & Clearing Co., Ltd.

Interbank Bond Market Dominated China's Bond Market (1999–2000)

Since 1999, as the scale of interbank bond market expanded, the OTC bond market has gradually played a dominant role in China's bond market.

Interbank bond market has become the primary place for China's bond issuance; in 1999, the Ministry of Finance and policy banks issued treasury bonds and policy financial bonds in the interbank bond market valued at RMB442.6 billion, accounting for 74 percent of the total issuance of bonds of that year in China. In 2000, the Ministry of Finance and policy banks again issued bonds valued at RMB390.4 billion in the interbank bond market, accounting for 62 percent of the total issuance of bonds in China of that year.

In October 1998, the PBC granted insurance companies access to the market; at the beginning of 1999, 325 urban and rural credit cooperatives became members of the interbank bond market; in September 1999, some securities companies and all securities investment funds started to trade in the interbank bond market; and in September 2000, the PBC permitted financial companies to enter the interbank bond market. By the end of 2000, 693 financial institutions became members of the interbank bond market as representative of China's wholesale bond market, which basically covered China's financial system.

In 1999, the turnover of bond repo in the interbank bond market rapidly increased. By August 2000, after the central bank started two-way operations in the open market, the daily trading volume of the interbank bond market stayed at around RMB20 billion, which is far beyond that of the exchange-based bond market (see Table 2.4). Innovation of the trading system enables the realization of large amount of bond trading, which greatly motivated banks to hold bonds. This not only reduces the bond issuance cost, expands the capacity of the market, and supports the implementation of China's positive fiscal policy but also meets the demand of commercial banks to improve their asset structure. Among the assets of commercial banks, the percentage of bonds surged from 5 percent at the end of 1997 to 17 percent at the end of 2001; the balance sheet of commercial banks that used to be dominated by loans had been diversified.

The rapid and steady development of the interbank bond market has provided a foundation for open market operations of the central bank and allowed it to become the major measures for the central bank to realize monetary policy and had also laid a foundation for the government to promote the interest rate liberalization.

Suggestions on the Development of China's Bond Market[4]

China's bond market in the future shall be an open market covering all investors, dominated by OTC bond market and supplemented by the exchange-based bond market. It must embrace the following five elements:

First, an integrated bond custody and clearing system. It consists of a central custody and clearing system and a custody and clearing system for smaller financial institutions. The former is responsible for the custody and clearing for financial institutions and other major investors; the latter provides custody and clearing services to small- and medium-sized investors. The bonds of exchanges are deposited in the central custody system on a uniform basis and trading is conducted via the trading systems of exchanges. The advantage of OTC bond market lies in diversification and low cost; however, a custody system for financial institutions that is available to all small- and medium-sized investors in the society needs to be established so that the trading will be mainly conducted by institutions where the bonds are deposited as it is convenient for clearing. The crux of the bond custody system is safety, which requires the formulation of specific laws that prevent the custodian from embezzlement of clients' bonds;

Second, the coexistence of OTC market and exchange market. The coexistence will continue for quite a long time in China. The custody should be unified, but it is undesirable for the trading methods to be unified, which means that under the precondition of a unified custody and settlement system, investors may choose freely between the OTC transaction or the exchange transaction;

Third, a unified issuance market. According to the international practice, treasury bonds will be issued by the central bank by means of auction, while corporate bonds will mainly be issued by means of underwriting. Regardless of the means of issuance, it will be available to all investors. The bonds will be under unified custody by the China Central Depository & Clearing Co., Ltd. after issuance, and investors may freely choose the market to trade on;

Fourth, a market accessible to all investors, including banks, insurance companies, social insurance funds, bond funds, and other institutional investors, as well as enterprises, individuals, and other noninstitutional investors. Among which, the establishment and cultivation of bond investment fund and money market fund are very important; and

Fifth, diversified financial instruments, including treasury bonds, financial bonds, and corporate bonds. The corporate bonds should become the major type of bonds traded on China's bond market.

In this section, I put forth the following systemic suggestions.

Suggestion I Facilitate the Development of Bond Investment Fund

The bond fund should be the core channel for nonfinancial enterprises and individuals to enter the bond market.

The advantages of OTC bond market are represented by its decentralized trading form and lower cost; the participants of the interbank bond market must therefore be extended to all financial institutions, nonfinancial enterprises, individual residents, and nonresidents to the extent that all investors that wish to make bond investment may participate in the interbank bond market.

The "OTC bond market" means that all investors of the society may use any means that is appropriate to them to purchase, sell, and trade bonds in the OTC bond market. To do this, designing a channel for nonfinancial enterprises and individuals to enter the bond market is the crux; at present, the bond fund would be a good choice.

China is a country with high savings rate. The savings rate in a broad sense has been over 35 percent for many years, among the highest level in the world. By contrast, the savings rate of the United States and Japan are 10 percent and 33 percent, respectively. As of the end of June 2001, the household saving deposits have aggregated to RMB7 trillion. This bulk saving deposits needs to be transformed into other forms of financial assets, and bond as a form of asset is safe with stable return and can be used to improve the structure of personal financial assets. However, for individual investors, the calculation of bond yield and picking from the various types of bonds are very difficult, and the knowledge acquisition cost is relatively high. In developed countries, the major method for individuals to invest in bonds is to purchase shares of bond fund, and the fund will invest in the OTC market. And individual investors are rarely seen in the bond market; the percentage of personal direct bond holding in developed countries such as US is ussually no more than 10 percent(see Table 2.5).

Different from developed countries, residents in China are more used to purchasing bonds directly. In recent years, despite the rapid development of the interbank bond market and the exchange market, the certificate treasury bond held by individuals still played an important role, and the percentage of certificate treasury bond in the quantity of issued treasury bonds in 2000 still reached as much as 40.78 percent. However, as residents' financial assets expand, the simple "holding to maturity" strategy, and the few types of certificate bonds cannot satisfy the needs of residents for financial management; but the custodian bond fund for trading may require professional investment service and also economies of scale. The economy of scale

Table 2.5 US treasury bond holding structure (Unit: USD1billion)

Year	*Individuals*	*Commercial banks*	*Insurance companies*	*Money market fund*	*Enterprises*	*State and local government*	*Foreign holders*	*Others*
1991	263.9	232.5	181.8	80	150.8	485.1	491.7	677.4
Percentage (%)	10	9	7	3	6	19	19	26
1992	289.2	294.4	197.5	79.7	192.5	476.7	549.7	760.2
Percentage (%)	10	10	7	3	7	17	19	27
1993	309.9	322.2	234.5	80.8	213	508.9	622.6	755.8
Percentage (%)	10	11	8	3	7	17	20	25
1994	333	296.4	256.8	67.6	230.2	540.2	688.1	785.5
Percentage (%)	10	9	8	2	7	17	22	25
1995	347.7	278.7	241.5	71.5	228.8	421.5	862.2	843
Percentage (%)	11	8	7	2	7	13	26	26
1996	356.6	261.7	235.9	91.6	258.5	358	1,131.8	717.1
	33%	10%	8%	7%	3%	8%	10%	21%

Source: Xiao Yu, China's Bond Market Development, Comparison and Foresight, China Social Sciences Press, 1999.

is reflected in two respects: first, large funds are able to enjoy the benefits of cost saving from bulk transactions with institutions in the OTC bond market; second, due to the expertise required in bond trading, bond investment may incur know-how acquisition cost, which, however, can be reduced after the expansion of scale in terms of reducing unit fund cost. Thus the bond fund can become a major channel for individuals to enter the OTC bond market.

Due to Chinese residents' tradition of "holding to maturity," individual investors will be playing an important role for a certain period; however, bond is a financial investment instrument that is appropriate for large-scale and long-term investors. We may continuously encourage the participation of retail investors, but a growing number of long-term investors are required to be in place. The bond fund is a good way to transform individual bonds into an institutional investment, with the establishment and operation of a bond fund, the proportion of individual investment in the total investment on bonds will gradually decrease, which gives rise to a more reasonable structure of institutions and individual investors in the bond market.

The bond fund is featured with safety and strong liquidity. The investors may purchase and redeem a bond fund from time to time and obtain a higher return than the interests of banks, therefore it is called as "temporary parking lot for funds" in overseas countries. Modern enterprises will invest in the bond fund for cash management and may also obtain some profits on the basis of fund safety. In this regard, enterprises mainly and indirectly enter the OTC bond market through the channel of the bond fund.

Enterprises and individuals investing in the bond fund will obtain stable returns with lower risk. According to the statistics of MORNINGSTAR in the United States, in the yield analysis of 899 bond funds, the long-term (10Y) annual yield averages at 6.68 percent, while in the volatility analysis for 3,539 bond funds, the average standard deviation is 4.4, which indicates a considerably low risk.

Meanwhile, establishing bond fund is conducive to attracting funds into the bond market, increasing the issue amount of different bonds, and stimulating the development of the bond market. Professional management of funds is also conducive to enhancing the liquidity of the bond market and establishing the benchmark interest rate of the bond market.

In addition to bond fund, social security fund may become another major investor in the bond market. In fact, compared with other funds, social security fund is characterized as having a high requirement for stability, with a long lock-up period and being able to make long-term investment; therefore, bonds that come with relatively low risk and relatively stable yield are its best investment vehicle. Taking Chile as an example of a developing country with successful reform of its pension system; the bonds (including government bonds, financial bonds, corporate bonds, etc.) held by pension insurance fund management companies still account for about 50 percent of the total amount of the fund. Most countries set a minimum level of bond investment for the social security fund; for example, France requires that 50 percent of the assets of its supplementary pension fund must be invested in government bonds; and in Denmark, the pension fund must hold domestic bonds at a value equivalent to no less than 60 percent of its funds, and Latin countries also set the pension's investment on bonds to a percentage of no less than 50 percent.

In China, the social security fund has just started to make financial investment. Even if 60 percent of assets of the social security fund is put into the bond market, the total amount is merely RMB54 billion. However, things will be greatly changed in 2002. With the upcoming sale of state-owned shares of listed companies, the assets of social security fund will greatly expand and may therefore grow up to be an important force in China's bond market.

Suggestion II Launch Bank OTC System

The direct purchase of the treasury bonds by enterprises and individuals may be realized by the bank OTC system.

In addition to making investment on bonds with bond investment fund, the direct purchase of treasury bonds by enterprises and individuals will mainly be realized through the OTC trading system of banks.

At the end of 2001, there are only 703 financial institutions in the interbank bond market (see Figure 2.4). It was impossible for nonmember institutional investors to invest in the interbank bond market before 2002. However, this situation will soon be changed fundamentally. On January 31, 2002, the PBC issued the Order of the PBC [2002] No. 2 to release the *Administration Rules on the Book-entry Treasury Bonds Trading over the Counter of Commercial Banks*, which marked the official launch of the OTC trading system for bonds. From now on, all nonmember investment institutions and resident individuals may purchase and sell bonds listed in the interbank bond market through the OTC bond trading system of banks. Member banks may quote the price for sales and purchases at their counters, and sell the outstanding bonds it held to resident individuals; in this way, the types and number of bonds that may be invested in by residents will be greatly increased. Member banks may provide bond transfer and fund settlement service to their OTC clients through their own bond agency settlement system so that investors may conveniently invest in the interbank bond market at low cost.

As a result, the room for the OTC bond trading market in China will be greatly expanded, especially that the bond trading volume is likely to grow by folds, which will further and fully improve the market efficiency.

Before 2002, most nonfinancial enterprises and resident individuals could invest in certificate treasury bonds(see Figure 2.5). Due to the fact that this kind of treasury bonds cannot be circulated, the nominal interest rate will generally be higher than the book-entry treasury bonds for the same period. That is to say, the treasury must pay extra cost to issue certificate treasury

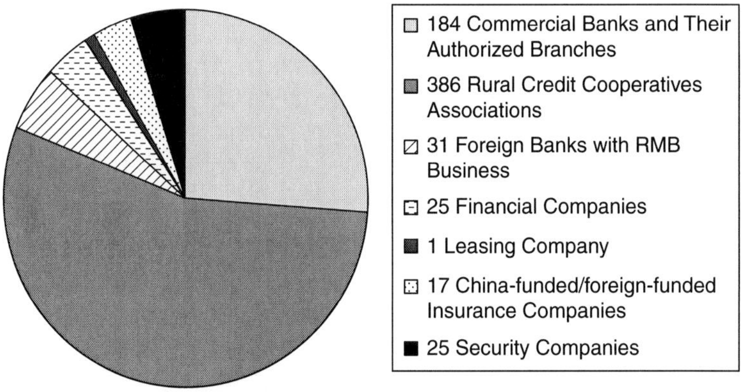

Figure 2.4 Structure of participants in interbank bond market.
Source: China Foreign Exchange Trading System (www.Chinabond.com.cn).

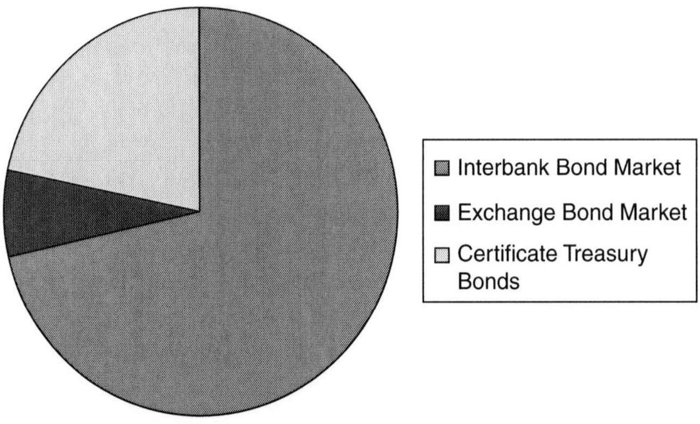

Figure 2.5 Structure of China's bond market.
Source: China Central Depository & Clearing Co., Ltd. (www.Chinabond.com.cn)

bonds. But the official launch of the bond settlement agency business system and OTC bond trading system will certainly change this situation. Since most nonfinancial enterprises and resident individuals may purchase or sell book-entry treasury bonds on the bond trading counters of member banks, therefore, it will not be necessary for the Ministry of Finance to issue certificate treasury bonds; instead, the Ministry of Finance may convert the quota of certificate treasury bonds into book-entry treasury bonds. This will not only reduce the issuance cost for treasury bonds but also greatly expand the scale of interbank bond market and exchange-based bond market, which will further satisfy the needs for market development to a greater extent.

It is estimated that, as the major purpose for residents trading bonds at bank counters is to cash in, the demand for such trading might not be too great at the beginning of 2002. Therefore, in 2002 when the bank OTC system was started, there were worries that the trading volume and activeness of trading might be very limited.

Suggestion III Include Corporate Bonds into the OTC Bond Market

Corporate bonds should be included into the OTC bond market as a trading vehicle. Banks and other institutional investors should be encouraged to hold corporate bonds, and insurance companies should be allowed to hold corporate bonds. Other matters of the corporate bond market can be solved on that basis.

At the beginning of 2002, Zhou Xiaochuan, the chairman of China Securities Regulatory Commission, said in a public speech that there was still much room for the development of China's capital market, including the corporate bond market. He admitted that the corporate bond market still had a long way to go. Coincidentally, relevant officials and scholars in different fields started to put forth their opinions on developing the corporate bond market recently. Despite the diversity of these opinions, people seem to reach a consensus that China's corporate bond market should be reinforced as soon as possible, and China's nongovernment credit system should be established and improved on that basis.

The issuance of corporate bonds by enterprises is conducive to improving the liability structure of enterprises, expanding the sources of funds for small- and medium-sized enterprises, establishing active financing channels and building up nongovernment credit. Corporate bonds are meaningful for investors as they may help diversify the investment portfolio with different levels of credit, risks, and returns. Different investors will assume different types of risks and obtain different types of returns.

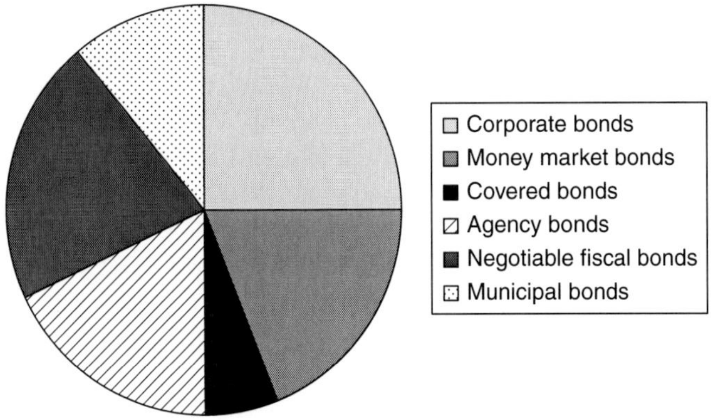

Figure 2.6 Structure of US bond market.
Source: Bloomberg.

In the bond markets of developed countries, corporate bonds account for a considerable percentage (see Figure 2.6). The risk of bonds can be broken into benchmark yield volatility and credit risk premium. Various institutions assume different risks and returns. Fund and other investors taking corporate bonds as their major investment target will set treasury bond yield as the benchmark for performance evaluation and only calculates the spread. The bond market will therefore grow more professional and rich in structure with multilevel investors and trading tools.

In China, the corporate bond market is undeveloped for now. All investors, including insurance companies and commercial banks, are assuming the risk resulting from the volatility of benchmark interest rate, and all are attempting to profit from predicting the change of benchmark interest rate. Yet the overconcentration of price risk intensifies the systemic risk of the whole market and increases the difficulty of bond clearing at the time of volatile interest rate and therefore enhances the liquidity risk. In this sense, the development of corporate bonds may decrease the liquidity risk and price risk of the bond market.

The number of investors and the variety of trading tools are closely associated with each other. Introducing more institutional investors may support the development of treasury bond and corporate bond market, and the expansion of corporate bonds can greatly enrich the trading tools in the market and attract more investors. The treasury bonds, especially short-term treasury bonds, has no credit risk and is therefore frequently used by financial institutions and other investors as a means for liquidity management.

The corporate bond is a typical capital investment tool. The development of corporate bonds is conducive to the transformation of China's bond market from money market to bond market. Without a sound corporate bond market, it is difficult to form an open bond market with expansive participation by investors, and the nature of China's bond market will be hard to change.

In developed countries, the corporate bond outstanding is usually three to ten times that of the stock market capitalization; the stock issuance amount in some countries is even negative; in other words, stocks newly issued are less than stocks delisted from the market, while the issuance volume of corporate bonds becomes larger and even exceeds GNP. For example, in 2000, there were 1,592 listed companies in the securities market of the United States that had issued corporate bonds, and only 199 listed companies had issued stocks. In China, the total capitalization of the securities market in 2000 was more than RMB640 billion, with the capitalization of treasury bonds, stocks, and corporate bonds being respectively RMB480 billion, RMB140 billion, and RMB20 billion. In 2001, the value of treasury bonds newly issued that year exceeded RMB460 billion, and the issuance of policy financial bonds in the nature of "quasi-treasury bond" also exceeded RMB300 billion, while the issuance of corporate bonds was less than RMB17 billion. Thus it can be seen that China's corporate bond market lags far behind developed countries.

The problem is caused by many reasons, including the approval system for issuance, lack of objective, and impartial credit rating agencies, lack of corporate credit, limitation on the interest rate of bonds due to incomplete liberalization, but there are two crucial restraints:

First, the listing and trading of corporate bonds in the exchange market impedes the circulation of corporate bonds. Usually, only bonds with little credit risk and simple property may be traded in the exchange bond market. In the United States, only the bonds of a few corporations may be listed on the exchange for trading, and the trading volume is small; the listing mainly serves for the purpose of price publicity because most of the corporate bonds are traded over the counter. Institutions with knowledge of corporate bonds will become the market makers to maintain the liquidity of the secondary market. At present, China only has ten corporate bonds traded in Shanghai Stock Exchange or Shenzhen Stock Exchange. Most of the corporate bonds do not satisfy the conditions for public listing, and therefore, the daily turnover of corporate bonds that have been listed and traded is less than RMB50 million. The trading is very inactive. The inactiveness of the secondary market will in turn raise the cost for issuing bonds in the primary market, which has restrained the development of corporate bonds.

Second, mature institutional investors are not in place. Among the current purchasers of enterprise bonds, individuals still take a considerable stake, which leads to two consequences: (i) insufficient supply of corporate bonds to another requesting party. Banks and other institutional investors cannot purchase corporate bonds, while enterprises and individuals lack the expertise to evaluate corporate bonds. Under the circumstance of lack of the external restraint from professional institutional investors, it is difficult to regulate the corporate bond market merely by relying on the self-discipline of credit rating companies. And (ii) the lack of banks or other institutional investors gives rise to the difficulty in expanding the scale of corporate bonds. In this case, if we do not expand the scope of institutional investors but continuously promote corporate bonds to individuals, the lack of external restraint from the trading parties will deteriorate, which will eventually increase the risk of corporate bonds. We can see that the rapid development of bond fund and other institutional investors in Taiwan in recent years has created robust demand for corporate bonds, increased the diversified fund-raising channels for enterprises, lowered the cost of issuance, and stimulated the issuing volume of corporate bonds, which shows the significance of the intervention of institutional investors in developing the corporate bond market.

In order to solve these two problems, we should include corporate bonds into the OTC bond market as a trading instrument, simultaneously promote banks and other institutional investors to hold corporate bonds, and lift the limitation on insurance companies' holding of corporate bonds. Institutional investors and OTC market are compatible. Therefore other problems relating to the corporate bond market may be solved on this basis.

First of all, the issuance of corporate bonds may be changed from the approval system to verification system. The existing issuance approval system is to transfer the credit risk to the government, which has distorted the risk assumption mechanism and increased the cost of companies to issue bonds. The reason for this is the worry over the social risk arising out of the problems concerning corporate bonds holdings by individuals. If corporate bonds are mainly held by institutions, the corresponding social risk will become much smaller and the capability of the society of undertaking credit risk of corporate bonds will become stronger.

Second, we should gradually liberalize the issuance interest rate and allow the price to be set by the market. Individual investors have only obtained limited information, which leads to a relatively higher cost, and have inaccurate judgment on interest rate as price takers. In developed countries, even if individual investors participate in treasury bond auction, they would usually participate in noncompetitive bidding, taking the price generated from the bidding of institutional investors; therefore, if we adopt the underwriting method to issue corporate bonds to institutional investors, it will create conditions for the liberalization of issuance interest rate. After the lifting of issuance interest rate, there will be different interest rate levels formed in the primary and secondary markets for corporate bonds with different credit levels and liquidity to reflect different risk premiums and liquidity premiums, and companies with good standing and credit will raise funds at an interest rate lower than the lending rate of banks, which will stimulate financing via bonds.

Third, we should formulate laws and regulations for the administration of credit rating companies and establish China's own objective and impartial credit rating companies. Institutional investors holding corporate bonds will boost the growth of credit rating companies, which is conducive to the establishment of the market status of credit rating companies with good reputation. We should build up the sound cycle of credit rating and development of corporate bonds.

Fourth, we may consider interest tax reduction and exemption to encourage the development of the corporate bond market.

Fifth, we should establish the corporate bond fund that takes corporate bonds as its major investment instruments and make use of the advantages of professional investment to provide a convenient way for investors to participate in corporate bonds.

So far, the conditions for developing the corporate bond market are in place, and if we could make breakthrough in the two basic aspects, China's corporate bond market may take a historic leap.

Suggestion IV Implement Treasury Bond Balance Administration System

As to the development of treasury bonds, growing supply of short-term treasury bonds may provide commercial banks with tools for liquidity management and fills up the gap in the bond yield curve. Since the primary instruments on the bond repo market are ultra-short-term repos with maturities up to seven days and the seven-day repos are traded most, the liquidity of bond repos with maturities over one month is poor; therefore there will be a lack of representation if we use the repo rates to build the yield curve (see Figures 2.7, 2.8, and 2.9). The growth of short-term treasury bonds will also vitalize the money market, enhance the enthusiasm of investors, and provide good tools for open-end funds.

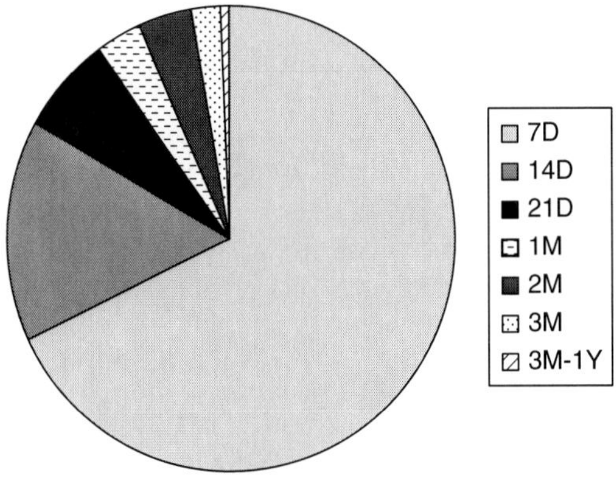

Figure 2.7 Trading volume of instruments with different maturities in the interbank bond market of 2000.

Source: China Foreign Exchange Trading System (www.Chinamoney.com.cn).

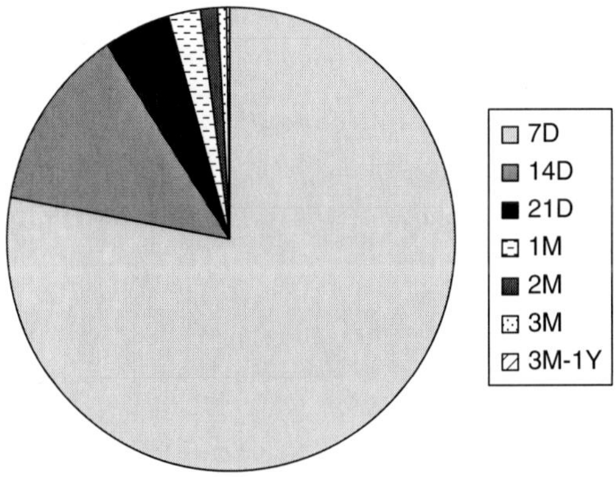

Figure 2.8 Trading volume of instruments with different maturities in the interbank bond market of 2001.

Source: China Foreign Exchange Trading System (www.Chinamoney.com.cn).

If treasury bond balance management is in place, short-term treasury bonds that are issued and repaid within one year will not be included in the treasury bond issue plan, which will provide a greater room for Ministry of Finance's to make rolling issuance of short-term treasury bonds. The issuance mechanism of US short-term treasury bonds by the Federal Reserve, in

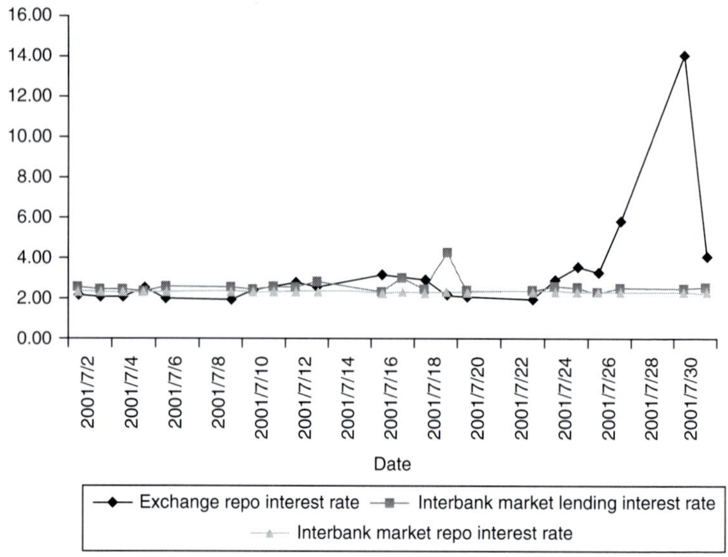

Figure 2.9 Comparison of repo interest rate between exchange and interbank market (%).

Source: China Foreign Exchange Trading System (www.Chinamoney.com.cn).

which public auctions are made for 3M T-bonds and 6M T-bonds at a fixed time each month or week to form reasonable benchmark short-term interest rates, may be taken as a reference.

Since the resumption of treasury bond issuance in 1981, the Chinese government has adopted annual quota management system to control treasury bond issuance. The system requires that annual treasury bond issues shall be determined upon the repayment of principle and interest as well as the fiscal deficits of that year. In other words, the amount of treasury bonds issued each year shall be equal to the amount of repayment of principle and interest of that year plus the fiscal deficits of that year. Once the issue scheme was approved by the National People's Congress, it will become a mandate so that no change is allowed.

Under this management system, the treasury bond policy objective for the Ministry of Finance is relatively dull, that is, merely to make up for the fiscal deficits; so it is difficult to take into account the demand of treasury bonds of the financial system and will obviously undermine the consistency of fiscal policy and monetary policy.

In the market economy, the treasury bond market is the most effective and the only conjunction point of fiscal policy and monetary policy.

Li Yang, director of the Institute of Finance & Banking of the Chinese Academy of Social Sciences, said that since treasury bond market has to generate the benchmark interest rate, to some extent, the financial property of treasury bonds is stronger and more outstanding than its fiscal property.

Take the US treasury bond market as an example. After World War II, due to production resumption and disappearance of the demand for issuing treasury bonds for war, fiscal surpluses emerged. Out of the consideration of prudent fiscal policy, the US government started to repurchase treasury bonds at net amount from the market. However, due to the fact that treasury bonds were assets of the highest liquidity in the provision of assets of financial institutions besides cash and have played an indispensable role, as a result of the shrinking volume of treasury bonds, nearly all financial institutions encountered the problem of liquidity shortage. The central bank was also in trouble, because it could not find any other financial instrument to serve as an instrument for open market operations as safe and efficient as treasury bonds. The efficiency of the US economy was greatly affected due to the unsound operation of the financial market. Thus the Treasury Department of the United States had to make an emergent issuance of treasury bonds.

Judging from China's treasury bond market, except for the 3Y and 5Y bonds that are mainly nonnegotiable certificate treasury bonds sold to the general public, the 3M, 6M, 1Y, 2Y, and 3Y book-entry treasury bonds are absent from the market, leaving a vacuum in China's benchmark interest rate system.

The problem is a result of the fact that Chinese treasury bonds are managed under the annual quota system and also a result of the inconsistency of fiscal policies and financial policies.

Generally speaking, the annual growth of fiscal revenue is limited; therefore, with a view to stimulating fiscal growth and the improving the solvency, treasury bonds administrator may only issue as few short-term treasury bonds as possible but to issue long-term treasury bonds as much as possible. As a result, the term of Chinese treasury bonds becomes longer and therefore distorts the structure of the bond market and also the financial market, which in turn reduces the efficiency of monetary policy.

It should be especially pointed out that, under the circumstance where the administration of treasury bonds adopts the annual issuance quota system, it is difficult for the Ministry of Finance to issue treasury bonds with maturities up to one year, because doing so will take up the quota of that year. This leaves a huge vacuum in the benchmark interest rate system.

There is a good reason to reform the current administration system of treasury bonds as soon as possible and transform the annual issuance quota management to the treasury bond balance administration.

The so-called treasury bond balance administration means that the Ministry of Finance must take the treasury bond balance as approved by the National People's Congress each year to be a nonoverriding indicator. As long as the issue volume of treasury bonds had not exceeded the set balance, the Ministry of Finance may flexibly control the issuance volume and term structure on the basis of the market situation.

In fact, treasury bond balance administration is a common international practice, which not only marks the maturity and transparency of the fiscal administration of a country but also provides more flexible means and diversified tools for fiscal policies and financial policies and lays the foundation for the consistency of macroeconomic policies. More importantly, the treasury bond balance administration will enrich the term structure of China's treasury bonds, set China's benchmark interest rate, and underpin the reform of financial system, especially the liberalization of interest rates.

As for the fiscal system, if treasury bonds are under the system of balance administration, the treasury bonds matured within one year will not take up the quota for the next year due to the fact that they will be repaid at the year they are issued; therefore, such bonds will not be required to be included in the treasury bond issuance plan of that year, which will greatly enhance the flexibility of fiscal measures. That is to say, the treasury bond balance administration creates sufficient conditions for the issuance of short-term treasury bonds.

First, when the fiscal account is in temporary deficit, the Ministry of Finance may rapidly issue short-term treasury bonds. Besides, for the 2Y T-bonds and 3Y T-bonds, the authority may at the time of their repayment increase the issuance of treasury bonds with maturities up to one year to offset the pressure of repayment in that year.

From the perspective of financial market, in the current treasury bond market, the bond trading of middle- and long-term treasury bonds produces middle- and long-term benchmark interest rate. And due to the fact that repo operations mainly involve the 7D or 14D ultra-short-term varieties, the yield curve formed thereby can only represent the instant interest rate level. In China's bond market, there is barely any repo trading for treasury bonds with maturities over one month; therefore, benchmark rates between 1M and 1Y generated from bond repos are not representative.

More importantly, the consistency and coordination of fiscal policies and financial policies demand for the balance administration system of treasury bonds.

Just take the United States as an example. In order to accurately obtain market information, the Ministry of Finance and the Federal Reserve Board work closely in public auction of the 3M and 6M short-term treasury bonds at a fixed time of each month or week. This rolling issuance mechanism not only brings more treasury bond to the market, increases fiscal revenue, and strengthens the macro control of fiscal policies but also allows the Federal Reserve to continuously test the market interest rate level and the fund supply and demand and further to rationalize its decision-making for more timely and accurate actions. In other words, accurate market information is the foundation for government's decision-making, and the rolling issuance mechanism of short-term treasury bonds exactly provided an effective measure for the government to obtain accurate market information.

It is the right time for the implementation of the balance administration for treasury bonds, which is the consensus of most of the experts, scholars, and market participants and the fiscal authority.

First of all, bank's saving and loan rates have not been liberalized for the time being, and this not only results from the commercial banks' lagging reform but also from the fact that China has no effective benchmark interest rate. That is to say, if the saving and loan rates are liberalized before the establishment of benchmark interest rate, it will bring chaos to the market and brew financial risks.

Second, the loose liquidity of China's commercial banking system has provided a good market foundation for the implementation of balance administration for treasury bonds. On one hand, the rolling issuance of short-term treasury bonds may solve problems concerning further improvement of the asset structure of commercial banks and create conditions for the market-oriented reform of commercial banks. On the other hand, the surplus fund of commercial banks may also provide strong support to the rolling issuance of short-term treasury bonds.

Third, China's treasury bond market is currently having bond liquidity shortage so that the yield curve formed by treasury bond trading is in doubt. However, once the balance administration for treasury bonds is implemented and the rolling issuance of short-term treasury bonds can be achieved, the bond trading volume of treasury bonds will be greatly increased and the creditability of the yield curve will be enhanced.

Therefore, the advantages far outweigh the disadvantages of the balance administration for treasury bonds, which carries a profound meaning for China's bond market and financial system.

Suggestion V Choose Complete Public Auction for Bond Issuance

For the mechanism of treasury bond issuance, transforming the underwriting system into the auction system is more than simple transformation of issuance mechanism.

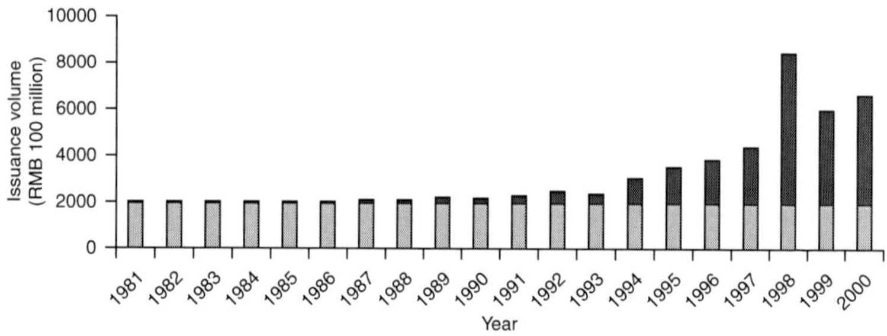

Figure 2.10 Issuance volume of China's treasury bonds (1981–2000).
Source: China Central Depository & Clearing Co., Ltd.(www.Chinabond.com.cn).

Since 1999, the Ministry of Finance (see Figure 2.10), policy banks and almost all bond-issuing entities have adopted the market-oriented issuance measures and achieved obvious effects. However, the current bond issuance process usually comes up with bid-winning interest rates via tendering within the underwriting group. That is to say, only underwriters may participate in the bidding, and nonunderwriters cannot participate in the formation of price but to passively accept the price. Thus, since the underwriters cannot completely represent all preferences of the market, the bond issuance market interest rate is not representative, and price discovery function is undermined, which entails great risks for underwriters.

The main methods for issuance of government bonds in developed countries include: auction, negotiated underwriting, underwriting, and sale of savings bonds at bank counters (in which the issuer sells nontransferable saving bonds through the counters of commercial banks, and this is also known as tap issue). We should say that these four modes have their respective advantages and disadvantages. Among which, auction is the fairest one and has the lowest cost and highest efficiency and is conducive to the liquidity of secondary market; underwriting is relatively simple, but it takes a longer issuance time and has a higher interest rate, and investors must pay underwriting fees. In the United States, this part of fees is usually 1.05 percent of the face value of bonds, so issuers and investors will both have to pay a higher cost; issuing saving bonds by means of tap issue will provide convenience to individual purchase of residents, but such nonnegotiable bonds have higher issuance cost.

The bond issuance in developed countries mainly takes auction and underwriting. Take the government bond issuance of the United States for instance. The US treasury bonds regardless of terms are all issued by auction. Through the Federal Reserve banking system, all investors may participate in tendering. The investors of nonunderwriters of treasury bonds must entrust underwriters of treasury bonds to bid, and the charge for each entrustment is USD50. Municipal bonds issue take the method of competitive underwriting or negotiated underwriting, while corporate bonds issue will mainly take the method of negotiated underwriting.

From auction, competitive underwriting to negotiate underwriting, the price discovery capability grows stronger, but the distribution difficulty grows larger. If bonds are of high quality and simple properties, do not require special information or intense promotion, are not particularly sensitive to the change of market interest rate, and without the need to choose the timing of issue, it is appropriate to take the method of auction or competitive underwriting. Otherwise, they had better choose negotiated underwriting. Therefore, auction issuance is the best method for issuance of treasury bonds.

The current issuance method of Chinese treasury bonds is basically competitive underwriting. Therefore it should gradually be transformed to the complete public auction method. Of course, the issuance of financial bonds by policy banks should also adopt the public auction method as much as possible. In the future, the issuance of financial bonds and corporate bonds of commercial banks may adopt negotiated underwriting or competitive underwriting.

Under the current issuance system, if investors do not open a bond account with China Central Depository & Clearing Co., Ltd., but instead open a custody account for secondary bonds with an underwriter, it is difficult for the regulatory authorities to implement effective regulation and control over them. If the public auction or agency bidding is adopted for the issuance of treasury bonds, then as a general practice, before the bidding, the underwriter must submit all the data of proprietary bidding and agency bidding must be submitted and reported to the regulatory authorities by the underwriters. Bonds of the bid-winning agents must be handed over immediately for custody, and the regulatory authorities may conduct spot inspection after issuance to verify the data submitted and reported by the underwriters so as to prevent the underwriters from conducting illegal financing in the disguise of purchasing bonds on behalf of clients.

For different bond varieties, the issuance method will also have different levels and categories. As for treasury bond issuance, transforming underwriting into an auction is not merely a transformation of the issuance method. It not only means returning the investment opportunities to investors but also may also help China's bond market grow into a mature and standardized bond market.

Suggestion VI Establish the Market Maker System

As the dominant platform in the bond market, the interbank bond market should improve the liquidity of the market and implement the market maker system and increase the number of market participants.

The market maker system is required for the development of OTC bond market. The development of secondary market lags behind the development of repo market in China (see Figures 2.11 and 2.12).The crux for developing the secondary market lies in improved liquidity. In China's bond market, the exchange-based bond market will maintain a considerable liquidity due to the fact that it mainly involves small investors. Interbank bond market as the dominant force of the bond market should above all introduce a market maker system while increasing its liquidity and expanding the participation. In theory and from the practice of developed countries, the quote driven method adopted by OTC bond market is considered to be the same as the market maker system in essence. Adopting quote driven method will naturally require market makers to help traders to search for bonds and negotiate for price. The implementation of the market maker system is required to be supported by bank counter trading and development of bond funds to bring in more trading parties; otherwise, if market making is only done among a few financial institutions, there will not be

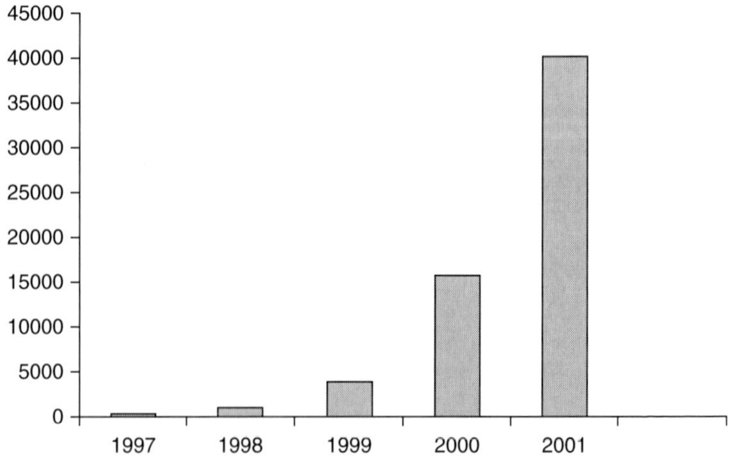

Figure 2.11 Repo trading volume in the interbank bond market (RMB100 million).

Source: China Foreign Exchange Trading System (www.Chinamoney.com.cn).

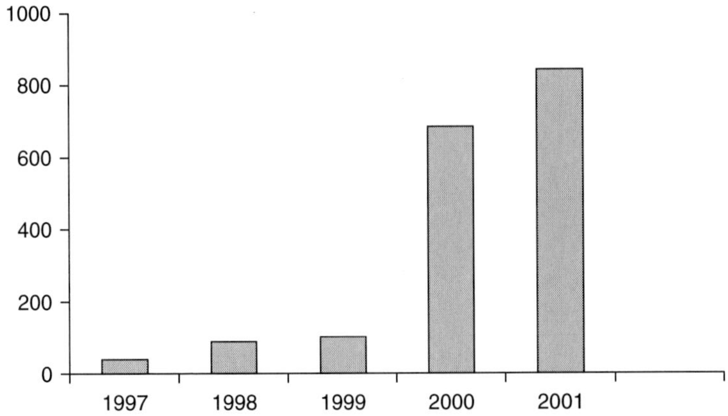

Figure 2.12 Cash bond trading volume in the interbank bond market (RMB100 million).

Source: China Foreign Exchange Trading System (www.Chinamoney.com.cn).

sufficient liquidity. Moreover, growing corporate bonds, enriching market instrument varieties, and developing derivative instruments are forceful and effective measures to support market making. The market maker system is the crux of solving OTC bond market liquidity; with growing number of market players, OTC market should be able to have reasonable turnover and liquidity.

Market maker system started to unfold at the beginning of 2000, with the release of the *Measures for Administration of the Bond Trading in the National Interbank Bond Market*, the concept of bilateral quotation was put forth for the first time and proactively promoted by the central bank. Up to August 2001, the Industrial and Commercial Bank of China, Agricultural Bank of China, Bank of China, China Construction Bank, and other five commercial banks have been officially approved as bilateral market makers, and the market maker trading system of China's OTC bond market was then officially established.

According to the regulations of the central bank on supporting bilateral market makers, the supportive measures mainly include the following four aspects: (i) bilateral market makers have the convenience in purchasing bonds in the primary market; (ii) the central bank will support the financing needs of bilateral market makers via open market operations pursuant to the needs of the monetary policies and the position of bilateral market makers; (iii) the central bank will support the needs of bilateral market makers on bilateral quotation for bonds via bond trading and margin trading of open market operations pursuant to the needs of monetary policies as well as the quotes and trading situation of bonds quoted by bilateral market makers; and (iv) the National Interbank Funding Center will provide technical support for continuous improvement of bilateral quotation system in accordance with the needs of the bilateral market makers in carrying out bilateral quotation business.

Bilateral market makers have rights but also obligations. According to the relevant regulations, the obligations include: (i) the quotes made by bilateral market makers must be of real price, and no false quote is permitted; (ii) the spread in the bilateral quotation for bonds made by bilateral market makers may not exceed the range as stipulated by the central bank, and the basis for the spread of bilateral quotation determined by them should be reported to the central bank; (iii) bilateral market makers undertake to maintain continuously daily bilateral quotation for at least one type of bonds, and such bonds should be addressed as "bilateral quotation bonds." Bilateral market makers have to report the bond variety to the central bank for filing and report the market turnover ratio to the central bank each week. The bilateral quotation bond may have different bilateral market makers; and (iv) bilateral market makers have to submit to the central bank the bond market analysis report and the trading report on a weekly basis, which will include their bilateral trading volume, number of trading, bilateral trading situation, and continuous trading situation. Bilateral market makers should timely report any material event in bilateral quotation and trading situation and report their business operation situation, fund position, bond holding, underwriting and trading situation, and other relevant materials on a quarterly basis.

The market maker system is necessary to ensure the liquidity of OTC bond market. However, we must realize that there is no guarantee of sufficient liquidity in the market even if we have the market maker system. There is still a matter concerning the expansion of institutional investors. Therefore, the implementation of market maker system requires the coordination of measures for the development of bank's countertrading and bond funds and expands the market participation to the maximum extent to enable bilateral market makers to explore the possibility of trading in a larger scope; otherwise the market making activity will be very limited if it is only conducted among a few financial institutions.

In securities market, investors may often encounter temporary imbalance of market supply and demand—cannot buy what they want to buy (or buy as much as they want) and cannot sell what they want to sell (or sell as much as they want). This situation will usually cause large volatility in the securities market price, and investors are forced to pay a price that is beyond their expectation in order to realize instant trading. The imbalance makes the market maker system important.

Financial institutions undertaking the function of market makers are willing to purchase and sell securities of sufficient amount at a price any time, which therefore realizes the balance of market supply and demand and enables continuous trading. This not only facilitates investors and guarantees the continuity of market price but also brings spread returns for market makers. In the bond market, the OTC bond market usually adopts quote driven method, that is, an investor makes a quotation and other investors decide whether to make a deal or not based on such quotation. This trading method of OTC trading market will naturally require the market maker system. From the practice of the bond market of developed countries, the market maker system is a common practice in the OTC bond market. There are 16 gilt-edged market makers (GEMMs), among which, eight of them are index-linked GEMMs (IGGEMMs). The GEMMs are subject to the authorization and approval of the FSA.

Stigler (1964) and Demsetz (1968) explained the role played by market maker system in the securities market. In their opinions, the market maker system provides instant response to the market, that is, the ability of swift trading, and provides a better market price for market participants and, under certain market conditions, provides service similar to auctioneer to maintain the order and fairness of the market.

However, the contemporary securities circle has a further understanding of the market maker system. They consider that the market maker system has an outstanding advantage, that is, it provides a relatively large liquidity for securities with a small outstanding amount. The success of "NASDAQ" provides exact evidence for this understanding. The "competitive market maker system" as implemented by the "NASDAQ" provides strong liquidity to the stocks of small ventures and at least provides such possibility (and it is impossible to have stocks with very high liquidity under other trading systems). As a result, under the persistent exploration by the securities operation institutions assuming the function of market maker, and through market trading, the value of the stocks of small ventures is constantly discovered, encouraging pre-IPO venture investors and becomes an effective way for venture investors to realize their investment profit. In addition, it makes "NASDAQ" the only successful growth enterprise market in the world.

In China, the market maker system was first put forward in 1994. In June of that year, the China Securities Regulatory Commission organized and convened the "Seminar on the Market Maker System of China's Stock

Market" in Shanghai. As Chinese securities industry did not know much about the market maker system, the concept of market maker system is debated in the conference. But the trading system of China's stock market has not been changed after this conference.

The market maker system did not come up in China until 2000 when the PBC adopted a series of measures to promote bilateral quotation operations of financial institutions in the interbank bond market, which prepared for the establishment of the market maker system.

In October 1999, the PBC started bond trading in its open market operations, which promoted the active trading of bonds in the interbank bond market. The PBC included the provisions concerning bilateral market makers in the *Measures for Administration of Bond Trading in the National Interbank Bond Market* in early 2000 to encourage financial institutions to make bilateral quotation on bonds. Meanwhile, the PBC intensified bond trading in open market operations to actually support the bilateral quotation operations. In March 2000, Shanghai convened the market maker system seminar and conducted study on issues related to bilateral quotation operations. In December 2000, the PBC convened some of the primary dealers of open market operations to hold a conference in Nanjing to discuss the specific issues concerning the promotion of bilateral quotation operations. The National Interbank Funding Center has developed the bilateral quotation trading system and put it in operation, and the websites of "www.chinamoney.com.cn" and "www.chinabond.com.cn" of China Central Depository & Clearing Co., Ltd. have also provided bilateral quotation service for members of the market. This has enabled a certain development of bilateral quotation operations of the interbank bond market, and Bank of China, Agricultural Bank of China, Beijing City Commercial Bank, Nanjing City Commercial Bank, and other financial institutions started to conduct bilateral quotation on some varieties of bonds. The PBC has issued the *Circular of the PBC on Issues Related to the Regulation for and Support to the Bilateral Quotation Operations of the Interbank Bond Market* in March 2001, which stipulates the requirements for financial institutions to qualify as bilateral market makers to be approved by the PBC, and specifies the business norms that must be observed by market makers and the supporting measures given to bilateral market makers.

In August 2001, the PBC approved the first nine bilateral market makers of the interbank bond market, namely, the China Industrial and Commercial Bank, Agricultural Bank of China, Bank of China, China Construction Bank, China Everbright Bank, Yantai Housing Saving Bank, Beijing City Commercial Bank, Nanjing City Commercial Bank and Wuhan City Commercial Bank. These banks will enjoy and undertake the prescribed rights and obligations.

Suggestion VII Develop Bond Derivative Financial Instruments

A mature bond market needs to develop derivative instruments that link bonds and other tools and financial variables. According to the types of linked assets, the derivative instruments of bonds may be divided into interest rate-based derivative instruments and derivative instruments closely related to other assets; the former is represented by bond futures, while the latter includes asset securities and convertible bonds, etc.

The launch of bond futures may help investors hedge interest rate risks. Bond as an interest rate-based financial instrument, its price is mainly subject to the influence of interest rate, which follows the economic circle and follows certain trend pattern. If the direction has been going up in a certain period, the bond price will definitely drop gradually, and the loss of bond investors will be inevitable. Currently, commercial banks and insurance companies in China have a large amount of medium- and long-term bonds with relatively low fixed interest rates. Once the interest rate goes up, there will be a great loss, and under the current trading system and trading means, investors will be unable to solve this problem. Certainly risks cannot be eliminated but can only be redistributed, which means that investors with a high risk appetite may assume more risk while risk-averse investors assume less risk. Therefore, the crux is to develop the trading system and tools for risk hedging. Developing bond futures, options, forward, and other bond derivative financial instruments, the market may provide risk-hedge means for investors (of course, it will also provide some other investors with the opportunity to opt for more risks). And this is very important for institutional investors who have made a lot of bond investments in the long run.

In 1995, the "327" treasury bond futures event triggered a financial earthquake, and China's treasury bond futures were suspended. It has almost been ten years since then, and now the call for reopening treasury bond futures rises again. Are the conditions for reopening the treasury bond futures ready given the development of China's bond market nowadays?

Today, China's bond market is quite different from the past. First of all, 1995 was the time when China improved and rectified its economic order, and its inflation and market interest rate were both at historical high and the continuous hiking of the inflation-proof subsidy rate of treasury bonds provided sufficient chance for market speculation. However, the macroeconomic conditions of that year have gone. What people see nowadays is low inflation and high growth of China's economy, and the interest rate is in a relatively stable level. The central government's ability in macrocontrol and regulation over the market has been effectively strengthened, and these provide foundation for stabilizing treasury bond futures.

Second, the scale of the bond market has also been quite different from the past. In 1995, one of the important reasons for the T-bond "327" event was that there was too much money but too few bonds traded. At that time, the total outstanding volume of China's treasury bonds was merely more than RMB30 billion; the scale of a single bond was at least RMB1 billion or RMB2 billion, and as many as RMB10 billion, while most bonds were held by the general public; therefore the market trading volume was very low. That is to say, when market speculation is large and reaches a certain extent (e.g., occurrence of "squeezing"), which requires the supplement of bonds by participants, there is no way for the undersized bond market to provide sufficient support. However, at the end of 2001, the outstanding volume of China's treasury bond market had reached RMB2.8 trillion, and negotiable treasury bonds were valued at RMB2.2 trillion. Meanwhile, the cash bond trading volume has reached more than RMB540 billion, which was greatly different from the situation prior to the end of treasury bond futures in 1995, and there is little possibility for manipulation of price.

Third, commercial banks, insurance companies, and other large investment institutions have become the major force of the market, and 70 percent of the negotiable treasury bonds are held by such institutional investors for a long period, which is an important precondition for the stability of the market. Or perhaps because of this, in order to prevent any possible change in market interest rate, institutional investors will need to take treasury bond futures for hedging. In fact, the most important reason for the higher demand for treasury bond futures by institutional investors in the market is exactly their worries for changes in interest rate, which will have adverse impacts on the fixed coupon treasury bonds they hold.

In specific design, given that investors would like to hedge against systemic risk of the bond market, for instance risks of interest rate volatility, and to avoid manipulation of the derivative instrument market, an authorized institution may study and issue an index for China's bond market to provide a benchmark for the market, and such index will serve as the basis for derivative products; in other words, there is only one or a group of index futures (options, etc.) in the bond market, in this way, it cannot be manipulated and risk management may be realized.

However, reopening the treasury bond futures market at this time will have many adverse impacts, for example, (i) China's bond market has not been integrated, the bond prices in the two markets may sometimes be inconsistent, and this will set the futures price trend at loose ends; and (ii) the current short supply in the bond market will distort prices of bonds and futures to disable the discovery function of the futures market price.

To sum up, China's treasury bond market has currently called for treasury bond futures; however, from the perspective of market conditions, it seems that the market needs to grow more mature.

For bond futures related to other financial instruments, the instrument related to commercial banks' long-term credit assets is asset bond, and the instrument related to stocks is convertible bond. Commercial banks have a fundamental problem concerning the mismatching of their long-term loan assets and short-term deposit liabilities, and to solve this problem, asset securitization occurred in the United States in 1960s. Commercial banks issue bonds backed by their credit assets. As an important financial innovation, it has changed the traditional assets and liabilities management model of commercial banks and provided an investment product with appropriate risk-return, and therefore has undergone a rapid development and formed a very sound system in developed countries. The assets for securitization are mainly four types of loans issued by commercial banks: individual housing mortgages, credit overdraft advance, car loan, and other commercial housing and office building loans. From the situation of developed countries, the major investors (purchasers) of asset-backed securities are institutional investors, including pension fund, insurance companies, commercial banks, mutual fund and foreign investors, etc. China's OTC-dominant structure based on institutional investors will provide sufficient demand for assets securities to support the healthy and stable development of asset securities. The volume of convertible bonds in China is relatively small, and so far there are only nine companies issuing convertible bonds. Convertible bonds can connect the corporate bond market and stock market, and are greatly demanded by listed companies and pre-IPO companies, and therefore have a great development potential.

Conclusion

Over twenty years of development, China's bond market has made remarkable achievements and laid a good market foundation for the next stage of development. At present, the prospect of China's bond market should be the establishment of a uniform and diversified multilayered bond market. We have reasons to believe that China's bond market will be developed into a mature market with China's entry into the WTO and integration with the global market.

CHAPTER 3

Foreign Exchange Market

Practice and Research on Foreign Exchange Open Market Operations of the People's Bank of China[1]

In 1994, China decided to undertake fundamental reform in its foreign exchange management system to unify the dual exchange rates, adopt the managed floating exchange rate regime of RMB, implement the compulsory settlement system of foreign exchange, and establish an interbank foreign exchange market. At the same time, China's central bank started its foreign exchange open market operations and has achieved some initial success.

I. Formation of China's Foreign Exchange Market and Evolution of RMB Exchange Rate Regime

Since the reform and opening-up to the outside world, China's foreign exchange market has gone through four stages from the launch of retained foreign exchange business, the foreign exchange retention market, and the open foreign exchange retention market to the introduction of the integrated interbank foreign exchange market (see Figure 3.1). Accordingly, the RMB exchange rate formation mechanism has undergone significant changes from the unilateral official rate to the coexistence of official rate and market rate and further developed into a single and managed floating exchange rate regime based on market demand and supply.

Before 1978, China's foreign exchange management system was a planned system with centralized collection and payment under government control. There was no real foreign exchange market in that period, and RMB exchange rate was merely a tool for internal auditing and was

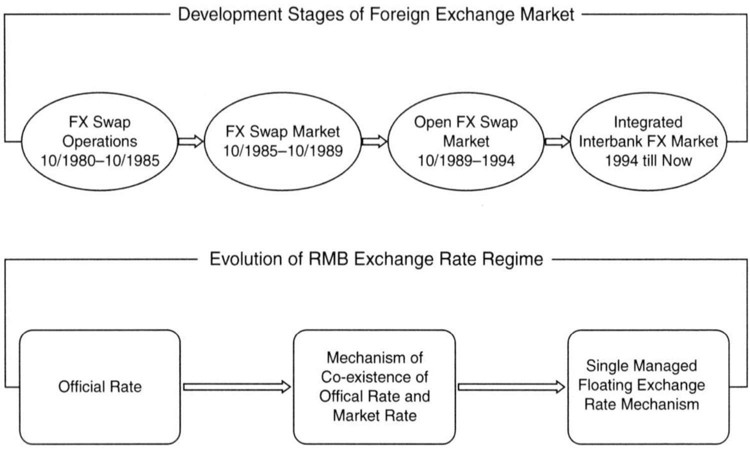

Figure 3.1 Development of foreign exchange market and RMB exchange rate regime.

determined by a government plan. After the reform and opening-up, China implemented the foreign exchange retention system in 1979, in which enterprises receiving foreign exchange may retain part of it, and hence give rise to the demand of trading retained foreign exchange. In October 1980, the Bank of China commenced the retained foreign exchange business, which marked the inception of China's foreign exchange market. In this period, the official exchange rate dominated the foreign exchange trading, and the market-based exchange rate had little influence; the RMB exchange rate formation mechanism was still in its infancy.

In November 1985, Shenzhen Special Economic Zone established the first retained foreign exchange trading center to collectively handle local foreign exchange transactions. In the following two years, other localities in China established foreign exchange trading centers one after another, and the retained foreign exchange transactions outstanding in this period increased and the price floating range was also expanded, so the foreign exchange retention market came into being gradually. However, different retention markets came up with different exchange rates, which resulted in the coexistence of official exchange rate and many other retention rates, but the official exchange rate still had a dominant role; the RMB exchange rate formation mechanism was far from perfect.

In September 1988, Shanghai created the first open foreign exchange retention market in China under a membership system through competitive bidding and collective clearing. At the end of 1993, 18 cities in China have run open foreign exchange retention markets, and approximately 80 percent of foreign exchange generated from international payments was traded in the market. In this period, the official rate and the market rates coexisted, and market force has taken up the leading role. However, due to the fragmentation of the retention market, what was traded on the market was still foreign exchange quota instead of spot exchange rate, and the market-based exchange rate had yet to form and was not regulated. Since July 1993, for the purpose of strengthening macrolevel management, the PBC started to intervene on local foreign exchange retention markets, which was later transformed into foreign exchange open market operations.

In 1994, China decided to carry out significant reform of its foreign exchange management system to unify exchange rates, adopt a managed floating exchange rate regime of RMB, implement the foreign exchange compulsory settlement system and establish an interbank foreign exchange market. On April 4, 1994, the China Foreign Exchange Trade System officially commenced internetwork operations, which marked the establishment of a single nationwide interbank foreign exchange market. Since then, China's foreign exchange market entered into a new era with a single exchange rate and market-based system. The foreign exchange market in the new era has taken a big step toward the unified and standardized market in terms of market structure, organization form, trading method, and price formation. As to market structure, the foreign exchange market has two levels: one is the retail market between authorized banks and enterprises, and the other is the interbank foreign exchange market comprising mainly of banks. As to the organization form, interbank foreign exchange market conducts trading through the market trading network of China Foreign Exchange Trade System. The trade center is headquartered in Shanghai that runs on a membership system with a national computer network. In terms of trading method, the interbank foreign exchange market adopts competitive bidding and computer matching based on the price and time of each order. Accordingly, the RMB exchange rate formation mechanism has undergone fundamental changes and has been developed into a single managed floating exchange rate system based on market supply and demand. The current RMB exchange rate is determined by market supply and demand, fully reflects the willingness of the trading parties, embodies the open, fair, and impartial market principles, provides price signal for domestic economy and external economic and trade relations, and improves resources allocation.

II. Practice of Foreign Exchange Open Market Operations of the People's Bank of China

In April 1994, following the establishment of the interbank foreign exchange market, the foreign exchange open market operations of the PBC were officially launched.

(I) Operational Mechanism of Foreign Exchange Open Market Operations

The Office of Open Market Operations of the PBC is an organic constituent of the basic structure of China's interbank foreign exchange market and serves as a foreign exchange control and management authority, which is independent from the State Foreign Exchange Administration and the China Foreign Exchange Trade System, with the former being the foreign exchange market regulatory body and the latter being the foreign exchange operational system. These three parties perform their respective duties and check each other as well as closely cooperate to guarantee the stable, efficient, and safe operation of the foreign exchange market.

In terms of the control and regulation over the foreign exchange market, the PBC aims at maintaining a relatively stable RMB exchange rate. The Office of Open Market Operations of the PBC, as instructed by the PBC headquarters and based on the changes of foreign exchange and through standardized and flexible operations, takes the opportunity to enter into the market to purchase and sell foreign exchange, adjust exchange rate, balance supply and demand, and stabilize the market to secure the RMB exchange rate.

The Office of Open Market Operations of the PBC currently carries out foreign exchange open market operations in Shanghai. It would participate in the foreign exchange market trading and has a dual status: an ordinary member of the China Foreign Exchange Trade System and also a special member responsible for control and management. As an ordinary member, it must observe the articles of association and trading rules of the China Foreign Exchange Trade System, participate in the market trading in accordance with the principle of "price/time priority" on an equal footing, and conduct RMB and foreign currency clearing in accordance with the unified clearing method, which is the same with other members. As a special member, however, it acts on behalf of the PBC to participate in foreign exchange trading to stabilize exchange rate and adjust market supply and demand.

(II) Prominent Features of Interbank Foreign Exchange Market and the Status of the RMB Exchange Rate

Since the establishment of China's interbank foreign exchange open market, one of the prominent features is the oversupply of foreign exchange. Oversupply of foreign exchange reflects the international balance of payments situation in China. Since 1994, China has maintained foreign trade surplus, and the foreign trade surplus in 1994, 1995, and 1996 was USD5.35 billion, USD16.7 billion, and USD12.24 billion, respectively; the foreign capital inflows for the same period have increased steadily, with foreign direct investment (FDI) utilized in 1994, 1995, and 1996 being RMB43.22 billion, RMB48.13 billion, and RMB51 billion, respectively. Therefore China's international balance of payments has continuously maintained a favorable balance with an increase in the foreign exchange supply.

Since April 1994, the oversupply of foreign exchange continued, which in turn led to a slight decline of RMB exchange rate and relative appreciation of RMB. The RMB/USD exchange rate broadly followed a five-stage trend:

1. From April 1994 to mid-April 1995. After the unification of exchange rate at the beginning of 1994, there was a large extent of RMB depreciation, stimulating a surge of export, increase of foreign trade surplus, and large oversupply of the US dollars in the foreign exchange market, and the weighted average price of the US dollars in the market gradually dropped from around 8.70 at the beginning of April 1994 to the 8.42 in mid-April 1995, representing an accumulative drop of about 2,800 points, a relative appreciation of RMB of 3.2 percent, and a downward slopping trend of the exchange rate.
2. From late April 1995 to mid-May 1995. Under the selling pressure of foreign exchange due to oversupply, there was a rapid fall in the US dollar exchange rate, which recorded an accumulative drop of 1,400 points from 8.42 to 8.28 within three weeks.
3. From late May 1995 to mid-February 1996. The US dollar exchange rate basically fluctuated within the range of 8.30 to 8.32, and depreciation slowed down.
4. From late February 1996 to mid-March 1996. In view of the implementation of national foreign trade reform policies, it was expected that there would be smaller export with larger import, which would then results in trade deficit and the inevitable depreciation of RMB. Because of the expectation, the pressure of oversupply in the foreign exchange market was eased, and the US dollar exchange rate presented a small upward trend from 8.31 to 8.33.
5. From late March 1996 to late December 1996. China's export trend was gradually reversed and moved upward progressively month by month after July, and the trade surplus was expanded with growing foreign capital inflows and increasing selling pressure in the foreign exchange market, and the US dollar exchange rate has gone downwards steadily from 8.33 to around 8.30.

III. Achievements of the Foreign Exchange Open Market Operations by the Office of Open Market Operations of the PBC

Since April 1994, with persistent oversupply of foreign exchange, the Office of Open Market Operations of the PBC has used indirect monetary policy tools to timely control and manage the foreign exchange market, smooth out any big fluctuations in the foreign exchange market, and maintain the relative stability of RMB exchange rate by carrying out foreign exchange open market operations. It was proven that the foreign exchange open market operations conducted by the Office of Open Market Operations of the PBC have made great achievements:

(I) The smooth implementation of foreign exchange compulsory settlement system is ensured. Since April 1994, it has carried out operations commensurate with the settlement requirements. Therefore, the foreign exchange market ran smoothly, and it is convenient and efficient for banks to manage their foreign exchange positions to guarantee smooth foreign exchange settlements and transactions.

(II) The growth in foreign trade is reinforced. The relative stability of the RMB exchange rate creates a favorable environment for the development of China's foreign trade, which is conducive to the growth of foreign trade. In 1994, 1995, and 1996, China's foreign trade increased by 20.9 percent, 18.7 percent, and 3.2 percent, respectively.

(III) The national foreign exchange reserves were increased. Since 1994, it has timely sterilized the exchange surplus through foreign exchange open market operations, which has greatly expanded the national foreign exchange reserves. By the end of 1996, China's foreign exchange reserves have reached USD105 billion, up USD83.8 billion compared with the end of 1993.

(IV) The central bank's allocation method for base money was changed. From April 1994 to the end of 1996, it had supplied a net amount of RMB777.5 billion to the market through foreign exchange open market operations, accounting for more than 70 percent of the base money increment for the same period, which has changed the asset structure of the central bank and strengthened the relationship between monetary policy and exchange rate policy, which marks a positive step toward indirect control and management by the central bank.

Comparative Analysis of Foreign Exchange Intervention by Foreign Monetary Authorities[2]

The Summit of the Industrialized Countries held in June 1982 at Versailles resolved to establish a "Working Group on Exchange Market Intervention" with economists to specifically study the issues on foreign exchange market intervention. In 1983, the Working Group released a "Report of the Working Group" (also known as the "Jurgensen Report"), in which foreign exchange intervention is narrowly defined as "any trading of foreign exchange against domestic currency which monetary authorities conduct in the exchange market"; it may take the form of foreign exchange reserves, swaps between central banks, or official loans, etc.

I. Decision-Making Institutions and Operational Institutions of Foreign Exchange Intervention

Exchange rate policy is an integral part of monetary policy, carried out by the central bank. Due to the Bretton Woods System and other historical reasons, the treasury departments of some countries are also involved in decision-making related to foreign exchange intervention.

In the United States, the Federal Reserve Board and the Treasury Department make joint-decision on foreign exchange intervention. Nominally, the Treasury Department is responsible for international policy and negotiates with the central bank upon decisions on foreign exchange market intervention, but actually the Federal Reserve has considerable decision-making power. In the times of Paul Volcker and Alan Greenspan, the Federal Reserve's Chairman and the Secretary of the Treasury usually had different opinions on US dollar exchange rate and would only make an intervention after they have reached some kind of consensus.

In England, the Bank of England and the Treasury jointly make decisions about foreign exchange intervention. In addition, according to the agreement set forth in the letter from the chancellor of Exchequer to the governor of the Bank of England on May 6, 1997, the Bank of England may also intervene in the foreign exchange market for the purpose of realizing monetary policy objectives.

The decision-making authorities for European foreign exchange intervention are the European Central Bank and the European Commission; the European Central Bank has considerably more decision-making power.

The decision-making authority for foreign exchange intervention in Japan is the Ministry of Finance, which will negotiate with the Bank of Japan in actual intervention.

The operational authorities for foreign exchange intervention are the Federal Reserve Bank of New York in the United States, the Bank of Japan in Japan, the European Central Bank in Europe, and the Bank of England in the United Kingdom. As seen from above, the central banks are usually the agencies actually making Foreign Exchange (FX) interventions.

II. Transparency of Foreign Exchange Intervention

The mainstream opinion suggests that transparency of foreign exchange intervention may help guide market expectation and enhance the efficiency of foreign exchange intervention. Usually, foreign monetary authorities will announce information on foreign exchange intervention after they take actions.

The intervention in foreign exchange market by the monetary authorities of the United States is of the highest transparency. The United States has announced intervention information since 1970. Within the first 20 minutes after the implementation of foreign exchange intervention, the US Secretary of the Treasury will make a statement to announce that the US monetary authorities have intervened on the foreign exchange market with explanations. The Federal Reserve Bank of New York publishes the intervention data of the previous quarter with a one- to three-month lag, including intervention data, the specific time of intervention, the intervention direction, the intervened exchange rate level, the intervention amount of the Federal Reserve Bank of New York, the intervention amount of the Exchange Stabilization Fund, and the total amount of intervention.

Japan has announced intervention information since April 1994 and would announce the total monthly intervention amount at the end of the month, and the intervention details of the quarter with a one- to three-month lag (recently approximately 40 days), which includes the intervention date and intervention amount without announcement on the specific intervention time and intervened market (Tokyo, London, or New York) and the impacted exchange rate each day.

Europe will not publish any information on foreign exchange market intervention but only provide partial data to researchers.

England has published intervention information since 2000, and if the Treasury or the Bank of England makes any intervention, it will announce the date and amount of intervention and explain the reasons for intervention.

III. Source of Funding for Intervention

The source of funding for intervention by monetary authorities in the United States includes foreign exchange held by the Federal Reserve and the

Exchange Stabilization Fund (ESF) of the Treasury mainly denominated in Euro and Japanese Yen. The ESF of the Treasury comes from sale of gold by the United States under the Bretton Woods System. The Treasury and the Federal Reserve will usually share the intervention quota equally at the time of intervention. For example, in an intervention against Euro on September 22, 2000, a total amount of foreign exchange equivalent to USD1.34 billion was used, and the Federal Reserve and the Treasury each contributed half, that is, foreign exchange equivalent to USD670 million.

The source of funding for intervention by the England monetary authorities comes from the Exchange Equalization Account (EEA) of the Treasury and the foreign exchange reserves held by the Bank of England. The EEA of the Treasury was established in 1932, and the primary source of funding came from gold and the revenue from sale of gold.

The source of funding for foreign exchange intervention by the Ministry of Finance of Japan comes from the Foreign Exchange Fund Special Account (FEFSA); the foreign exchange was accumulated by the Ministry of Finance from foreign exchange intervention over the years, and Japanese Yen was raised by the Ministry of Finance through issuance of 3M financial bills. The foreign exchange in the FEFSA is mainly used for investment in the three-month T-bond of the United States, and due to the fact that the interest rate of the Yen is much lower than that of the US dollars, the FEFSA has made a big profit from the spread.

IV. Intervention Methods and Counterparties

The methods of foreign exchange intervention may be, according to different classification standards, divided into Entrusted Intervention and Reverse Entrusted Intervention ("Entrusted Intervention" means that a monetary authority entrusts the local monetary authority to conduct intervention when intervention is conducted in the overseas market, while "Reverse Entrusted Intervention" means that a monetary authority is entrusted by a foreign monetary authority to conduct intervention at the locality), Joint Intervention and Independent Intervention, Sterilized Intervention and Unsterilized Intervention, Spot Market Intervention and Forward Market Intervention, and Direct Intervention and Indirect Intervention ("Indirect Intervention" refers to the intervention of the exchange rate by administrative means such as capital control and foreign exchange control.)

The intervention methods of foreign monetary authorities are relatively flexible, and the intervention is usually made through transactions in the broker market, or through commercial banks under the entrustment of the central bank or through foreign exchange transactions between central banks and market members directly.

In the United States, the Federal Reserve Bank of New York has established a comprehensive foreign exchange dealer system and may also enter into the broker market sometimes, but usually it will simply conduct foreign exchange transactions with foreign exchange dealers. Although the Federal Reserve Bank of New York rarely intervened on the foreign exchange market in recent years, it has acted for the central banks of many countries to conduct foreign exchange transactions; therefore, its daily foreign exchange transactions are relatively frequent. As such, a foreign exchange dealer system with regular trading counterparties is necessary. On February 11, 2003, the Federal Reserve Bank of New York announced a new foreign exchange dealer system as an update of the system in 1992. The new system requires that foreign exchange dealers must be efficient and professional when implementing the orders of the Federal Reserve Bank of New York at a competitive price, and they must provide market information and analysis report to the Federal Reserve Bank of New York at any time, with good performance in the market and having joined the clearing system of the Federal Reserve Bank of New York.

The main form of intervention adopted by the Bank of Japan is to entrust commercial banks to conduct transactions. The Ministry of Finance will request a commercial bank through the Japanese Bankers Association to trade at the price designated by the Ministry of Finance, and this bank will purchase US dollars in the market, and after the completion of the trading, the Ministry of Finance of Japan will clear with the bank and this trading will be recorded by the Ministry of Finance and be included in the statistics of the monthly intervention amount for public release. The entrustment method of the Bank of Japan can keep intervention activities confidential; therefore it will not release the list of entrusted banks. The entrustment method is rather flexible; for example, currently the Bank of Japan has adopted the "all-or-nothing" intervention, that is, when other banks know that a bank is representing the Japanese government to purchase US dollars, they will also purchase US dollars so as to take advantage of the rising trend of US dollars driven by the intervention; at that moment, the Ministry of Finance will withdraw its order because US dollar has appreciated. Due to the withdrawal of order, the intervention will not be recorded in the official data. Afterwards, as Ministry of Finance and the Bank of Japan have withdrawn their orders, the bank that was ordered will sell US dollars at the rising exchange rate and obtain substantial return.

The United States will make intervention on the global foreign exchange market. Japan mainly conducts intervention on the Tokyo foreign exchange market and will only intervene in overseas foreign exchange markets jointly with other countries.

V. Intervention Frequency and Intervention Amount

The intervention frequency of major monetary authorities in the 1990s was much less than that in the 1980s, but the intervention amount was slightly increased.

From 1990 to 2002, the United States has made interventions in 74 days, among which, intervention on USD/JPY market was 39 days, while intervention on USD/DEM market 48 days and intervention on USD/EUR market 1 day. From mid-September 1995 up to now, the Federal Reserve has only intervened twice, and each lasted for only one day. The biggest single-day purchase of US dollars by the Federal Reserve was on November 2, 1994, when the Federal Reserve purchased USD1.6 billion, and the biggest single-day sale was on September 22, 2000, when the Federal Reserve sold euros equivalent to USD1.34 billion.

Japan has made interventions for 200 days within the decade in the 1990s, among which, it has made interventions for 165 days prior to June 20, 1995, and interventions for 35 days thereafter. The biggest single-day sale of US dollar by the Bank of Japan was on April 10, 1998, when USD20 billion was sold; while the biggest single-day purchase of the US dollar was on April 3, 2000, when USD13.5 billion was purchased.

Since its inception, the European Central Bank has intervened on the market for only four days, as follows: one day in September 2000, and three days in November 2000. However, the European Central Bank did not release the intervention amount.

From 1973 until now, central banks of industrial countries have made six joint interventions of a relatively large scale: (i) from 1976 to 1979, the United States worked with central banks of Germany, Switzerland, and Japan to make large-scale long-term intervention to boost weak US dollars, which ended up in failure; (ii) in September 1985, the United States, the United Kingdom, France, Germany, and Japan jointly conducted an intervention on the foreign exchange market and published the well-known "Plaza Accord" on September 22, which is effective as seen by many; (iii) in 1992, central banks of the United States and European countries respectively conducted large-scale interventions twice on the foreign exchange market to support US dollars on July 20 and August 11, which was a failure in the middle to long-term; (iv) in September 1992, the member states of the European Monetary System conducted a joint intervention on the foreign exchange market to maintain the European Monetary System, which eased the contradiction within the European Monetary System, but nonmember states have been alienated from the system; (v) in April 1998, the United States and the Bank of Japan jointly supported the Japanese Yen with obvious effect; and (vi) in September 2000, the Group of Seven (G7) intervened on the global foreign exchange market to support the euro and achieved short-term effect.

VI. Gains from Intervention

It is widely believed that the gains from foreign exchange intervention include three components: (1) real gains, referring to the actual proceeds generated from the sale and purchase of the same amount of foreign exchange at different exchange rates; (2) nonreal gains (gains from revaluation of market value), calculated by comparing the average cost of foreign exchange reserves and the difference of the current market exchange rate at the end of the observation period; and (3) interest margins, referring to the interest margins between the interest on the source of funding for foreign exchange intervention and the interest on the gains of foreign exchange reserves.

As of the late twentieth century, the real gains from foreign exchange intervention of the Bank of Japan is JPY981 billion, while the nonreal gains are JPY3,665 billion, and the interest margins are JPY3,958 billion, with total gains of JPY8,604 billion.

The amount of the foreign exchange intervention of other countries is relatively low and the corresponding gains or losses are relatively small. For example, as of the end of 2000, the gains from foreign exchange intervention of the United States Treasury and the Federal Reserve are respectively USD258.1 million and USD253.6 million.

VII. Intervention Strategy and Intervention Targets

The foreign exchange intervention strategy is usually divided into two groups, namely leaning against the wind and leaning with the wind. The former refers to the invention made by the central bank to counter short-term trends of the market to stabilize the market. The latter refers to the situation that when the short-term trend is contrary to the dominant trend, central banks will align the former with the latter via foreign exchange intervention; for example, the joint intervention by the monetary authorities of the United States and Japan in 1998 was considered to be a typical leaning with the wind.

Due to the fact that these two concepts are perplexing, the Federal Reserve Bank of New York does not apply them but categorizes intervention into narrow target intervention and broad target intervention; the former is to

Table 3.1 Foreign exchange operation strategies with different targets

	Targets of Foreign Exchange Intervention	*Strategy of Foreign Exchange Intervention*
Policy Targets	1. Determine the policy targets of exchange rate under the floating exchange rate mechanism; 2. Send the signal for change of macroeconomic policy in the future	• Announcement • Joint invention • Macroeconomic policy support • Leaning against the wind
Strategic Targets	3. Lower the fluctuations of exchange rate or resist short-term tendency; 4. Reverse the long-term tendency of exchange rate; 5. Combat monetary speculation and prohibit one-way bet.	• Confidential • Leaning with the wind • Large Amount • Timeline for the maximum effect

smooth out the fluctuations of the exchange rate while the latter is to reverse the exchange rate trend. The distinction between these two interventions is that the former will enable all market participants to make profits while the latter will in general bring about losses to market members so that they will rethink and rejudge the market trend and allow the market force to drive the exchange rate back to a normal track. In recent years, the Federal Reserve has only conducted broad target intervention, and a deputy governor of the Federal Reserve said: "[E]ach intervention will give a big surprise to the market."

The targets of foreign exchange intervention are divided into policy targets and strategic targets. The policy targets are long-term targets, which mainly focus on the impact of exchange rate on the economy. The strategic targets are short-term ones that mainly focus on the operation mechanism of foreign exchange market. Monetary authorities shall apply different operational strategies under different intervention targets (see Table 3.1).

Reform of RMB Exchange Rate Regime and Selection of Foreign Exchange Market Transaction Modes[3]

On January 4, 1994, China established a unified national interbank foreign exchange market and implemented a single managed floating exchange rate regime based on market supply and demand. It has been proved that the trading mode of interbank foreign exchange market over the past ten years has guaranteed the fundamental stability of RMB exchange rate at a reasonable and balanced level, and it is a success in general. The Third Plenary Session of the Sixteenth Central Committee of the Communist Party resolved to further improve the RMB exchange rate formation mechanism, which requires corresponding reform of the trading mode of the foreign exchange market.

I. Existing Trading Mode of Foreign Exchange Market

China's foreign exchange market consists of two tiers formed by interbank foreign exchange market and foreign exchange sale and purchase market at bank counters. Due to the mandatory foreign exchange settlement as well as the restriction of bank counter FX position, enterprises passively settle their foreign exchange balance at the bank counter and banks passively manage their position in the interbank foreign exchange market.

The interbank foreign exchange market adopts the exchange-based trading mode with four trading pairs, namely, RMB/USD, RMB/EUR, RMB/JPY, and RMB/HKD. The China Foreign Exchange Trade System runs upon a membership system, and members issue orders through spot or remote trading terminals, and orders of all members will be matched via the electronic trade matching system as per the principle of "price/time priority." The China Foreign Exchange Trade System is responsible for the collective clearing of funds in foreign and domestic currencies.

II. Reform of RMB Exchange Rate Regime Calls for Reform of Foreign Exchange Market Trading Mode

The exchange rate regime determines the foreign exchange market system and therefore decides the trading mode of the foreign exchange market. The long-term target of the RMB exchange rate formation system is to implement a managed floating exchange rate regime, and the RMB exchange rate shall be two-way floating. The floating of RMB exchange rate will change the expectation of dealers and influence their trading activities.

In the context of narrower floating band of exchange rate at present, dealers only have expectations of the long-term trend of exchange rate instead of short-term exchange rate adjustment, and their foreign exchange trading activities are irrelevant to the short-term exchange rate but only restrained by their quota on sale and purchase of foreign exchange and driven by their own liquidity needs, hence a substantive demand and supply in the market.

Once the exchange rate floats, especially after the two-way floating, dealers will immediately form expectations of short-term exchange rate, and there comes the concept of trading strategy. In addition to the substantive demand and supply under fixed exchange rate, there will also be an increase in expected and speculative demand and supply in the market. (i) Expected demand and supply. The dealers will adjust the trading volume with reference to their trading strategies and the daily trading volume might fluctuate widely. For example, Bank A purchases USD100 million from clients every day and then sells USD1 billion within ten days. Under fixed exchange rate, Bank A will sell USD100 million per day. However when it comes to floating exchange rate, Bank A might expect that the US dollar would keep appreciating, therefore it will not sell any US dollar on the first nine days but sell USD1 billion on the tenth day at one time. In this case, the change in foreign exchange market supply and demand will be relatively larger than that under fixed exchange rate. And (ii) speculative demand and supply. The short-term exchange rate expectations will also generate speculative foreign exchange demand and supply of dealers. Taking the said Bank A as an example, it could also purchase US dollars on the first nine days and then sell all of them on the tenth day so as to make attempted influence on the price. The existence of speculative demand and supply will make foreign exchange demand and supply in the market more volatile.

Following the inclusion of expected and speculative demand and supply in market demand and supply, the fluctuations in foreign exchange demand and supply will increase and brings more volatility. Any random fluctuations in exchange rate within a short period is disadvantageous to market participants, monetary authorities, and the real economy. As a result, the two-way floating of exchange rate requires that the foreign exchange market should have a reservoir mechanism, which is able to cushion short-term fluctuations in foreign exchange supply and demand. This reservoir mechanism is the market-maker system.

Under the market-maker system, the marker makers make bilateral quotation to absorb the foreign exchange supply and demand of clients in order to maintain the relevant stability of exchange rate. In assuming their obligations of bilateral quotation, market makers will have their corresponding rights in addition to their status as market makers and direct benefits brought about by bilateral quotation that are attractive to clients, and they are usually the counterparties of central banks. After China has introduced market makers to the foreign exchange market, the restriction of foreign exchange position may be relaxed for market makers to encourage them to take their responsibility.

The market-maker system requires a new trading mode of the foreign exchange market. In fact, the market-maker system and the OTC trading mode are consistent. The primary mode of OTC is that each market participant looks for a counterparty, while the mature OTC mode will implement the market-maker system, for example, as in the current international foreign exchange market and bond market. Each market maker is a node that collects client price information, and the wholesale transaction among market makers would turn into the benchmark exchange rate of the market, and the exchange rate formation mechanism of the market is in essence a mechanism driven by the quotes of market makers. The market-maker system and the exchange mode are contradictory; under the exchange mode, the exchange rate formation mechanism is driven by the orders of market members. In addition, under this mode, traders have no idea of their counterparties.

The reform of foreign exchange trading mode from exchange mode to the OTC mode may also solve the problem of credit risk assumed by the China Foreign Exchange Trade System under the current system so as to prevent any individual credit risk from developing into a systematic credit risk.

III. Trading Modes of International Foreign Exchange Markets and China's Selection of Foreign Exchange Trading Mode

The trading mode of international foreign exchange market is divided into the OTC mode and exchange mode. Due to technical progress, both modes process transactions through electronic network; we therefore could not interpret these two trading modes simply by their means of trading, for example, phone calls, counters, biding, etc. The essential differences between these two trading modes include: (i) in OTC mode, traders know who their counterparties are, while traders in the exchange trade do not; and (ii) OTC implements bilateral clearing, while exchange requires each trader to clear with the exchange.

International foreign exchange markets mainly adopt the OTC mode, while the foreign exchange OTC market is of a typical two-tier structure. The first tier is the market for transactions between dealers and clients, and the second tier is the market for transactions among dealers. The two-tier structure of China's foreign exchange market is similar to that of international foreign exchange markets, and the interbank foreign exchange market is the market for transactions among dealers. Hence, we mainly study the trading mode of the second-tier market, that is, the dealer market.

In the foreign exchange OTC market, the trading methods among dealers can be categorized into two types, namely direct dealing and trading through brokers. The trading through brokers may be further divided into two types, namely voice broker and electronic brokering system, while the latter is also known as automated order-matching systems. Since 1992, electronic brokering systems have seen a rapid development. In 1995, electronic brokering accounted for 18 percent of total broker-facilitated trading, and in 1998, this number increased to 57 percent. There are two major companies providing electronic brokering service: the Reuters and the Electronic Broker System (EBS).

In electronic brokering, dealers would first provide to the electronic brokering companies their own credit limit, and the electronic brokering companies will preset the same in the system. More specifically, after the dealer issued an order, the electronic brokering system will match the order within the credit limit of such dealer, and the dealer may know from the computer screen soon after the match is completed. Thereafter, the dealer would contact the trading counterparty, and the two parties will go through bilateral fund clearing in their respective bank once they have passed the credit risk check conducted by the risk management department. For example, Citibank (CB) issues an order to purchase US dollars at an amount of USD2 billion, and Bank of America (BOA) issues an order for the sale of US dollars at an amount of USD2 billion so that the prices are matched. However, the USD/JPY credit limit provided to EBS for BOA is USD1 billion, and the electronic brokering system will close the deal at USD1 billion. After CB and BOA see the matching on their own computer screens, they will settle the deal after their own risk management departments finish the credit check. If CB's risk management department considers the credit risk of USD1 billion is too great and allows trading at USD500 million only, then the deal will be closed at USD500 million.

In view of this, the role of electronic brokering systems is to enhance the matching efficiency of dealers' orders via the electronic system, and they do not change the essence of the OTC trading mode, and the trading parties know who the counterparty is. This guarantees the control over credit risks. As such, the development of science and technology and the extensive application of the Internet have enhanced the market trading efficiency, however, the basic concept that dealers must conduct risk management by themselves has not been changed (see Table 3.2).

Table 3.2 Comparison between OTC mode and exchange mode

	OTC mode	*Exchange mode*
Motivation	Strong Each Trader Is Motivated to Facilitate Active Transactions.	Weak Only the Exchange Cares About the Vitality of Transactions.
Risk	Low Traders Have Bilateral Credit Authorization. Risks Are Controllable and Dispersed.	Very High When There Is any Credit Risk, the Exchange Will Face Bankruptcy, Bringing about Systematic Risks.
Efficiency	Very High Dealers May Conduct Direct Trading or Trade through Voice Brokers or Electronic Brokering Systems.	Relatively High Dealers May Only Trade through the Electronic Matching System.

Electronic brokering systems have an edge to handle very active "currency pair" trading and small trades (USD/JPY and USD/EUR are the two most important trading pair of electronic brokering systems); in respect to other currency pairs and bulk trading, dealers will usually conduct direct transactions. Under the exchange mode adopted by China's interbank foreign exchange market, it is rather difficult for large orders of state-owned banks to be matched through the electronic system.

If the RMB exchange rate regime is reformed in the future, and the exchange rate becomes floating, in addition to the relaxation of foreign exchange control and expansion of foreign exchange market membership, the credit risks in foreign exchange trade will grow higher. At present, the interbank foreign exchange market applies the exchange mode, and the credit risks are assumed by the China Foreign Exchange Trade System. It is proved that the risk management of China's financial institutions has yet to improve; if there is any institutional deficiency in terms of risk problems, the participants will take advantage of loopholes, which will eventually lead to huge systematic crisis. As for interbank bond market, due to its adherence to the OTC mode pursuant to the international practice, there is no credit risk since its inception in 1997. The market adopts one-to-one transaction, one-to-one bond pledge, one-to-one negotiation on bond pledge ratio, one-to-one clearing, and all risks are borne by commercial banks themselves. The successful experience of the interbank bond market should be followed. In this regard, after the reform of the RMB exchange rate regime, it is necessary for the existing trading mode of the interbank foreign exchange market to be reformed and gradually move toward the OTC mode (see Figure 3.2).

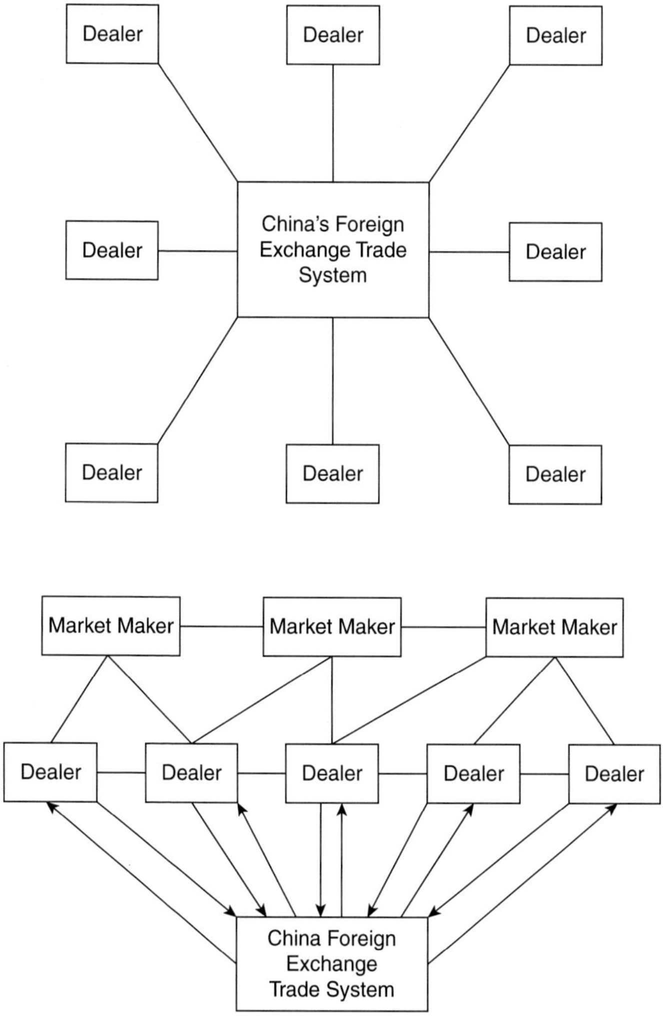

Figure 3.2 Diagram of the original mode and diagram of the mode after reform.
Note: The "arrow" means quotation information and "line" means trading and clearing.

Subprime Mortgage Crisis Prone to Evolve into a Major Global Crisis[4]

I. Federal Reserve's Strategy Brings about Great Changes to the Way of Asset Bubbles Burst

In recent years, the Federal Reserve has supplied much liquidity that has first driven up asset price and then pushed up commodity price. Consumer prices are also being pulled up now. Once the trend of rising consumer price is present, the Federal Reserve should be forced to raise interest rate, hence crunching the global liquidity and bursting the global asset bubbles. However, when the global inflation pressure was on the rise since 2007 and central banks of key currency countries represented by the Federal Reserve entered into the preliminary stage of tightening, the sudden outbreak of subprime mortgage crisis in the United States disrupted the market and changed the course of events. The asset bubbles did not burst due to interest rate hike but busted due to its own risks instead.

The underlying reason is the change of attitude of central banks toward asset bubbles. Before the Asian financial crisis, central banks usually contained the bubbles by means of raising interest rate, however, the public opinion laid the blame on central banks for the bubble burst; after the Asian financial crisis, the Federal Reserve headed by Alan Greenspan learnt the "lesson" and decided to play the role of a good person instead of a bad person and changed his attitude toward asset bubbles to "ex ante indulgence + ex post remedy," leading to growing risks, and the cause of price adjustment was changed from interest rate hike to the rational devaluation of assets.

The reason for the outbreak of the subprime mortgage crisis was the adjustment of ultra-low risk premium instead of changes of interest rate or exchange rate. The Federal Reserve headed by Ben Bernanke wanted to follow the old path of Alan Greenspan, but insurmountable difficulty was encountered.

II. Federal Reserve in a Dilemma

At the initial outbreak of crisis, the Federal Reserve, together with the European Central Bank and the Bank of Japan injected liquidity into the market in the hope of stabilizing it and maintaining asset bubbles. However, the situation was no longer the same; the old way could not solve new problems, and this crisis evolved into a great global crisis.

First, the asset bubble was excessively big. The stock market bubble in the United States found its way in the 1990s, and in 2001, the stock market bubble did not burst after the 9–11 events given the Federal Reserve's support to the stock market, which on the contrary had stimulated the expansion of the real estate bubble in the United States and the global asset bubbles of all kinds; however the accumulated risks have been too high for the Federal Reserve to maintain, even if it had spent all its efforts to inject liquidity. Second, the inflation pressure was rising. In order to prevent any future hike in inflation rate, the Federal Reserve should also be well-prepared to raise interest rates or at least should not lower the interest rate easily; this is exactly why recently the Federal Reserve lowered the rediscount rate instead of the federal funds rate.

In this case, the Federal Reserve was facing a dilemma between inflation control and financial market stability. If it lowered the interest rate to bail out the financial market, there was a fear that would lead to uncontrollable inflation. If it raised the interest rate to prevent inflation, there was a possibility that would lead to the collapse of the financial market, which was beyond control, eventually wrecking the economy. In mid-2007, the Federal Reserve struck an interim balance between the two options, and once the situation of any or both of them was firmed, the Federal Reserve made its decision: to raise or lower the interest rate. When the subprime mortgage crisis actually evolved into a severe global crisis, the Federal Reserve definitely cut interest rate substantially.

III. Formation of Currency Competition Pattern

After 9–11, the Federal Reserve reduced the interest rate in succession to inject massive liquidity into the market, and excess US dollars flowed to other countries, which is indicated by the increase of foreign exchange assets (including foreign exchange reserves) and local currency liquidity of other countries and global excess liquidity. Excess liquidity will necessarily give rise to a global asset bubble, which later adds to inflation pressure. However, Japan's protracted deflation absorbed the pressure from excess liquidity, eased global inflation pressure, and mitigated the risks resulting from the strategy of the Federal Reserve. With the end of Japan's deflation in 2005 (the Bank of Japan ceased its quantitative easing monetary policy in early 2006), the United States tried to replace Japan's deflationary economy and shifted its focus onto emerging market economies.

If the exchange rates of emerging market economies appreciate substantively, it will lead to exchange rate overshooting, which will finally guide emerging market economies to deflation. This will stabilize the global consumer price, including that of the United States, and also enable the Federal

Reserve to fulfill its responsibility to contain the inflation brought by excess US dollar liquidity. In the currency war, if emerging market economies largely appreciate their currencies, a large amount of US dollars will continue to flow inward and withdraw after they profit from asset bubbles, leaving the emerging market economies to suffer from long-term deflation; if emerging market economies realize inflation to some extent to pull up global consumer price, the Federal Reserve will be driven to raise interest rate substantially along with other key currency issuing economies. In this case, the US dollars will flow back to the United States, and Yen-denominated interest arbitrage fund will also flow back to Japan, thereby sterilizing the global excess liquidity so that inflation will naturally drop. However, whether the inflation in emerging market economies can bring about a rise in global consumer prices remains uncertain, and there exists difference in inflation tolerance between the United States and other developed countries. So this option of emerging market economies entails great risks. Emerging market economies may only moderately appreciate their currencies on the one hand and contain inflation by means of domestic monetary policies on the other hand. When the subprime mortgage crisis went worse and evolved into a major financial crisis, which drives the Federal Reserve to lower its interest rate, the economic crunch brought about by financial crisis also eased the inflation pressure.

Currency Swaps, Overseas Use of RMB, and Development of Foreign Exchange Market[5]

Since the outbreak of the international financial crisis, the PBC has proactively engaged in international and regional cooperation to cope with this crisis. On the G20 Summit on Financial Markets held in November 2008, President Hu Jintao stated: "[W]e will encourage regional financial cooperation, strengthen the ability to give mutual liquidity aid, speed up regional financial infrastructure development and fully utilize the regional funding relief mechanism." After the Summit, the PBC made an active response to the needs of neighboring countries and studied and promoted bilateral currency swap, turning it into an important means for enhancing the capability of mutual liquidity assistance. In recent time, the State Council has approved Shanghai, Guangzhou, Shenzhen, Dongguan, and Zhuhai to carry out RMB international settlement pilot projects, which has attracted wide attention and extensive discussion of various parties on RMB internationalization. I would like to take this opportunity to introduce RMB internationalization and bilateral domestic currency swap between monetary authorities and share with you about the relationship between RMB internationalization and foreign exchange market development.

I. Bilateral Domestic Currency Swap by Monetary Authorities

From the history of economic and financial development of great powers, internationalization of currency is a key step of financial internationalization strategy. As to RMB, internationalization refers to the process in which RMB becomes a generally accepted and recognized unit of account, medium of exchange and store of value in the world. If RMB internationalization requires a relatively long process, regionalization, in which RMB is used for regional trade settlement, would be the preliminary stage. At the beginning of 2009, the foreign trade volume of China ranks second in the world, and the demand for RMB for price denomination and settlement in cross-border trade is also growing. The State Council has now approved RMB internationalization settlement pilot projects and resolved to facilitate Shanghai to establish "two centers," which are conducive to trade and investment. The bilateral domestic currency swap agreements between China and the other economies will be an important catalyst for promoting the overseas use of RMB.

We often hear the word "currency swap," which is also known as "FX-swap," a financial product extensively available in the international financial market, which usually refers to the market activities that two transaction counterparties holding different currencies on the market exchange currencies at equivalent value at the beginning of the period as agreed, and then exchange their principals at the end of the period and pay corresponding interests to each other. Currency swap could be dated back to 1970s, originally carried out among commercial institutions for the purposes of comparative advantage to reduce their respective financing cost and hedge against their respective exchange rate risks. Recently, central banks of different countries have commenced using currency swap in regional financial cooperation, implementation of monetary policy, and meeting the needs for financial stability. For example, since 2001, the PBC has joined the currency swap network established among the ten countries in Association of Southeast Asian Nations (ASEAN) plus China, Japan, and Korea (10+3). Since November 2005, the PBC and commercial banks have carried out RMB foreign exchange currency swap in order to adjust the liquidity of foreign and domestic currencies. Since late 2007, in order to cope with the financial crisis and solve short-term US dollar liquidity problems of relevant countries, the Federal Reserve has carried out currency swap with several central banks.

The execution of currency swap agreement was intended to address short-term liquidity problems, effectively deal with financial crisis and maintain the stability of the financial system, but in the currency swap agreements entered into by the PBC and other monetary authorities, in addition to providing short-term liquidity support to stabilize the financial market, another important purpose of swapped currencies is to support bilateral trades. Bilateral monetary authorities may provide the swapped currencies to local financial institutions, which in turn would provide liquidity to local enterprises for import payment. This innovation is conducive to promoting the RMB valuation and settlement in international trade.

To date, the total amount of bilateral domestic currency swap agreements entered into by the PBC is RMB650 billion, including RMB180 billion/ KRW38 trillion framework agreement with the Bank of Korea on December 12, 2008; RMB200 billion/HKD227 billion formal agreement with the Hong Kong Monetary Authority on January 20, 2009; RMB80 billion/MYR 40 billion formal agreement with the Bank Negara Malaysia on February 8, 2009; RMB20 billion/BYR8 trillion formal agreement with the Belarus National Bank on March 11, 2009; RMB100 billion/IDR175 trillion formal agreement with the Bank Indonesia on March 23, 2009; and RMB70 billion/ARS38 billion formal agreement with the Argentine Central Bank on April 2, 2009. Besides, the PBC is negotiating with other monetary authorities in demand of RMB with respect to the conclusion of bilateral domestic currency swap agreements.

The economies that have entered into such agreements with China may be categorized into three types in respect to the economic and financial development status, currency convertibility, exchange rate mechanism arrangement, bilateral trade relationship with China, and the scale of financial institutions operating in China and other indicators. The first category includes developed market economies, including the Hong Kong region. Hong Kong has an open financial market where Hong Kong dollars can be freely converted. In 2008, the total exports from Mainland to Hong Kong were USD190.7 billion, while the total imports from Hong Kong to Mainland were USD12.9 billion. The second category is emerging market economies with relatively large bilateral trade volume with China, that is, Korea, Indonesia, Malaysia, and Argentina. They respectively imported from China USD73.9 billion, USD21.4 billion, USD17.2 billion, and USD5 billion in 2008, while exporting to China USD11.2 billion, USD32.1 billion, USD14.3 billion, and USD9.4 billion. The third category is developing countries with relatively small trade volume with China, that is, Belarus, which has imported from China USD400 million and exported to China USD500 million in 2008 (see Table 3.3).

Table 3.3 China's trade with bilateral currency swap economies (Unit: USD100 million)

	Type of economies	*Export by China*	*Import by China*	*Balance of trade*
Hong Kong	Developed market	1,907	129	1,778
Korea	Emerging market	739	1,121	-382
Indonesia	Emerging market	172	143	29
Malaysia Argentina	Emerging market	214	321	-107
	Emerging market	50	94	-44
Belarus	Developing country	4	5	-1
Total		3,086	1,813	1,273

Source: People's Bank of China (www.pbc.gov.cn).

II. Bilateral Domestic Currency Swap to Promote Overseas Use of RMB

Under the circumstance that China has a long-term trade surplus, the commercial incentive for RMB outflow to overseas countries by means of import payment is relatively weak. In the context of the financial crisis, financing activities among overseas and domestic financial institutions are suppressed, therefore the RMB outflow by means of creditor's right and the RMB outflow by means of trade can be integrated to jointly facilitate the overseas use of RMB. The currency swaps among monetary authorities are conducive to overcoming difficulties at the time of crisis such as the shrinking of trade and the financing market, excessive risk aversion of market participants, and underdeveloped financial market within the region. Since other monetary authorities assume credit risks, the credit risks for the direct provision of RMB financing by China's domestic banks under the crisis may be limited, which is conducive to creating an initial low-risk environment for trade settlement. So far, the PBC has entered into currency swap agreements with Korea, Hong Kong, Malaysia, Belarus, Indonesia, Argentina, and other monetary authorities at a total amount of RMB650 billion and have abundant funds available, which allow trade payment by domestic currency to start at a high point in an eased credit environment.

As estimated by an international research institute, the global trade amount in 2008 is USD 13–14 trillion and trade financing is approximately USD10 trillion, that is, about 75 percent trading in the world is supported by trade financing. Due to the deleveraging of financial institutions in crisis economies, the World Bank estimated that the global trade financing gap at present is USD100 billion, and new gaps will come up when old gaps are filled. The total exports from China to the said economies are USD308.6 billion; so if calculated at the global average of 75 percent, trade financing of around USD230 billion, that is, RMB1,500 billion is needed. The counterparties of bilateral domestic currency swaps are mainly emerging market economies, which are subject to greater influence by the global US dollar credit crunch and trade financing gaps may be higher than the average level in the world. RMB swap funds will also substitute part of US dollar trade financing in addition to filling its trade financing gaps. In this case, in bilateral domestic currency swap agreements, a certain amount may be actually used, thereby affecting money supply and promoting the development of offshore financial market. In addition, with an increase of the scope of signatories to domestic currency swap agreements and the use of RMB in regional trade settlement, the scale of RMB fund use under currency swap agreements may be increased and the influence will be further reinforced.

III. Overseas Use of RMB to Accelerate the Development of China's Foreign Exchange Market

Due to the mismatch of fund surplus and deficiency of different market participants in the regional use of RMB, exchange, financing, and other financial services are required. The administrative requirements for exchange rate and interest rate risk management will also bring about a growing demand for RMB derivative market. China's domestic financial market, as the primary market of RMB-related financial products, needs to serve the full function of the pricing center of RMB-related financial products in the RMB internationalization process and take a dominant role of RMB pricing through continuous enhancement of its competitiveness.

First of all, the balance must be sought between the demand of market development and risk control requirements in the development the RMB derivative market. Hence, the problems exposed in this international financial crisis must be fully analyzed, especially the risk disclosure and risk control mechanism in the development of OTC market, and we must study and establish the central counterparty clearing system, give full play to the flexibility and convenience of OTC market, enhance the transparency of the market, and establish a systematic risk control mechanism.

Second, the overseas use of RMB demands market intermediaries to accelerate the full extension of their services. In line with the overseas use of RMB, the varieties, scope, and geographical location of RMB trade in the international market will continuously be extended, and overseas RMB offshore markets will also achieve rapid development. Market intermediaries will face competitive pressure and proactively "go global" and establish the global RMB transaction platform, extend the scope of services to cover trade, custody, settlement, and information, as well as provide different kinds of services in connection with RMB transactions for international market participants.

Third, financial institutions must strengthen the set-up of the "price transmission mechanism," "liquidity management mechanism," and "risk prevention mechanism," and enhance the capability in independent pricing and risk management. In recent years, financial institutions have made remarkable progress in the development of the three mechanisms, with a higher degree of integration of foreign and local currencies and an enhanced risk management and control capability; therefore there is basically no sign of liquidity risks and currency mismatch risks as exposed by other emerging market economies in this global financial crisis. In the future, as the important participants for the overseas use of RMB, financial institutions will play a key role as the developer, price setter, and liquidity provider of RMB financial products. Whether RMB can effectively serve its function as a medium of exchange, a unit of account and a store of value depends on the development of China's economy and whether RMB-related financial products can satisfy the diversified demand of market players in terms of payment, settlement, risk management and value store, and increase. Accordingly, financial institutions need to further strengthen the three mechanisms, enhance independent pricing and risk management capability, and promote the healthy development of RMB market.

Challenges Posed by Capital Flow to Emerging Market Economies[6]

I. Brief Review of International Capital Flow since 2002

From 2002 to 2007, under the long-term globally ease monetary environment, emerging market economies have experienced unprecedented large-scale capital inflows, which basically followed the pattern: in terms of mid- and long-term capital flow, East Asian countries and Middle Eastern countries provide financing to the United States, which is reflected in their rising global foreign exchange reserves; in terms of short-term capital flow, capital continuously flowed to emerging market economies from developed countries, which is reflected in the massive Yen carry trade. From 2008 to 2010, under the international financial crisis, the global capital flow changed its previous tendency and presented new features of massive volume, fast speed, and high volatility: first, global financial deleveraging causes the swift withdrawal of a large amount of capital from emerging market economies, which can be seen from a dramatic diminishing of current account surplus, withdrawal of direct investment and securities investment and massive profit repatriation. However, the emerging market economies have long been accumulating foreign exchange reserves after the Asian financial crisis and have a more rational foreign debt structure, so their financial systems are more flexible. Given that the capital accounts of most economies have not been completely opened up, and such economies have maintained an effective control over international capital, especially short-term capital flow, emerging economies possess a certain capability to mitigate the impacts of capital outflow. Since the second half of 2009, the economic situation of emerging market economies has been revitalized, stimulated by quantitative easing of major developed economies, a large amount of capital flowed back to emerging market economies.

II. Challenges to Emerging Market Economies Resulting from Recent Huge Capital Inflows

In August 2010, Federal Reserve Chairman Ben Bernanke revealed a second round of quantitative easing, or "QE2," in Jackson Hole and the alleviation of Euro zone sovereign debt crisis has weakened the demand for safe-haven US dollars, which contributed to the rapid depreciation of US dollars after mid-September. The liquidity of US dollars has started to spill over prior to the implementation of QE2 by the Federal Reserve, which mainly flowed to commodity market and emerging market economies that have better economic fundamentals than the United States. This contributed to the rapid rise of international commodity price, which was completely uncorrelated to the fundamentals. From mid-September to early November, crude oil futures have recorded a rise of 15 percent and the CRB (Commodity Research Bureau) Index, measuring a basket of bulk commodity prices, has also recorded a rise of 16 percent. A large amount of international capital simultaneously flowed to emerging market economies. In accordance with the survey of the Emerging Portfolio Fund Research, a global fund research institute, the fund flowing to the stock markets of emerging market economies in the first week of October has reached up to USD6 billion, a record high in the past 33 weeks.

Since mid- and late November, with the spread of the European sovereign debt crisis, US dollars slightly rebounded under the demand of safe haven, and the capital inflows to emerging market economies slowed down. However, given that the global economy has been on the track of a mid- and long-term moderate recovery and subject to high unemployment rate and financial deficit, major reserve currency issuing countries still maintained and even extended the scale of quantitative easing policy, and the depreciation of major reverse currencies might be a long-term tendency and capital continued to flow to emerging market economies. The Washington-based Institute of International Finance expects that the net capital inflow to emerging economies in 2010 and 2011 will exceed USD800 billion.

The quantitative easing monetary policy of developed economies had a strong spillover effect through the asset portfolio channel, information channel, and liquidity channel, especially when a large amount of liquidity was injected. The commodity market and emerging market economies recovered at a relatively fast speed, resulting in imported inflation and short-term capital inflow and pressure on the monetary authorities of such emerging market economies. The pressure comes from four respects. First, imported inflation and rapidly rising inflation expectation; second, rapid appreciation of domestic currency, which has adverse impact on the export sector; third, a rise in asset price, which leads to the risk of an asset bubble; and fourth, exacerbation of currency mismatch in which the private sector, including the financial sector, holds assets in domestic currency and has liabilities in foreign currency. All these impacts may result in a dilemma for emerging market economies in their selection of macroeconomic policy: if they tolerate the appreciation of domestic currency, the export competitiveness will be weakened; if they restrain the appreciation of domestic currency, the imported inflation will rise; interest rate hike will attract capital inflow but credit expansion and asset bubble will also be stimulated, which will expose hidden problems accompanying an overheating economy, and once major reserve currency issuing countries tighten their monetary policies, capital outflow and rapid depreciation of domestic currency in emerging market economies may be triggered, and even worse, a monetary crisis may happen due to severe currency mismatch in the private sector. According to IMF's incomplete statistics, from 1980s to 2008, emerging market economies have experienced 109 capital inflow cycles. In 87 inflow cycles, nearly one-third of them ended up in sudden reversal or monetary crisis.

Since the Federal Reserve announced QE2 in August 2010, the capital inflow of emerging market economies has increased substantially, which leads to appreciation of currency and asset bubble and increase of the risks of the financial system. The emerging market economies have applied traditional foreign exchange intervention and monetary policy tools one after another, while some of them have turned to macroprudential policies to protect their Achilles' heels that are vulnerable to the capital inflow impact. Taken together, these measures can be categorized as follows:

The first category includes traditional tools such as interest rate, reserve requirement ratio, loan quota, and open market operations. For example, Indonesia, Malaysia, and some other countries have enhanced exchange rate flexibility, and their currencies appreciated to a greater extent; many countries have made foreign exchange intervention to increase the accumulated foreign exchange reserve; the central banks of Indonesia and some other countries have also strengthened the administration on liquidity, and the Bank Indonesia has raised the statutory deposit reserve ratio from 5 percent to 8 percent, requested commercial banks to hold the Bank Indonesia Certificates (SBI) for at least one month and issued nonsecurities monetary instruments (certificate of deposit) and 9 months SBI and 12 months SBI.

The second category is to guide the overseas capital flow directly through the relevant foreign exchange measures to restrict capital inflow or encourage capital outflow. For example, India raised the investment limit of government bonds and corporate bonds by overseas investors respectively to USD10 billion and USD20 billion; the Bank Indonesia strengthened the restriction on the net foreign exchange position of banks; Korea has lowered the ceiling of foreign exchange derivative position of banks, restricted overseas lending, requested foreign exchange loans to be used overseas, and strengthened foreign exchange liquidity management by banks; the Philippines' central bank did not allow banks to sell and borrow foreign exchange on the spot market, allow enterprises to make prepayment, increase the quota for purchase of foreign exchange by residents (no documentation requirements), and impose new requirements that the investment period must exceed five years and the investment instrument must be infrastructure corporate bonds.

The third category is the macroprudential policy measures that restrict the side-effects of capital inflow as much as possible. These measures mainly focus on housing price and bank credit loan, which are believed to be of the highest possibility in producing liquidity-driven bubble. The frequently used policy tools include loan balance ratio, liability/income ratio, mortgage down payment ratio, taxes and expenses on transactions or capital gains, direct intervention into housing supply, etc. For example, Brazil raised the rate of financial transaction tax against fixed income investments by overseas investors from 2 percent to 4 percent on October 4, 2010, and further raised the rate to 6 percent on October 18, and at the same time the rate of foreign exchange derivatives transaction tax was raised from 0.38 percent to 6 percent. Thailand has relevied taxes at a rate of 15 percent against overseas investors. The Bank of Korea has prepared to levy taxes on overseas investors' purchase of government bonds. Hong Kong and Singapore believe that the main problems rest with the rising housing prices, and their governments have therefore issued measures to curb the rise of housing prices.

Some other countries believe that capital inflows will bring about great opportunity to develop their domestic financial markets. For instance, India hopes to take advantage of foreign capital inflows to develop the domestic bond market and facilitate infrastructure development, so they instead increase the scale of investment on local government bonds and corporate bonds by foreign investors to USD5 billion.

III. Characteristics of Capital Inflows in China and Countermeasures

At present, since China's economy has rebounded and has a relatively large market, it has come under the pressure of capital inflow to some extent. However, the situation in China is obviously different from other countries. China's foreign exchange inflows mainly come from current accounts and FDI channels, which account for approximately 90 percent of the total foreign exchange inflows into China. China still exercises control and regulation over capital and financial account and imposes strict quota control over nonresident securities investment and resident overseas financing. Therefore international capital mainly flows into China through legal channels under current accounts such as goods trade, service trade, and current transfers, in which enterprises disguise arbitrage activities in order to save financial cost, by means of export prepayment and deferred import payment, replacing the purchase of foreign exchange by foreign exchange loans and intercompany trade credits, and handling long-term settlement of exchange. The inflow can also be detected from the fact that the net settlement of exchange from enterprises' goods trade has been higher than trade surplus and the net settlement of exchange from foreign direct investment has all along been higher than FDI. In addition, there is no obvious feature evidencing the entry of abnormal foreign exchange funds in China is on a short-term basis. They are mainly seeking return from the prospects of middle- and long-term economic growth of China, even if China has experienced the once-in-a-hundred-year international financial crisis; there is no sight of continuous large-scale capital outflows. It is therefore difficult for China to simply adopt the measures commonly taken by emerging market economies, whether it being taxes hike or investment restrains.

In response to capital inflows, China has on the one hand strengthened foreign exchange administration, for example, strengthening the administration on short-term foreign debt for financial institutions, restricting the forward settlement of exchange of enterprises through foreign exchange settlement position administration, implementing quota administration over the RMB settlement business in foreign trade, etc., to prevent the inflow of any speculative foreign exchange funds. However, China mainly adopts the measures for aggregate hedge by means of increasing the statutory deposit reserve ratio and intensifying the issuance of central bank bills and other measures to freeze RMB liquidity caused by speculative foreign exchange inflows, which may be comprehended as putting all short-term inflow funds into a "pool," thereby reducing the impact of abnormal fund inflows to China's economy.

Besides, China is also considering including the administration of capital inflows into the framework of macroprudential administration, in addition to traditional measures such as strengthened regulation, examination, and restriction. China is also considering strengthening administration over assets and liabilities of banks in response to capital flow. In addition, China will continuously expand overseas investment channels and encourage capable enterprises to carry out cross-border operations, allow different types of institutions to engage in the Qualified Domestic Institutional Investors (QDII) business, lift the restriction on individuals' overseas direct investment, allow individuals to invest in overseas securities and real estate by means of market-based purchase of foreign exchange, etc.

Milton Friedman said: "Inflation is essentially a monetary phenomenon anytime and anywhere," and we could interpret the current large-scale of flow of international capital as a monetary phenomenon in essence by following the logics of Friedman. The capital flow problems faced by emerging market economies stem from the spillover resulting from the ultra-ease monetary policies of developed countries, and the challenges faced by economic development and financial stability will become more serious, no matter what measures are taken, they could only ease but never really avoid the impacts of the frequent flow of overseas capital. As such, major international reserve currency issuing countries should adopt responsible monetary policy to prevent the flooding of liquidity of reserve currency and maintain the stability of major currency exchange rates.

European Debt Crisis Continues to Evolve[7]

The debt issue of the United States and the European debt crisis are correlated. It seems that the United States is willing to see the spread of the European debt crisis. This may be one of the factors driving the continuous growth of the European debt crisis. The United States faced the pressure of rising inflation and tightened monetary policies of other countries, so the Federal Reserve was expected to announce the end of QE2 at its meeting in June 2011. If there is a strong expectation, the rise in interest rate and the liquidity crunch are likely to happen in United States in the second half of

2011. The fact is that the US dollar interest rate and exchange rate dropped after the Federal Reserve announced QE2 in August (the official launch is in November). The Federal Reserve was absolutely unwilling to see this happen, which was precisely why the Federal Reserve has not yet taken a firm stand on the monetary policy direction by the middle of 2011.

The European debt crisis has temporarily relieved the United States from its own debt problem. On the issue of government debt problem, the United States and Europe seem like two people chased by one tiger—what matters is running faster than the other to leave him to the tiger. Hence, we could see that US credit rating agencies will always lower the credit rating of Euro zone countries such as Greece when the timing is right, and so far, the US government and the US-dominated international financial organizations have not expressed any views on the European debt crisis. In this regard, the market had heard talks about a US exit from QE2 since late April, and the discussions on the US government debt ceiling problem were also heated up; however, due to the fact that capital flows back to the United States in fear of European debt crisis, the U.S. market interest rate had actually gone downwards before the end of May 2011—the benchmark 10-year treasury bond yield has dropped 18 points in May. It seems that the European debt crisis was more effective in lowering the U.S. interest rate than that of the QE2. The European debt crisis mitigated the adverse effect over the U.S market resulted from market expectation of QE2 tapering and the worries over U.S. government debts.

From the perspective of Europe, the economic growth of Germany, France, and other major European countries was strong in the first quarter of 2011, among which export was a significant driving factor, whereas Germany and France benefited from the depreciation of the euro against the US dollars in light of the European debt crisis; that may be the reason why Germany and France have not given any specific views. As for periphery countries such as Greece, either debt restructuring or bailout would be a good outcome. Therefore, developed economies are not pushed hard enough to solve the crisis fundamentally. In the face of the European debt crisis, the emerging market economies and developing countries are the only victims, which in fact have no say and capability to find solutions to this issue. Hence, since the financial market has always been expecting a bailout, the European debt crisis is likely to further evolve.

From the history, culture, and politics of Europe, the pursuit of unification of Europe is a dream of politicians and the general public for many years; the political cost for the exclusion from the Euro zone is not a result any of the parties can bear; therefore, the chance of Euro zone breakdown is slim, and this crisis will finally be solved. Nevertheless, in the short run and from the present situation of Greece, the issue is quite a problem. Greece will be required to sell state-owned assets of EUR50 billion to repay its debts; however, it is hard to sell state-owned assets under poor economic conditions; coupled with the abovementioned external environment, the European debt crisis was extended to other countries and continue to evolve into a real crisis. The nature of the global financial crisis is deleveraging: in the past, there were a very high level of private-sector debt; but after the crisis, the leverage ratio has to be reduced by two methods: (i) the traditional asset sales; and (ii) replacing private-sector debt with government debt and then replace government debt with central bank liabilities. The traditional method would result in a drop in their price and then more assets have to be sold, thereby giving rise to a vicious cycle. It has been proved in practice infeasible. Central banks of developed countries abandon the method and often use the second method, which has resulted in inflation.

After the breakout of the financial crisis, assets of the private-sector were purchased, replaced, or guaranteed to save the whole financial system. As a result, private-sector debt has been transformed into public debt. Upon developing, this process has triggered severe consequences: as economic growth becomes poor, the financial return drops and results in sovereign debt crisis; if expenditure is reduced, the vicious cycle of economic downturn is started. And the governemnt debt is then replaced with central bank liabilities, for example, quantative easing monetary policies adopted by the United States, Britain, and Japan in which their central banks directly purchased government debt. However, restrained by the political structure of the Eurozone, the European Central Bank has been very prudent in purchasing government debt. But if a real crisis occurs, it has to follow the footstep of US and other countries. Therefore, the private-sector debt is transformed into government debt and then central bank liabilities. In the end, it is likely that the crisis has to be settled by debt monetization.

Cross-Border RMB Business and Markets

The discussion about cross-border RMB business and markets has three parts: cross-border RMB business, RMB offshore market, and RMB direct trading.

I. Cross-Border RMB Business

Background

Over the past twenty years, China has achieved a phenomenal twentyfold increase in its GDP, from less than USD400 billion in 1990 to over USD8 trillion in 2012. China's trade and foreign direct investment have also grown significantly from around USD100 billion to nearly USD4 trillion during the same period.

China is now the second largest economy and trading country in the world. The International Monetary Fund (IMF) has projected that China will contribute to about one-third of global growth by 2017. As China's economy becomes increasingly integrated with the rest of the world, it is a natural trend for its currency, RMB, to become more widely used in trade and investment activities.

Key Benefits and Triggers of Using RMB to Do Trade and Investment in China

The key benefits of using RMB to trade with Chinese businesses and make investment in China include: improved pricing competitiveness from avoiding currency exchange costs and risks involving a third currency; enlarged client base and business partners in China to include customers and suppliers who prefer to settle transactions in RMB; and shortened settlement cycle, which allows business to be done more efficiently.

According to a survey conducted by HSBC in 2012, "hedging foreign exchange fluctuation risk (72%)" and "more convenience in daily business operating and accounting practice (44%)" are two key triggers of doing RMB cross-border business. Besides, the number of companies who choose "holding more RMB in the view of RMB appreciation expectation" has dropped significantly in 2012. This implies that holding RMB for speculative purposes is declining as more and more use of RMB is driven by real needs of the economy.

Cross-border RMB Business typically refers to the following business activities including goods and service trade settlement, RMB purchase and sale, foreign direct investment (FDI) and outward direct investment (ODI), foreign investment in China's interbank bond market, the investment by RMB Qualified Foreign Institutional Investors (RQFII), and the bilateral currency cooperation.

RMB Cross-Border Trade Settlement

In the 1980s, RMB was first brought to neighboring regions, such as Hong Kong and Macau, mainly through personal transfer, tourism, and border trade. Since the 1980s, RMB has been widely used to settle border trade with neighboring countries, including Vietnam, Myanmar, Mongolia, Russia etc. Since the 1990s, especially after joining the WTO, China gradually relaxed restrictions on RMB cash outflows. RMB cash within a certain limit can be brought out of China freely. Since January 2005, the limit of cash brought out of the border by individuals was raised from RMB6,000 Yuan to RMB20,000 Yuan. In July 2009, a pilot program on trade settlement in RMB was introduced to facilitate trade and investment.

The pilot program on cross-border trade settlement in RMB experienced three phases of development. In July 2009, the pilot program only permitted the settlement of goods traded in RMB and covered Shanghai and four cities in Guangdong province with 365 designated exporters involved and no restrictions on importers. The eligible offshore counterparties were restricted to those in Hong Kong, Macau, and ASEAN countries. In June 2010, the pilot program extended to 18 other provinces (autonomous regions, municipalities), such as Beijing, Tianjin, Xinjiang, etc., and involved 67,724 designated exporting enterprises by December of that year while still posing no restrictions on importers. The restriction on eligible offshore counterparties was also lifted, and all current account transitions were allowed to be settled in RMB. After adjustments made in August 2011 and June 2012, the pilot program covered the entire country with all exporters and importers permitted to settle transactions in RMB. But a negative list of enterprises (typically with prior violations) was subject to intense supervision. All current account transactions and some capital account transactions (FDI, ODI, project financing) were permitted thereafter.

Since then, cross-border RMB business has been developing rapidly. Enterprises in all provinces and cities in China can now settle their trade transactions in RMB with any part of the world. An overseas company can receive RMB payment through a bank in the rest of world from its trade counterpart in Mainland China. The RMB proceeds can be deposited with a bank in the offshore market, invested in a wide range of RMB financial products or converted into other currencies.

Transactions can be settled in RMB through three channels. 1) Agent bank channel: an overseas bank could open a RMB settlement account (RMB interbank current account), send cross-border settlement information through SWIFT, and overseas participating banks would settle the transaction with the domestic agent banks in RMB through the PBC's High Value Payment System (HVPS); 2) Clearing bank channel: an overseas bank directly or indirectly connects with HVPS through an overseas clearing bank and carries out cross-border RMB settlement using the RMB settlement account (agent account) opened with the clearing bank; 3) NRA channel: an overseas institution could open NRA in domestic banks, which could be used for cross-border settlement. The businesses are free to choose any one of the three channels for RMB settlement.

From January to December 2012, total cross-border RMB settlement registered RMB 2.94 trillion Yuan, a YoY increase of 41 percent, among which, settlement for trade in goods stood at RMB2.06 trillion Yuan, a YoY increase of 32 percent and accounting for 8.4 percent of all goods import and export during the same period. From July 2009 to end-2012, RMB cross-border settlement totaled RMB5.5 trillion Yuan. By the end of 2012, enterprises in 206 countries or regions have carried out RMB deposit and payment business with domestic counterparties. And accumulated RMB settlement with Hong Kong, including deposit and payment, accounts for 55.7 percent of the total.

From January 2010 to December 2012, the monthly volume of goods and service trade settled in RMB settlement increased considerably, from nearly zero to about 300 billion Yuan combined (about 200 billion Yuan for goods trade and 100 billion for service trade).

The share of China's goods trade settled in RMB was up steadily by 2.2 percent in 2010, 6.6 percent in 2011, 8.4 percent in 2012. In 2012, Hong Kong took the lead with 55.7 percent of the total RMB settlements, followed by Singapore, Taiwan, Japan, Macau and Germany. The rising proportion reflects a bigger role and growing importance of RMB in the international arena.

RMB Purchase and Sale

Overseas participating banks could purchase or sell RMB with domestic agent banks or clearing banks, mainly to satisfy overseas enterprises' demand for initial RMB fund and to facilitate conversion between RMB and other currencies once overseas enterprises acquire RMB. The short and long position of agent banks or clearing banks caused by such buy/sale business could be cleared in China's domestic interbank foreign exchange market. In 2012, total RMB buy/sale business by clearing banks and domestic agent banks reached RMB267.1 billion yuan, involving 77 countries and regions over the world.

RMB FDI & ODI Settlement

In October 2011, foreign investors were allowed to make RMB-denominated investment in China's mainland. Foreign investors and foreign-invested enterprises could go to banks to make inward remittance of RMB funds related with investment, outward remittance of RMB profits and RMB funds obtained by means of capital reduction, liquidation, and equity transfer, and borrow RMB after getting the approval/registration certificate from competent authorities. And there is no need to apply for another approval from the PBC or SAFE before doing such business. In 2012, China's FDI inflows settled in RMB totaled RMB253.58 billion, accounting for 36 percent of all the FDI inflows.

In January 2011, the PBC released the Administrative Measures for the Pilot RMB Settlement of Outward Direct Investment, allowing domestic institutions to make outward direct investment in RMB. After obtaining the approval certificate/document from competent authorities, domestic institutions could go to banks to handle the outward remittance of the RMB funds for the outward direct investment or for upfront expenses. In 2012, China's ODI outflows settled in RMB totaled RMB30.44 billion, accounting for 6.3 percent of the all the ODI outflows.

The FDI & ODI flows settled in RMB indicate that there are already some RMB settlements under the capital account in addition to the early use the RMB for current account items.

Investment in China's Interbank Bond Market

On August 16, 2010, three kinds of institutions including foreign central banks, monetary authorities, Hong Kong, and Macau clearing banks and participating banks were allowed to make investment in the domestic interbank bond market.

In practice, investors were expanded to include foreign insurance companies, international financial institutions, sovereign wealth funds, and RQFII participants. By the end of 2012, a total of 100 foreign institutions had entered China's domestic interbank bond market, including 18 foreign central banks, 3 international financial institutions, 2 sovereign wealth funds, 2 Hong Kong and Macau RMB clearing banks, 48 overseas participating banks, 7 foreign insurance companies, and 20 RQFII participants.

The inclusion of more overseas players into the interbank bond market is an important step in the opening-up of China's capital markets and the opening-up of financial markets such as the bond market in particular.

RQFII Investment

In December 2011, qualified foreign fund management companies and securities companies were allowed to make investment in China's security market on a trial basis. From the beginning of the pilot program until January 2012, a RMB20 billion Yuan's quota has been distributed among 21 pilot institutions. In April 2012, another RMB50 billion Yuan's quota was added. And the first A-share ETF was listed on the stock exchange of HK, focusing on direct investment in domestic A-share market. In February 2013, accumulated RQFII quota reached a total of RMB270 billion yuan, after another increase of RMB200 billion Yuan.

Bilateral Currency Cooperation

By March 2013, 19 central banks and monetary authorities have entered into bilateral currency swap agreements with China, with over a RMB2.0 trillion liquidity line. By March 2013, nine central banks and monetary authorities have signed bilateral local currency settlement agreements with China. Fifteen countries have included RMB assets into their reserve portfolio.

II. RMB Offshore Market

The Connection of Onshore and Offshore Markets

The onshore market is the market located in China's mainland for RMB transactions. RMB funds from trade settlement, FDI, foreign investment in bond market, RQFII investment, and RMB sale will flow into the onshore market. The offshore market is the market for RMB transactions outside of China's mainland. RMB funds from trade settlement, ODI, lending from China's market, bank financing, bilateral currency swap, and RMB purchase will flow into the offshore market. The onshore and offshore markets are closely linked, and the RMB funds can flow into each other through several channels.

So far, a wide range of cities (including potential ones), such as Hong Kong, Macau, Taipei, Singapore, London, Dubai, Sydney, Johannesburg, Moscow, New York, and Saint Polo, have already built RMB offshore markets, and each covers different geographical areas in terms of the business operation. The establishment of offshore RMB markets in more cities around the world will help further boost the international use of RMB.

Development of Offshore RMB Business in Hong Kong

Offshore RMB business was initiated as early as 2004. In January 2004, the personal RMB business was permitted in the Hong Kong market. Over the last decade, the offshore RMB business in Hong Kong developed very fast, accomplishing many milestones, as is shown by the table. Undoubtedly, Hong Kong is the biggest offshore RMB market and plays the most significant role, while offshore RMB markets are also being diversified.

Hong Kong RMB Market

Hong Kong market engages in many types of RMB business, including RMB retail and corporate banking, RMB capital market, RMB money, and foreign exchange market, as well as RMB insurance. RMB retail and corporate banking: deposits, currency exchange, cheques, bank cards, remittance, financing, and wealth management products; RMB capital market: debt origination, investment funds, commodity-linked products, real estate investment trust, exchange-traded fund and equity financing; RMB money and FX market: spot FX, deliverable forwards and futures, nondeliverable forward and FX options; RMB insurance: insurance plans and products.

Hong Kong hosts the largest pool of RMB liquidity outside mainland China. At the end of 2012, RMB customer deposits and certificates of deposit issued by banks in Hong Kong together amounted to RMB603 billion Yuan. About 70 percent of the RMB customer deposits were held by corporates, and over 15 percent of which were from overseas. This sizeable liquidity pool is meeting the increasing global demand for RMB financing and investment.

The Hong Kong market of RMB bonds (dim-sum bonds) is the largest outside mainland China. Over the years, the range of issuers in the RMB bond market in Hong Kong has diversified from predominantly the sovereign (Ministry of Finance of China) and banks in Mainland China to international financial institutions and companies from different parts of the world. Since 2011, the scope of issuers further expanded to include non-bank institutions in mainland China. In 2012, 78 issuers issued 110 billion yuan of RMB bonds.

Apart from issuance of RMB bonds, bank borrowings, and other forms of RMB financing are also available to companies. The outstanding RMB loans in Hong Kong reached over RMB70 billion Yuan at the end of October 2012. RMB shares were first listed in Hong Kong in October 2012.

Hong Kong has a wide range of RMB financial products ranging from currency futures, investment funds to insurance policies to meet different needs of investors.

Other Offshore RMB Markets

In August 2012, in China-Singapore Free Trade Agreement (FTA), relevant parties agreed to establish local RMB clearing mechanism. In April 2013, the PBC signed RMB clearing agreement with ICBC Singapore. In August 2012, the PBC signed MOU with the monetary authority of Chinese Taipei to set up direct cross-strait currency clearing mechanism. In January 2013, the PBC signed RMB a clearing agreement with Bank of China Taipei.

HSBC issued the first RMB denominated bond in London in April 2012, for a total amount of RMB2 billion.

Prospect

China's fast economic development provides huge potential and solid foundation for developing offshore RMB markets. The favorable conditions are many. For example, China's imports are expected to reach USD8 trillion in the next 5 years; China is expected to rank number four in the world in terms of ODI; internationally, a more stable, sustained, and balanced economic development will create a sound environment for the RMB to be used more widely. Domestically, Chinese enterprises going global, the globalization of financial institutions, and the development of the stock and bond markets will all boost the development of RMB offshore markets.

And as the Chinese financial market is not yet fully developed, it means more room for development in the future. First, it is a market to be opened further. In the domestic stock market (A shares), foreign investors only hold 2.9 percent of the total shares. Considering all the Chinese companies listed both at home and abroad (A, B, and H shares), foreign investors hold 15 percent of the total equity. So there is huge room for further opening. Second, it is also a market to have more financial instruments. The stock market may allow short selling in the future. For the bond market, municipal bonds, and securitization may be introduced. The FX market may introduce more instruments to hedge foreign exchange risks. And for other markets, credit-enhancing instruments, government debt futures and commodity futures denominated in RMB may become available in the near future.

And there is more to be done to build a robust financial infrastructure. A more resilient financial system should be pursed. More banking services should be rendered. More RMB products should be provided. A more internationally adapted payment system, namely the CIPS (China International Payment System), should be built.

III. RMB Direct Trading

Since foreign exchange reform in 1994, after nearly 20 years of development, China's foreign exchange market has been established to contain multilevel markets with different trading modes and a variety of participants. It is a two-tier structure: the first tier is the market between the banks and its customers, which is the base of China's FX market. The second is the interbank market. Two types of trading modes: bilateral trading and anonymous trading (matching). China Foreign Exchange Trading System (CFETS) located in Shanghai, as market intermediate, provides an integrated and efficient e-trading system for the interbank market. Interbank FX market adopts a membership system with 333 members, including 295 banks, 37 nonbanking financial institutions, and 1 nonfinancial enterprise.

China's FX market involves three types of players, including CFETS, banks, and customers of banks, and has a two-tier structure, that is, the interbank market and OTC market. CFETS provides a bilateral trading and anonymous trading platform.

Direct Trading between RMB and AUD

The direct trading between RMB and AUD in China adopts a market-maker system, with 12 market makers classified into three types. Seven Chinese domestic banks: ICBC, ABC, BOC, CCB, Bank of Communications, CITIC Bank, and China Guangfa Bank; two Australia banks: ANZ and Westpac; three global banks: HSBC, CITI, BMO (Bank of Montreal). Why do we need three types of market makers instead of just one? That's because different market makers can provide liquidity in different currencies to make sure there is abundant liquidity so that the market can function well. For example, Chinese banks can mainly provide RMB liquidity, and Austrilian banks can mainly provide liquidity in AUD while global banks can provide liquidity in other currencies. With the various ample liquidities, the market will thus be invigorated.

The formation mechanism of the central parity of RMB against AUD will be improved. Prior to the direct trading, the central parity is calculated on the basis of the cross rates between the central parity of CNY/USD and the exchange rate of the AUD/USD. After the direct trading, the central parity will be calculated on the basis of direct quotations offered by the market makers. The improved formation of central parity is an important step in the market-based reform of the RMB exchange rate regime.

The Benefits of AUD/CNY Direct Trading

What are the benefits of direct trading? Direct trading between two currencies can streamline the exchange process, thus lower the cost. Taking AUD/CNY trading, for example, without direct trading, banks have to exchange the AUD position formed from doing business with customers into the USD position, and then sell/buy the USD position in the interbank FX market. With direct trading, banks can exchange the AUD (CNY) position formed from doing business with customers into the CNY (AUD) position in the interbank FX market in one step. The launch of direct trading between AUD and RMB effectively reduces the transaction cost for both businesses and individuals.

Currency Pairs Traded in CFETS

There are nine currencies against CNY and nine foreign currency pairs being traded on CFETS: five direct trading currency pairs: CNY/USD (1994.01), MYR/CNY (2010.07), RUB/CNY (2010.11), JPY/CNY (2012.06), AUD/CNY (2013.04); four others: CNY/HKD (1994.04), CNY/EUR (2002.04), CNY/GBP (2006.08), CNY/CAD (2011.11); and nine foreign currency pairs: EUR/USD, AUD/USD, GPB/USD, USD/CHF, USD/HKD, USD/CAD, USD/CAD, USD/JPY, EUR/JPY, and USD/SGD.

The Connection between RMB & AUD Markets

Direct trading between RMB and AUD involves a CNY/AUD market in China and a CNY/AUD market in Australia. Branch of Australian banks in China can provide AUD liquidity for the CNY/AUD market in China. Branch of Chinese banks in Australia can provide RMB liquidity for the CNY/AUD market in Australia. Going forward, more currencies will be directly traded with RMB. The diversification may help RMB gain more importance and become a central currency in the international FX markets in the future.

Conclusion

Generally speaking, progress has been made in promoting the international use of RMB. However, there is still a long way to go before RMB becomes a truly international currency.

CHAPTER 4

Stock Market

Inevitable Reform of IPO Method[1]

The existing IPO process has three steps: (1) to set the price at a designated PE ratio of 15 (or below) that is obviously lower than the average PE ratio in the secondary market; (2) to freeze the funds of investors according to how much IPO stocks they would like to bid for; and (3) to require the investors to transfer their funds to appointed accounts. This issuance method has adversely affected the development of the stock market and the economic growth. Therefore it must be reformed.

I. Existing IPO Method

When an investor purchases a given stock, whether from underwriters or other investors, the stock price should be similar, because they are identical and represent the identical shareholder's rights and obligations. In developed countries, the price of new shares is jointly determined by underwriters and stock issuers (the entrepreneurs). The pricing method is that underwriters will first recommend the new shares to potential investors and collect the information about the acceptable price and determine the IPO price accordingly with a slight discount. The entrepreneurs have assumed the risk of startups and therefore may convert net assets into shares at par value, and new shareholders may only purchase the shares at market price higher than the face value. These two groups of investors obtain the same shares at different prices, and the return gained from the price differential is the return for entrepreneurship.

At present, the average PE ratio in the secondary market of China is 30–40, and the PE ratio of IPO is stipulated by the regulatory authority as not exceeding 15; therefore new shareholders may obtain shares at a "discount price" that is far lower than the market price. The price of new shares will generally double on the day of listing, allowing its PE ratio to converge on the secondary market immediately.

According to the basic principles of economics, risks and returns are correlated; high returns must be accompanied by high risks. The bidding for new shares generates high profits, while it is almost risk-free. The reason lies in the man-made price differential between the primary market and the secondary market, thereby state-owned enterprises can issue new shares at a price obviously lower than the market price.

The new shares purchased at the primary market are the same as the existing shares purchased at the secondary market. The large amount of fund frozen at the primary market for the bidding of new shares is not because new shares are preferred but because the primary market has seen the lower stock price. The primary market price is planned to be low, while the secondary market price is higher as decided by the market. The dual-track pricing system of the stock market will definitely attract capital to the primary market for sale at market price on the secondary market after bidding for newly listed stocks. If the price of new shares is market-oriented, the "law of one price" will have the prices of the two markets converged. However, the price of the primary market is planned, which makes the spread exist between the two markets and leads to the short supply of new shares (the price spread of the two markets was temporarily eliminated when the SHSE dropped to 333 points and the SZSE dropped to 95 points in 1994). It is in nature like the arbitrage of steels under the "dual-track pricing system" when China started reform and opening up. In order to solve the contradiction between demand and supply, it is very important to know how to allocate new shares among market players.

If the price is not liberalized, it is difficult to find solutions for supply shortage. After a series of experiments, the administrative authorities have finally adopted the method that is convenient for operation: freezing subscription funds to calculate the subscription ratio for new share. However, although the method is economic in that new shares are distributed according to the bank deposits, the social cost is obviously too high. The funds raised from new stocks are merely several hundreds of millions, but hundreds of billions of deposits are frozen.

Since the freeze of fund is required to determine the quantity of stocks to be purchased by each investor, it is necessary to verify the amount of fund, and this requires capital verification. Given their worries over false figures provided by banks, the administrative authorities require all local dealers to deposit the subscription fund of their clients into the special accounts of the SHSE and the SZSE opened at the Shanghai and Shenzhen branches of the ICBC and the PBC. In this case, the account opening banks of all dealers have to make actual transfer of reserves at the People's Bank of China (PBC) to designated banks.

These three steps are interconnected, and the fundamental problem is the ultra- low price of stocks on the primary market. However, price differential in the first step does not mean that the second and the third steps must follow, and the latter two steps involve technical problems. There are plenty of technical solutions for the supply shortage caused by the planned pricing system, such as "food coupons." Now we have discovered that problems associated with these three steps, that is, one fundamental problem and two technical problems, have done much harm to the macroeconomy.

II. Hazards of Existing IPO Method

1. The high return from subscription of new shares caused by the low price on the primary market has twisted profit distribution and lowered social investment.

From the statistics of the past few years, the return from subscription of new shares throughout a year was around 50 percent; if the frequency of IPO decreases, a yield of no less than 30 percent can also be guaranteed, which is much higher than the average profit ratio. This will form a vortex that takes in a large amount of funds. In order to promote investment, the state has adopted a series of policies including interest rate cut; however, subscription of new shares can generate such a high return without any risks and can accommodate a huge amount of funds, while nonfinancial investment is of higher risk and lower return, unappealing in comparison. A large amount of fund is unresponsive to an interest rate cut by the central bank because it is stuck in the primary stock market. The low interest rate brought about by the low price of new shares is one of the reasons that investment supply drops in the first half of the year.

2. The freeze of clients' fund has sterilized liquidity from production and circulation, leading to the reduction of money supply and results in deflation.

Currently, M1 is of around RMB3.5 trillion, among which a considerable amount is noncirculating. Judged from the total retail sales of consumer goods of RMB2.6 trillion, the quantity of money that is circulated is not large. Therefore, since more than RMB200 billion is used for IPO subscription in the primary market and frozen, it is likely to be the major cause of deflation.

Currently, the deposits involved in the subscription of new shares is not counted as money supply; therefore, on June 30, 1998, due to the issue of new shares on the SHSE, a large amount of funds was frozen, which led to the abnormal drop of the money supply growth in these two months. In practice, the frequency of IPO is usually high, and a large amount of fund is frozen for a long time. Even if securities administrative departments no longer issue new shares at the end of the month and the money supply counted at the end of the month was not affected by IPO, money supply was reduced de facto. Even in the interval of IPOs, the subscription fund is usually retained instead of being used for other purposes. By then, this portion of fund is included in money supply count; but in fact, it is circulated. Its negative impact on the economy is the same as the direct cut of money supply. The fund freezing has adversely affected money supply, thereby affecting price stability and the normal growth of the macroeconomy.

3. The subscription method of fund freezing reduces the fund in the secondary market and brings about tense relationship between the primary market and the secondary market, which also affects the issuance of new shares.

In fact, the fund raised in IPO is very small, but the method to distribute shares according to the fund frozen will attract a large amount of fund (approximately RMB200–250 billion) to this risk-free "speculative" activity, hence sterilizing the liquidity in secondary market. A PE ratio at 15 times corresponds to around 500 and 600 points of Shanghai Composite Index. As long as the stock index does not fall into this interval, the planned stock price will be different from the market price and is therefore profitable. There will always be conflict between the primary market and the secondary market.

At the time of IPO, some investors will sell stocks in the secondary market to subscribe for new shares in the primary market. Under the method of IPO fund freezing, this impact is amplified by several hundred times. For example, issuance of 100 million new shares at the price of RMB5, the total amount, that is, the total fundraise is merely RMB500 million, and the influence on the secondary market will be no more than RMB500 million. While under the method of fund freezing, RMB100 billion may be involved in the application for subscription, and the influence on the secondary market will be amplified 200 times, which turns the issuance of new shares into an important factor that affects the liquidity of secondary market. Once IPO is more frequent, the liquidity on the secondary market will be sterilized so the issue of new shares must be postponed. If new shares are priced by the market, or the method of fund freezing is abandoned, even if we make ten IPOs a week, only thousands of millions of fund will be withdrawn from the secondary market at most, and the impact on the secondary market will largely be contained and the relationship between the primary market and the secondary market will get better.

4. The capital verification mechanism, under which funds are required to be transferred to appointed accounts, has adversely affected the total quantity of base money of commercial banks and therefore largely weakens the lending capability of commercial banks. It has a negative impact on national economic growth.

The fund being frozen for the issuance of new shares at the two exchanges are around RMB235 billion, and the daily average volume in this year is RMB263 billion. Among which, one-fourth is frozen at the Shenzhen branch of the PBC, which cannot be used by commercial banks. The remaining is frozen at the Shenzhen and Shanghai branches of the ICBC. The base money deposited in the banks with dealer accounts is substantially reduced. Although the Shenzhen and Shanghai branches of the ICBC are free to use the base money transferred to their accounts, in reality, the freezing period is only one to three days, which means the use of the fund is impossible. Currently the base money available (i.e., excess reserves) that is held by state-owned and joint stock commercial banks is about RMB480 billion, which means that nearly half of the excess reserves of commercial banks is frozen and cannot be used due to the issuance of new shares, thereby seriously influencing the normal liquidity management and the lending activities of commercial banks.

In fact, the issuance amount of each stock is relatively small at no more than RMB2 billion. The huge amount of deposit transfer and freezing at the PBC by commercial banks is merely to secure an allotment rate threshold, that is, the amount each investor can purchase. But the mechanism renders a great amount of base money idle. Its impact is equal to the withdrawal of central bank loans at RMB235 billion by the PBC or 3.5 points hike of the reserve requirement ratio.

The interest rate trend of the interbank lending market and the interbank bond market has proved the adverse impact upon liquidity of IPO. When the SHSE and the SZSE issue new shares, the interbank lending and repo interest rates will go up, which reflect the tight position of banks. In the first half of the year, the frequency of issuance of new shares was comparatively high, the positions of commercial banks were tight, and the lending was relatively inactive. In July, the issuance of new shares was basically stopped, and the commercial banks had a better supply of liquidity so that the lending activity has accelerated. Seven new shares were issued in August, fewer than the previous period, so that the positions of commercial banks were less tight, and the lending growth stayed at a relatively higher rate.

III. Reform Implications

The fundamental solution to the problems is to change the current issuance method with IPO price fixed at low P/E ratio to market-oriented issuance mechanism. The underwriters and the sponsors will jointly determine the IPO price, and the underwriters will make stock recommendation to the public. The price of new shares will be slightly lower than the market price. In this case, no huge amount of fund will be frozen in the primary market, and the influence on base money will be greatly contained. If the issuance method cannot be changed to be more market-oriented, we may consider raising the PE ratio to minimize the differential between the planned stock price and the market price. In this way the difference between the subscription fund and the fund raised from IPO will be smaller, and the subscription of new shares with more than RMB200 billion of fund will be no more. As such, even if the second and third steps of IPO remain unchanged, the problems will be contained within an acceptable scope.

If it is difficult to give up the planned pricing mechanism for the issuance of stocks in a short time, it is now required to immediately change the second step of the subscription method, that is, to cancel the fund freezing, and a lot of experts and investors have put forward suggestions in this respect.

As for the third step of the IPO mechanism, namely, the capital verification method under which actual transfer of fund to banks has to be made, Hong Kong once adopted this method. However, the Hong Kong Monetary Authority (HKMA) observed that this method has brought about too many problems to the monetary policy in practice. If the subscription fund is of a relatively large amount, the HKMA will have to urgently inject liquidity to banks, which results in an extreme waste of social resources; therefore the HKMA reformed the capital verification method. The banks no longer have to conduct actual transfer of funds, rather, they issue promissory note to verify the fund. If the second step cannot be changed in a short time, the top priority is to use a promissory note for capital verification, which is relatively easy.

2000 Points in Year 2000—How Bubble Begins[2]

I. Strong Rise of China's Stock Market Promoted by the Flow of Fund Despite Its Lack of Investment Value

Since this year, China's stock market has been rising. The Shanghai Composite Index has climbed from 1,366 points at the beginning of 2000 to 2,023 points at the end of July, up by 48 percent. In the same period, the Shenzhen Component Index jumped 55 percent. The seven-month continuous hike has hit new record of China's stock market. In the mean time, the P/E Ratio also keeps rising. In July 2000, the average P/E Ratio of A Shares in Shanghai Stock Exchange is 58.21, while that in Shenzhen Stock Exchange is 57.89. Over the threshold of 2,000 points, the P/E Ratio of China's stock market has approached 60. Compared with European countries and the United States, as well as the emerging markets, the P/E Ratio of China's A Shares is far higher. In history, only the P/E Ratio of Japan and China's Taiwan at the peak of their bubble economy are comparable.

However, the problem reflected by the unreasonable P/E Ratio of 60 is just the tip of an iceberg. The P/E Ratio of China's stock market is not the same as that of international markets, and the P/E Ratio used to understand the investment value of China's stock market would fail to show the whole picture.

Profits go to the listed companies, but not the investors. Taking the profits of companies to be the value indicator of stocks would fail to show who the real beneficiary are. The proceeds to listed companies must be distributed as dividends so that the investors can share the corporate profit. Among three ways of profit distribution by the listed companies in China, stock dividend is merely the adjustment between the items in the shareholders' equity, and its nature is share split; rights offering is an increase in both the left and right sides of the balance sheet, that is, the simultaneous increase of assets and shareholders' equity; only cash dividend is a decrease in both the left and right sides of the balance sheet, that is, the simultaneous decrease of assets and shareholders' equity. Investors and listed companies are two entities. The assets of investors increase while the assets of the listed companies decrease. Only when the assets of the listed companies are transferred into the pocket of the investors will investors share the corporate profit. Obviously, cash dividend is the only way to increase the proceeds of investors rather than the other ways. In international stock markets, the profits of listed companies are closely related to the cash distribution. Therefore, the P/E Ratio may represent the cash distribution level to some extent. However, in Chinese stock market, the P/E Ratio is not closely related to cash distribution, thus it has lost its function in analyzing the investment value, and we cannot compare it with the P/E Ratio of the stock markets in other countries.

According to the calculation based on the data of annual reports, the cash distributed to the shareholders in the A-share market in 1999 was merely RMB2.4 billion. And on average, each share may have RMB0.028 pre-tax cash dividend, or RMB0.022 after-tax. Based on the average price

RMB14.4 of the A shares in China in July 2000, investing RMB1 in the stocks in the secondary market will generate RMB0.0016 in cash return a year later, that is, "dividend yield" is 0.16 percent, and its inverse is 635, which indicates that after purchasing the stocks, investors have to wait 635 years to take back their investments from cash dividends. Such investment recovery period is more than ten times that of the P/E Ratio. Take the stock market of Hong Kong as example. Since this year, it has standing at historical highs. From January to July of 2000, the average P/E Ratio of all common shares is 13.97 with an average dividend yield of 2.34 percent, an inverse of 42.73 and a third of profits have been distributed by cash dividends. Currently, the dividend yield of the S & P 500 Index stocks of the US stock market is around 1.4 percent, 8 times than that of China's A-shares. Back to 1929, the average dividend yield of the US stock market before its crash was 3 percent. Compared with that, the 0.16 percent dividend yield of China's stock market can be totally disregarded by the investors (the cash dividends proceeds of RMB2.4 billion going to the investors each year is less than the stamp taxes they pay in a month), and in fact, the investors of China's stock market do ignore it. Financial instruments should have been developed for investors to get return from investment. If stocks cannot bring returns for investors, it will lose its fundamental profitability as a financial instrument.

China's stock market has been rising continuously (see Figure 4.1); why is that? It is easy to find answer if we look at the growing financing volume (the amount of fund in the secondary market) in the stock market. Since May 1999, the financing volume of China's stock market has started to increase and was robust in 2000. The monthly average turnover of the Shanghai Stock Exchange and the Shenzhen Stock Exchange was RM 196.2 billion in 1998 and RMB260.9 billion in 1999. And in the first seven months of this year, the monthly average turnover doubled and reached RMB572.9 billion, with an average annual growth rate of 71 percent. The fund freezing in IPOs has repeatedly made new records. In 1998, the average fund required to be frozen in each IPO was RMB68.6 billion, peaking at around RMB100 billion; in 1999, the number was RMB74.5 billion, peaking at RMB200 billion; and in the first seven months of 2000, the number was RMB86.8 billion, indicating an uptrend year by year. In 1998, the largest amount of fund freezing in a single IPO was RMB150–250 billion. However, the amount of fund freezing for the new share "Angel Yeast" issued earlier this year was nearly RMB330 billion, and the highest freezing fund level this year is around RMB500 billion, more than a double of that in 1998. The rising stock price driven by capital inflow embodies the feature that the stock price's movement has been deviated from the performance

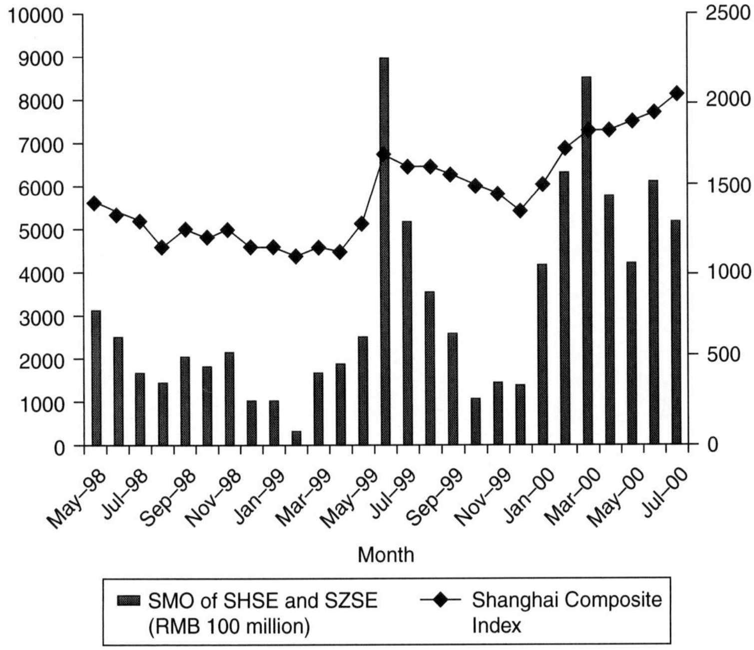

Figure 4.1 AMO and index of Shanghai stock exchange and Shenzhen stock exchange.

Source: Shanghai Stock Exchange (www.sse.com.cn) and Shenzhen Stock Exchange (www.szse.com.cn).

and other fundamental variables; nothing is able to press down the surging price, whether it being that the number and percentage of loss-making listed companies are hitting historical records or the release of an administrative regulation that sets the ceiling of price hike and removes the floor of price fall for PT companies.

II. Excess Money Supply and Low Interest Rate Policies

The continuous rise of stock price and the continuous fall of commodity price make a sharp contrast. Since 1998, the money supply has grown rapidly, the M2 has maintained a growth rate of no less than 13 percent, but the inflation has remained suppressed(see Figure 4.2). This cannot completely be explained by monetization, because the growth rates of money supply and inflation diverge absolutely and directionally.

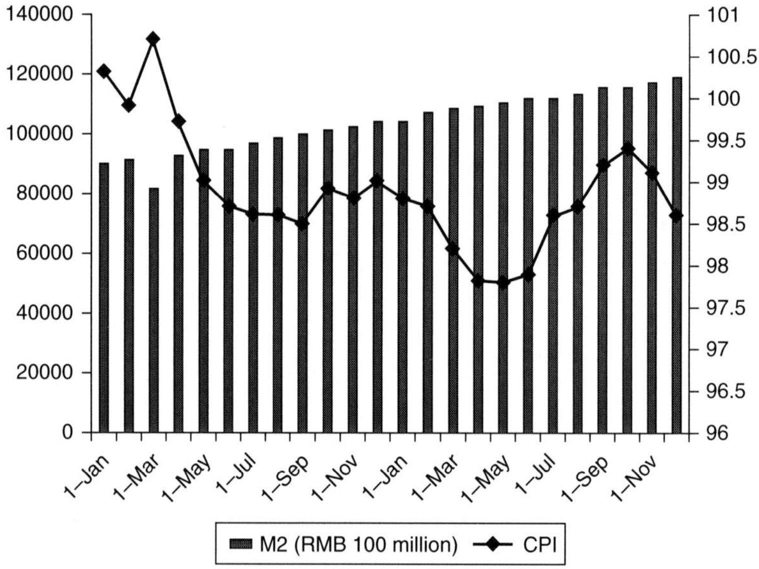

Figure 4.2 M2 and CPI on year-on-year basis.

Source: People's Bank of China (www.pbc.gov.cn) and National Bureau of Statistics of People's Republic of China (www.stats).

Let's analyze the issue based upon a new money demand formula, $M = P_cT_c/V_c + P_fT_f/V_f$, that is, money supply = money in the goods market + money in the financial market. There are multiple causes of the phenomena that the inflation was not boosted by growing the money supply; on the one hand, the velocity of money circulation in the general market has slowed down, and on the other hand, a large amount of money has flown into the financial market, which creates new money demand and absorbs the expanding money supply.

Inflation is a monetary phenomenon in essence, and the change of money is different from that of price, but the trend will definitely be convergent. In the inflationary period, the common rise of price level is difficult to sustain for a long time without rapid growth of money. Similarly, if there is no slowdown in the money growth, the continuous decrease of price level is difficult to last for a long time. Therefore, under the condition that the aggregate money supply is growing rapidly, there is no real deflation. The trend of money supply will not deviate from the trend of price for a long run, and there are two possible results. The price stays low, effective demands are insufficient and enterprises' performance gets worse, resulting in the insufficient effective loan demands and therefore banks find it difficult to issue loans so that the growth rate of money supply has to slow down to be consistent with deflation. In this case, the real deflation would take shape. Japanese economy is a typical case. From 1995 to 1997, the base money growth of Japan reached 7.9 percent, indicating the urgent need of the central bank's expansionary monetary policy. However, due to insufficient effective demand, the enterprises and individuals were unwilling to borrow money, and the banks' lending shrunk. And as a result, the annual growth of M2+CD was merely 3.2 percent, which was significantly lower than the growth rate of base money but was consistent with the inflation, which was less than 1 percent. The other possibility is that under the condition of deflation, the continuous injection of money inconsistent with the inflation rate would slow down the velocity of money circulation. And when this process develops to a certain degree, the money supply passively accepted by enterprises and individuals will reach a considerably high level, and driven by external shocks, the money circulation velocity will suddenly accelerate, which is going to cause rapid inflation. And this will boost consumption and investment, further accelerating money circulation. Finally, the money circulation velocity will overshoot to a level higher than normal. However, a large amount of money flowed into the stock market, so none of the said two possibilities stand in China. The loan demands are still strong. The expanding money supply is aimed to boost domestic demands to bring up inflation, but instead, the money supply actually drove the stock price up. In the first half of 2000, the money supply was growing fast. At the end of June, the balance of M2 was RMB12.7 trillion, with a year-on-year growth of 13.7 percent; while the balance of M1 was RMB4.8 trillion, with a year-on-year growth of 23.7 percent. The loan demands were thriving, and the balance of loans of all financial institutions recorded a year-on-year growth of 13.8 percent. And the growth of household deposits greatly decreased. At the end of December last year, the growth of national savings of urban and rural residents was 11.6 percent; while at the end of April this year, the growth rate dropped to 7.1 percent, and at the end of May, June, and July, the growth rates were respectively 5.5 percent, 6.2 percent, and 6.3 percent. The household consumer price index only posted a 0.1 percent year-on-year growth, while the stock market index had soared approximate 50 percent compared with the beginning of the year. The growth rates of M2 and M1 were, respectively, 5.4 percent and 15.4 percent higher than the sum of the GDP growth and the consumer price growth. Compared with the economic growth and the inflation, the money supply is obviously too much. The ratio of M2/GDP of China was 1.31 in 1998 and 1.46 in 1999. By contrast, the ratio of M2/GDP of the United States is 0.67 in 1998,

South Korea 0.7, India 0.5, and Japan 1.2. Therefore, China had the most excessive money supply.

When the stock market has no investment value, the excessive money supply cannot alone drive a large amount of money into the stock market. The yield spread is an important variable for the public to decide whether to invest in the real economy or stock market. The interest rate is so low that the funds swarm into the stock market, thereby stimulating the rise of stock price. Since 1996, China has lowered the deposit and loan interest rates seven times. Take 1Y deposit rate as example. It has dropped to 2.25 percent after the June 10, 1999, from 10.98 percent at the beginning of 1996 (after deducting the 20% interest tax, this rate is just 1.8%). The interest rate of 1.8 percent is equal to 16 percent of 10.98 percent. From 1980 to 2000, the time weighted average value of the 1Y time deposit rate is 6.73 percent in China, which is at a considerably lower level compared with the average interest rate of the same period (see Figure 4.3).

Low interest rate may stimulate investment to some extent, but an ultra-low interest rate has a distorted price signal on the money market, disrupts

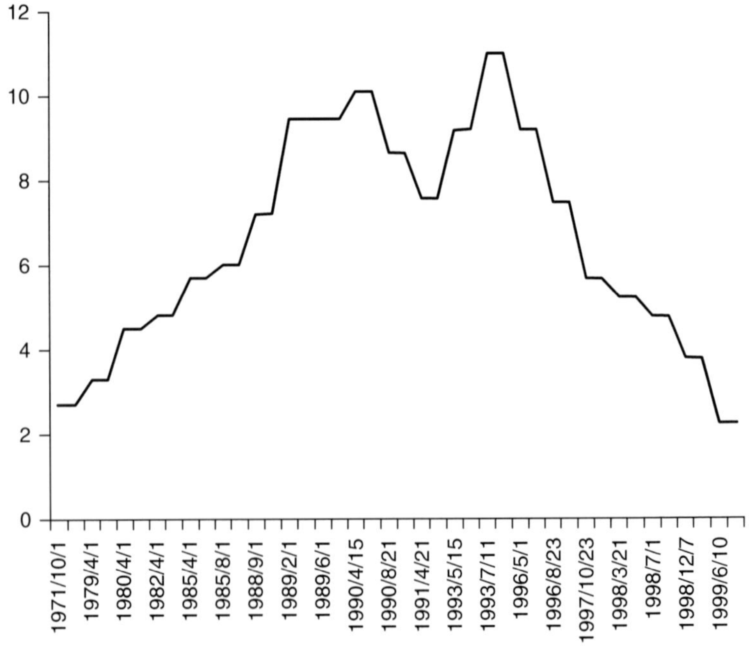

Figure 4.3 Change for 1Y deposit interest rate (%).

Source: People's Bank of China (www.pbc.gov.cn).

the allocation of social resources, and lowers market efficiency. The lower level of interest rate greatly reduces the income of depositors, so the residents reduce consumption, and the high return of the stock market has become more attractive. In order to make up for losses, residents invest in the stock market. Thanks to the low interest rate, enterprises are able to obtain loans easily and put their money into the stock market. Both the residents and enterprises push the stock market price up, developing the "effect of sheep flock." The continuous rise of stock price raise the expected return and made the public underestimate the risk. The return of the stock market is the highest in the whole society, leaving other financial investment and real economy investment far behind.

The bubble economies happened in the United States, Japan, China's Taiwan, and other places also prove that. From January 1923 to May 1928, the US government had controlled the monthly call loan rate of stock exchange at no more than 5.7 percent to maintain the short-term interest rate and the so-called orderly status of money market, which stimulated a large amount of money to flow into the stock market. And the loan balance of stock brokers rose from the USD1.86 billion at the end of 1922 to USD2.78 in March 1928. The stock price greatly rose in the wake therewith. It is after June 1928 when the monetary authority allowed the short-term interest rate up to 6.32 percent and in December 8.86 percent. However, it was so late that the stock market bubble had taken shape. On October 4, 1929, the stock price of the United States slumped, and the stock market crashed.

In 1985, in the conference participated by the finance ministers and central bank governors of the United States, Japan, France, the United Kingdom, and Germany in the Plaza Hotel, launched by the United States, the five countries decided to intervene in the foreign exchange market. As a result, the USD/JPY exchange rate declined from 360:1 to 200:1 (representing a sharp appreciation of JPY), which heavily undermined the export sector of Japan. Japan then adopted the expansionary monetary policy to stimulate domestic demands. Since January 1986, the discount rate has lowered five times, dropping to the extra low level of 2.5 percent in 1987 from the original level of 5 percent, which lasted to May 1989. The monetary supply (M2+CD) from 1987 to 1997 exceeded 10 percent. The low interest rate and growing money supply made the money flow into the stock market and real estate market, which caused the rapid development of bubble economy. And the Nikkei had risen rapidly from 12,000 points in 1985 to the 39,000 points at the end of 1989, and the land price in 1990 became five times that in 1985. Since October 1989, the central bank started to hike up the interest rate, which rose to 6 percent in August 1990. The stock market started to drop since January 1990, and in May 1991, the stock market had dropped by two-thirds. By 1995, the housing price had dropped by two-thirds.

The peak of China's stock market return is not only supported by the rising price of the self-reinforcing secondary market but also the high return of IPO in the primary market, which is different from other countries. For a long time, the stock issuance price in China has been greatly lower than that of secondary market, which leads to the riskless high return. Since 2000 the regulatory authorities have taken some reform measures, and the stock issuance price and P/E ratio have been raised, but still with a large spread compared with the secondary market. The average P/E ratio for the new share issued in the first half of 2000 was 25.1, still less than half of that in the secondary market. Because it is risk-free, the high return of IPO is comparable to the savings rate. The riskless return in the primary stock market intensifies the hoarding of funds in the stock market.

The stock market bubble may only be addressed as a "bubble economy" when it leads to the large-scale change of monetary structure and enables the bubble to dominate the economy of a country, which is supported by money supply and low interest rate. Therefore, there are two preconditions and one characteristic of the bubble economy. The preconditions are excessive money supply and an ultra-low interest rate, and the characteristic is that the rising of stock price makes the stock market lose its investment value, and the purpose for investors to enter into the stock market is for speculation. The monetary policy of the central bank to boost economic growth and maintain commodity price is greatly undermined by the bubble of stock market.

III. Dangers of Bubble Economy

Money insufficiency in the real economy restricts the consumption and investment demands. Usually, the analysis on the dangers of the bubble economy focuses on the losses brought to investors due to the burst of the bubble. However, losses have already occurred in the early stage of the bubble. The prosperous stock market attracts money. Residents reduce consumption to invest in the stock market, which causes insufficient consumption demands. Enterprises use bank loans or fund for production to invest in the stock market. Any unused fund will flow to the stock market, causing insufficient investment on equipments and technologies. The rapid growth of funds in the stock market means the money supply to the real economy is lower than that of the monetary aggregates. Therefore, a considerable part of the money supply injected by the banking system flows to the stock market instead of the real economy; therefore it is difficult for such money supply to have an impact on price. This is why the current money supply in China expands greatly but the price is continuously going downward. As we can see, a bubble economy seems to be a privilege for the United States, because its stock market bubble is supported by foreign investors, including foreign direct investment in the US stock market and indirect support via foreign government's purchase of the US treasury bonds and holding of dollar deposits. Therefore, the bubble in the US stock market does not affect its equipment and technology investment as well as consumption demand So the performance of the listed companies are not affected, thereby restricting the stock market bubble to spread to the whole economy.

Tremendous investment in the stock market is not good for real investment. The public financial investment is no real investment demand. Taking stock market as an example; the trading in the secondary stock market by the public does not change the number of stocks nor the quantity of money. For individuals, putting money into the stock market is to make an investment, but their purchase of stocks is based on the sale of stocks by others, thus the aggregates of stocks as a financial investment instrument does not increase. The public purchases financial assets from the primary market to transfer money from people with surplus fund to people in need of liquidity, but there is no demand of investment formed. Only when the enterprises issuing stocks use the fund raised to invest the total demand is then boosted. Thus, fund flow to the stock market doesn't mean the increase of investment. Since the state-owned enterprises in China go public mainly to reform their corporate governance structure, and in addition there exists the quota examination and approval system hampering investment, the fund raised in IPO doesn't necessarily have underlying investment projects. And the fund raised from IPO by many listed companies enters into the stock market via different channels, including but not limited to strategic placement, equity participation in dealers, self-investment and entrusting investment, instead of being transformed into investment demands.

The money-driven bubble economy invalidates supply-demand law of stocks and regulatory measures. The trading of stocks, whether in the primary market or the secondary market, does not change the money quantity. Generally, the increase of stocks supply leads to the decrease of the stock price. However, in the bubble economy, stocks are the first options for residents and enterprises to hold as assets, and the attractive return has made money of different forms all participate in the stock market. Even the money from issuance of new shares will reenter into the stock market. Similarly, sale of state-owned equity, taxation on the stock market, and issuance of treasury bonds do not change the money quantity. And entity obtaining this part of money will thereafter transfer to the enterprises and residents, and driven by the public's assets selection, the money will flow back to the stock market from different places. In the first half of the 1980s, the manufacturing industry in Japan issued stocks with an average value of JPY800 billion every year, and JPY5 trillion in 1989. From 1987 to 1989, Japanese enterprises raised fund of JPY21 trillion via issuance of stocks and corporate bonds. However, this huge amount of stocks did not cool down the stock price, which indicated that only enhancing the savings interest rate and narrowing the yield spread between stocks and other investments may curb the bubble economy.

The bubble economy intensifies injustice in wealth distribution. Stock trading changes the distribution of money but not the quantity. The small- and medium-sized investors are disadvantageous groups in market, so money is usually transferred from residents to enterprises or from low-income to high-income residents, which is proved by the development of stock markets at home and abroad. The low-income residents accounts for the largest percentage of the social population, so such transfer not only reduces the overall consumption trend but also damages the social order.

The further harm of bubble economy lies in discouraging the citizens' innovation spirit, investment enthusiasm, and work initiatives. These are exactly the fundamental forces for the development of a country. In the past, the United Kingdom, Sweden, Japan, China's Taiwan, and other countries and regions experienced a bubble economy, and all people are involved in the stock market. As a result, the national competitiveness is weakened; the leading status of some countries in international economy is lost, and the loss of national spirit makes the largest loss for a country.

What Interest Rate Liberalization Will Bring to the Securities Market?[3]

In recent days, Dai Xianglong, governor of the PBC indicated that China will complete the overall liberalization of interest rate in the next three years. First, interest rate of foreign currency has been fully liberalized; second, interest rates of interbank lending and interbank treasury bond market are being liberalized; third, the interest rates of lending and deposit in countryside are ready to be liberalized; and finally, the interest rates of lending and deposit of banks in cities will be liberalized. The floating ranges of loans are expanded, the interest rates of large value deposit are loosened, and then interest rates of other deposits can be modestly liberalized. The central bank will adjust interest rates through central bank lending and open market operations. All of these can be completed in about three years, which means China has been accelerating the process of interest rate liberalization.

Under the circumstance of interest rate liberalization, the central bank would make its asset/liability interest rate as the benchmark interest rate and implement monetary policy via open market operation, rediscount, required reserves, and others instruments. The financial institutions will determine lending and deposit interest rates and interest rates of various financial assets at their own discretion as per the supply and demand of funds and their operation conditions. The interest rate liberalization will has deep influence on Chinese securities market, which is in accelerated development.

I. Background of the Interest Rate Liberalization

With reforms, the framework of the socialist market economy of China is taking its shape, and the market becomes the main platform of resource allocation. But interest rate, the price of funds that plays a key role in the market allocation of resources, has not yet been liberalized and becomes the bottleneck of further improvement of the market economic system. In recent years, the central bank has carried out reform on the liberalization of interest rate, which is mainly reflected in (i) liberalizing interest rates of financial market and expanding the floating range of the lending and deposit interest rates. China's interest rate liberalization started from the money market. On June 1, 1996, PBC decided to remove the cap for the interbank lending rate to realize the complete liberalization of interbank lending. After the establishment of the interbank bond market in 1997, the bond repo interest rate and bond trading price were completely decided by the trading parties. In 1998 and 1999, PBC started market-oriented issuance of treasury bonds and policy financial bonds. The issuance rates of bonds in interbank lending market, the leading market of Chinese bond market, are determined by the market. The liberalized interest rate system of China's money market and bond market has basically formed to provide the foundation for the liberalization of interest rate. In the meantime, PBC enlarges the floating range and scope of lending interest rate for enterprises. It widened the floating range of lending interest rate for SMEs all to 30 percent in 1999 and allowed commercial banks to run pilot scheme on the contracted deposit with insurance companies. Such measures make necessary preparation for further liberalization of lending and deposit interest rates. (ii) Actively developing the financial market. An important premise of implementing interest rate liberalization is that the central bank has the capacity to control lending and deposit interest rates, which requires a financial market with considerable width, depth, and efficiency to act as intermediary of monetary policy. Since 1997, the central bank has vigorously regulated and developed the interbank bond market and interbank lending market. So far, the daily turnover of these two markets is about RMB10 billion, becoming the principal place for commercial banks, securities companies, and other financial institutions to adjust fund and make investment. (iii) Reforming the instruments of monetary policy. At the beginning of 1998, PBC cancelled loan size management and started to change to indirect monetary policy operations. On May 26, 1998, the PBC restored open market operation of bonds and achieved monetary policy objective through regulating the interest rates of base money, money market and bond market. In the year of 1999, the capital lent by the PBC via bond open market operations amounted to RMB707.6 billion and the base money supplied being RMB190.7 billion, accounting for around 50 percent of the newly increased base money of the central bank. Therefore, open market operations became the main monetary policy instrument of the central bank. Open market operations play a significant role in terms of supplying base money and regulating money market and interest rates of the bond market. The central bank has been equipped with sufficient measures to regulate interest rates. All these create the conditions for comprehensive implementation of interest rate liberalization.

Based on changes of objective conditions, the central bank accelerates interest rate liberalization, which is a visionary measure. The following five years are the key period for realizing the development strategy of "Three Steps" as set forth by Deng Xiaoping and also the five-year transition period upon China's entry into the WTO. The interest rate liberalization will not only provide necessary preconditions for the commercialized operation of national banks through comprehensively enhancing social economic vitality and social efficiency and optimizing funds allocation but also increase the competitiveness of financial institutions of Chinese bank against those of foreign ones. In addition, interest rate liberalization is inevitable for commercial banks to compete with security companies and for indirect financing to compete with direct financing.

In recent years, the competition between banks, security companies, and insurance companies has been intensified. The public are calling for higher profitability of financial instruments. Deposit, investment fund, and insurance products are more like investment instruments now. Especially, investment funds have growing advantage compared to banks. In developed countries, financial services are far less intermediated. Under such circumstances, mixed operation of financial services agencies has become an irresistible international trend.

In developed countries, interest rate liberalization has been finished; commercial banks have difficulty in competing with securities and insurance industries and instead, adopt mixed operation based on their advantages. Having no decision power on the price of the main asset and liability (lending and deposit) of the commercial banks of China, the commercial banks of China cannot cope with the challenges from international and domestic securities and insurance industries. The obvious decrease of residential saving rate this year reflects this trend to some extent. The competition between securities industry with banking industry is not yet obvious since China has not yet joined WTO and relatively low liberalization of domestic capital market. But with the high-speed development of the securities market of China and large-scale initiation of open-ended fund, as well as the fact that foreign banks are allowed to engage in securities business and mixed operations, Chinese banks will face big challenge from the securities industry. Before studying mixed operation and joint supervision, the bank industry shall first be released from the constraints on its operations. Therefore, to accelerate interest rate liberalization is the only way for commercial banks to compete at home and abroad.

II. Influence of the Interest Rate Liberalization on the Securities Market

(I) Promoting the Market-Based Reform of the Stock Market

With the promotion of interest rate liberalization, the price of assets and liabilities of the banking system will be determined by the market. Commercial banks have more autonomy in providing the credit and related service to enterprise clients and enterprises have more options. The competition between indirect financing and direct financing becomes more and more intense. In the secondary stock market of China, the prices are determined by trading parties with lesser intervention of the securities supervision departments, thereby the market reform was basically completed. However, the primary stock market has not yet been fully liberalized, in which the issuance prices of stocks are much lower than that of the secondary market. The regulatory authority introduces "strategic investors," and direct subscription of security investment funds allows listed companies to determine IPO price within the price range approved by CSRC and implements other reform measures. However, because the method of "strategic investors" is simply to alter the current public distribution of new shares by the original pricing method, it only strengthens the rent setting and rent seeking in IPO. After the interest rate liberalization, the long-term government-controlled interest rate system will be changed to the market-oriented interest rate system, which is an external shock to the capital market. The competition pressure from banks that provide enterprises with all-round services will facilitate market-based reform of the IPO procedure.

(II) Interest Rate Liberalization Significantly Benefits the Development of the Bond Market

In developed countries, short-term interest rate level is determined by interest rates of interbank lending and bond repo in money market, while long-and-medium-term interest rate is determined by the yield to maturity of bond in the bond market, and commercial banks make decision of the lending and deposit interest rates according to both the interest rate levels of various maturities in money market and bond market and their own operating conditions. Now China deregulates the interest rate in the money market and bond market but regulates the lending and deposit interest rates of commercial banks. Because credit asset and deposit liability are a large proportion of the balance sheet of the banking system, the range of interest rates on the money market and bond market are largely determined by the lending and deposit interest rates. Therefore, the range is narrow and the interest rate is an incompletely market-oriented rate. The trading activities of interbank lending, bond transaction and bond repo are restricted. Interest rates of money market and bond market fail to influence the expected interest rate. After liberalization of interest rate, the range of bond price and bond repo interest rate in the bond market will be expanded and the market transactions tend to be more active. The liberalization of interest rate is not only conducive to the development of treasury bond and financial bond markets, but also a strong push to corporate bond market. In accordance with the current regulations, the issuance interest rates of corporate bonds are not allowed to be higher than the sum of the government-controlled deposit interest rate and a fixed margin. The issuance interest rates of corporate bonds usually reach this upper limit. The rigid issuance interest rate of corporate bonds detains the expansion of corporate bond market. The liberalization of interest rate will enable enterprises to broaden the channels of fund raising through bond issuance and will differentiate the interest rates of bonds issued by different types of enterprises with different credit level, being helpful to form an active corporate bond market.

(III) Expanding the Financing Channels for Listed Companies and Facilitating the Structural Optimization of the Listed Companies

Usually, commercial banks make overall judgment of risks and profits before lending to enterprises. When lending interest rate is fixed, banks fail to attract clients with sound credit status and adequate repayment capacity by favorable interest rates and make loans to and cultivate those clients with unsatisfactory credit standing, but with great potential to improve, by raising lending interest rate and reinforcing their credit standing. At present, many state-owned enterprises, high and new-tech enterprises and private enterprises with great prospect fail to raise funds as necessary for their development due to the constraint of policy and government-controlled interest rates. After the liberalization of interest rate, commercial banks enjoy more autonomy in providing loans and related services to enterprises and may set reasonable lending interest rate to match the risks. The commercial banks increase their capacity of developing clients, which is conducive to some well-developed listed companies to get lending from banks and increase profits. In the meantime, it will change the situation that enterprises thread their way to go public or make share offering to raise fund. According to the pecking order theory in the Western financial theory, the sequence for the source of fundraising shall be after-tax profits, debt financing, and public offerings. The financial cost for debt financing is low and is subject to financial leverage effect, while public offerings have higher cost and may dilute interests and rights of existing shareholders. As a result, debt financing is preferred to public offerings. After the liberalization of interest rate, it will be easier for enterprises to get loans from banks and the channels of financing via issuance of enterprise bond will be broadened, facilitating enterprises to form reasonable financing structure, supporting good enterprises, and limiting the bad ones to optimize the structure of listed companies.

(IV) Capital Flow in the Financial Market Will Become More Smooth and the Yield of All Markets Will Experience Co-movement

Since 1999, thanks to a series of policies launched by the central bank, security companies and investment funds are allowed to enter the stock market, and banks can provide securities traders with stock collateral loans to open up the financing sources for the financial institutions and connecting the money market, bond market, and stock market. For the time being, the interest rates of banks are government controlled and thus are relatively stable, so it is the capital of the money market and bond market that flows to the stock market. After the liberalization of interest rates, the prices of the above three financial submarkets are more market oriented, thus the scale of the capital flow will grow enormously and the flow direction and method will be more diversified. For the purpose of profit maximization, the investors will compare and select among different investment instruments in various markets and continuously adjust asset structure. By way of the high efficient flow of capital, the return in all markets will be balanced effectively, thereby promoting effective allocation of funds in the financial market.

(V) The Trading Instruments of the Securities Will Be Greatly Enriched

After the liberalization of interest rate, the central bank will make more fine-tuning of the interest rate, mainly achieved by regulating the money market and bond market. Commercial banks will also adjust lending and deposit interest rates for the clients based on comparison between and expectation of their costs and revenues during the operational course. The frequency of interest rate fluctuation will increase. The financial institutions and nonfinancial public are eager to use derivative financial instruments of interest rate to avoid and mitigate the risks of interest rate fluctuation to secure stable cost and benefit and cushion the impact of interest rate volatility. At the same time, the valuable financial variable signals generated from the trading in derivative market will improve the efficiency of capital in the whole society and provide the macroeconomic regulatory authorities with necessary information to make decisions. Forward, swap, and treasury bond futures, interest rate futures, and other derivatives seem ready to be in place, all of which may provide a very great potential for the improvement and deepening of the securities market.

(VI) The Influence of the Central Bank's Monetary Policy on the Securities Market Will Be Obviously Enhanced

The liberalization of interest rate is not to abandon the power to influence the interest rate but to reform the interest rate adjustment mechanism. Based on government-controlled interest rates, the central bank directly determines the lending and deposit interest rates of commercial banks. After the liberalization of interest rate, the central bank will influence the interest rates of the money market and the bond market via monetary policy such as open market operations, and consequently influence the adjustment of commercial bank balance sheet to lead them to change the lending and deposit interest rates. Moreover, from the experience of developed countries, the monetary policy operations of the central bank will cast larger and larger and more and more direct influence on the financial market, which even surpasses the influence cast by the fluctuation of lending and deposit interest rates of commercial banks. In addition, the influence of direct adjustment of lending and deposit interest rates by the central bank would be very great on every aspect of society. Therefore the central bank cannot use it randomly, rendering the forward-guiding function of monetary policy ineffective. After the liberalization of interest rate, the central bank mainly use monetary policies such as open market operations to regulate and control interest rates of money market and bond market, fine-tuning the market conditionally, and selecting the force and direction of regulation. As a result, the monetary policy signals from the central bank will be greatly amplified. Because the main way of the central bank achieving the operation objective is to conduct open market operations in money market and bond market, monetary policy operations will affect the securities market in a very direct way. Based on the experience of developed countries in recent years, central banks start to pay attention to the prices of financial assets. Some of them even include the asset prices as the reference of judgment, in which way monetary policy has become an important variable that affect the trend of the securities market.

Can China Avert a Bubble Economy?[4]

The ratio of cash dividends of Chinese listed companies to their profits is 1/10, while the number in developed countries is around 1/3. Therefore, compared with the P/E ratio of stock markets in developed countries, the P/E ratio of China's stock market is underestimated by more than 2/3. By the end of May 2001, the average P/E ratio of China's A shares was 56, which is equivalent to no less than the 170 P/E ratio in developed countries and had in fact been the highest in the world. Under this circumstance, the stocks have lost one of the fundamental characteristics as financial instruments, that is profitability, and become the intermediary tools for the reallocation of funds among investors of the secondary market. And it is obvious that China's stock market has a bubble. If the stock market bubble continues to develop, the economy of the whole country will be undermined and therefore becomes the "bubble economy." Will China's stock market bubble brings China into a "bubble economy"?

I. The Nature of Stock Market Bubble

Stock trading is the exchange of stocks and money. You may assume a stock market with only two investors that we call A and B. A has RMB100 and 1 share while B has RMB100. The issuance price of the stock is RMB1 per share, so the nominal fortune of them is RMB201 in total. Now, B purchases the 1 share from A at the price of RMB2, and thus A has RMB102 while B has RMB 98 and a share with the market value of RMB2. The nominal fortune of A increases from RMB101 to RMB 102, and A's money has truly increased by RMB2, so A is definitely much richer than before. B loses RMB2 but has a share valued at RMB2, so B has no feeling about his loss. And then A may purchase the 1 share from B at the price of RMB5, and B may repurchase the same from A at the price of RMB10. And if they keep trading at higher price, then at a moment when A has money of RMB150 while B has money of RMB50 and a share valued RMB50, the nominal fortune of A is equal to his money and thus A's real wealth increases, while B gives RMB 50 to A but feels nothing about the reduction of fortune because he has a share valued at RMB50. In this way, A and B both feel the growth of fortune.

However, such fortune is actually the "wealth illusion," because the stock trading never changes the quantity of money. In the example above, the fortune of a resident includes money and stock, and no matter how the stock price changes, the money quantity remains the same. Money can be used for payment or exchanged for commodities and labor service; but stock itself cannot be used to purchase goods and as a financial instrument; its real purpose is to get monetary return. If the listed companies do not give monetary return to the shareholders, the stock is just a tool that redistributes money between A and B. Let's suppose that A and B are locked in a room together with RMB200 and a share. If this stock does not produce any return, then no matter what trading activity occurs between A and B and at whatever price, when the door is opened, there will just be these two persons coming out, together with RMB200 and a share. The only difference is the distribution of wealth.

In the said example, the purpose of B holding the stock is to convert it into money in the future. The market capitalization of stocks is used to evaluate the fund he may obtain when selling the stocks at the current closing price in the market. As for B, the stock is valued at RMB50 because he bought it from A at the price of RMB50 per share, thus he expected to sell at the same price. If there are other investors in this stock market, C, D, and E may think that the stocks can also be sold at the same price. Every investor expects himself or herself to sell the stocks at market price and obtain the money, whereas, it is impossible for the investors to all obtain money at the market value, since the investors in general cannot sell all the stocks. In 1936, Keynes pointed out in his *The General Theory of Employment, Interest, and Money* that, "every investor thinks that his stock has liquidity while in fact it is impossible for the entire investors to realize it." It is impossible for all the stock holders to sell off their stocks at high price, and the market value and the corresponding nominal fortune of the stocks held by the general investors are doomed not to be realized. As a result, the nature of the stock market bubble is that some investors keep more money while some give up their money in return of high-priced stocks to enjoy wealth illusion. In this process, neither the real economy nor the money has changed; the feelings of the investors are the only thing changed.

II. From Stock Market Bubble to Bubble Economy

In reality, the stock market is continuously fluctuating. If there are not many participants and not much funds inflow, the formation or burst of the stock market will not generate a big impact on the economy. The funds of the whole society are like water and each market is a separate water container connecting with each other. The variation of the return in each container causes waves of capital flow, and the stock market bubble forms the spiral pitfall on the water in other containers. The bubble economy takes shape when this pitfall is so large that capital of the whole society flows to the stock market. In the bubble economy, no matter what external force attempts to pull capital out of the stock market, the capital will quickly flow back due to the gravity of the bubble market, just like the black hole in the universe.

In China's Taiwan, the stock market started to boom since 1986 and experienced two crashes in October 1987 and September 1988 due to policy reasons. But after a break, the capital of the whole society still flowed back to the stock market. In 1990, there were 4.6 million accounts in the stock market and 4.7 persons share one stock account on average. Almost all families entered into the stock market, which pushed the capital to its peak. Finally, the stock market thoroughly collapsed at 12,600 points in February 1990.

In Japan, the average shares issued by the manufacture industry was JPY800 billion per year in the first half of the 1980s and reaching JPY5 trillion in 1989, increased by more than five times. From 1987 to 1989, capital raised by enterprises via shares issuance and corporate debt amounted to JPY21 trillion. Such an enormous amount of stocks and debt issuance did not cool down the stock price at all. The capital raised flowed back to the stock market through "special funds" and investment funds promptly, fueling the rapid rise of the stock market.

Because of the nature of self-replication and self-growth of the bubble economy, since its birth, the course to bubble economy is difficult to change. Moreover, there are no opponents to bubble economy. It requires opposing force to change the course of movement. Any governmental policy will benefit some interest groups while harming others. The unique characteristic of bubble economy is that it is difficult to use the concept of "interest group" to analyze the beneficiaries of the bubble economy, because the whole society is the "interest group" of the bubble economy, with every one enjoying illusionary wealth. There is no opponent to the bubble economy, and the only terminator to the bubble economy is the bubble economy itself.

As the representative of the long-term interest of the general public, the government can adjust the basic conditions of the macroeconomy to some extent to contain the bubble economy. However, the government is not exogenous to the society since it represent the interest of a group of people or the general public, and the expansion of the bubble economy may be in line with their interests. In addition, it is difficult for the government to actively eliminate the bubble during the formation of the bubble. In most cases, the bubble bursts incidentally when austerity measures are launched by the government to solve other economic problems at the peak time of the bubble. The financial elites of Japan pointed out that it has been ten years since the burst of the bubble economy of 1990, but the minority in political circles that proposed to eliminate the bubble economy was still reproached by the public who thought intervention was too late or regarded the measures as too drastic. In a word, the opponents to the bubble are usually held accountable for the burst of bubble. In fact, the bubble will burst itself even without any external shock. In the stock market of the United States in 1926, the public blamed the two horrible hurricanes from the Caribbean Sea in the autumn for the collapse of speculation instead of the speculation itself. In case of external shock, the bubble will burst at a touch, which cannot be solved by any gentle measures.

The advices of a few sober economists are usually ignored, which is well described in the *A Short History of Financial Euphoria* written by John Kenneth Galbraith: "In euphoria is the condemnation that the reputable public and financial opinion directs at those who express doubt or dissent. It is said that they are unable, because of defective imagination or other mental inadequacy, to grasp the new and rewarding circumstances that sustain and secure the increase in values. Or their motivation is deeply suspect."

III. Dangers of the Bubble Economy

People usually consider the drop of market value of stocks and nominal fortune after the burst of the bubble economy as the main danger of the bubble economy. Based on such misunderstanding about the bubble economy, it is believed that people are delighted to see the increase of nominal fortune of the public created by the bubble economy, since they can enjoy the growth of wealth as well as avoid the misery of loss of wealth. Their wealth can grow out of nowhere, can't it?

The fact is that when the bubble economy forms, neither the real economy nor the amount of money changes, but the wealth illusion is created. People get no additional money from the bubble economy, and they lose little due to the burst of the bubble economy. The real fortune never increase at the beginning the bubble, so the real fortune of the general public does not decrease when the bubble bursts. The nominal fortune boasted by the stock market surge is doomed to crash.

The dangers of the bubble economy exist in its formation and burst. In the formation of the bubble economy, a large amount of capital is stranded in the stock market instead of being invested in the real economy, which reduces the demand of investment and consumption, aggravates the uneven distribution of wealth allocation, and discourages the citizens' innovative spirit, investment enthusiasm, and work initiatives (see *How Bubble Begins* written by the author and published in the *Caijing* Magazine No. 9, 2000).

The major dangers when the bubble economy bursts are as follows:

1. The Fracture of Bank Credit Chain

The stock cannot be used for consumption or monetary return. The holders of expensive shares have to sell their shares to get money so as to realize the wealth illusion in reality. And thus the purchaser of such shares will lose his money. In the upsurge of the bubble economy, all investors want to share the advantage of the rise of nominal fortune, so they pledge the stocks or directly loan from the banks for consumption. In the course of rapid rise of stock price, many people will recklessly obtain bank loans to invest in stocks. All these make the bubble economy closely linked with bank credit. No matter the loan is for stocks or for consumption, the foundation of credit is the wealth illusion that cannot be realized. They need money to pay back the loan. Actually, before the burst of the bubble economy, the large-scale lending by the banks in connection with the stocks are doomed to be unrecoverable, for the reason that the loans are far beyond the actual repayment capacity of the general investors. Once the bubble bursts and the problems are exposed, the general public is unable to pay back the loans, thereby leading to the fracture of bank credit chain and even a financial crisis under extreme conditions.

2. Blow to the Confidence of General Public

The sound operation of economy relies on the confidence of the general public. It is true that the bubble economy does not change real wealth, but the general public will lose confidence after such a big rise and fall. If you tell a person that he won the lottery and later tell him that he did not, he must be more frustrated than he was at the very beginning, though his conditions do not change at all. When people get used to the illusion of wealth, the break of such illusion will be a severe blow to the confidence of the general public, and that may even result in extreme distrust of the stock market. It took a very long time for people to rebuild confidence after the British South Sea Bubble in 1720 and the US stock market crash in 1929.

China has two characteristics; one is a high starting point of the stock market bubble. The starting points of stock markets in other countries are P/E ratio of ten or so, and the bubble bursts when the P/E ratio reaches 50 (except for Japan), while the P/E Ratio in China is more than 50, equivalent to a P/E ratio of 150 in developed countries. If the bubble economy takes shape, the stock price will keep going up, causing heavy damage when it does burst. The other one is that China is a big country. Viewing from the history of the bubble economy, the bubble economy tends to occur in small countries, such as the United Kingdom, France, Sweden, and Japan, in which speculation is easy to spread among small population. Therefore, the bubble economy is much more difficult to take shape in China, one of the most populous countries in the world. However, once it does occur, the destructive power will be much larger. There is precedent of bubble economy in large county, for instance, the stock market bubble of 1929 and 2000 in the United States.

IV. Can China Avert a Bubble Economy?

By the end of 2000, there have been 58.01 million investors in Chinese stock market, accounting for 4.6 percent of the total population of China. The funds in the primary stock market are around RMB500 billion and assuming that the secondary stock market has around RMB500 billion, thus the total volume of the stock market is around RMB1 trillion, less than one-tenth of the aggregate money supply. The stock market bubble has considerable negative effects on the macroeconomy but has not yet dominated the entire economy of China, so there is no bubble economy so far.

However, it is worth noticing that from the macro background, after the rapid growth of 20 years since the reform and opening-up, the enterprises and residents have possessed abundant funds. Due to the constraint of economic structure and policy environment, as well as the insufficient aggregate demand resulted from export shrink since the Asian financial crisis in 1997, there are few channels to real economy investment for social funds, so the investors have great incentive to enter the stock market. In the meantime, because of the slowdown of export and for the purpose of expanding internal demand, the government has to adopt gentle macroeconomic policy; in addition, the regulation system for stock market supervision is to be improved. The foundation for a bubble economy has been laid. From the performance of the current stock market, the tendency of bubble economy has shown up, SOEs put the money raised from loans or shares issuance into the stock market via entrusted investment or others; laid-off employees and retired employees also put their pension into the stock market. According to regulations, a part of the social security funds raised by the reduced holding of state-owned shares will flow back to the stock market through investment funds management institutions. The large-scale flow of social capital from all channels into the stock market is taking its shape. At the same time, the stock prices in Shanghai Stock Exchange and Shenzhen Stock Exchange show an upward spiral by self-reinforcement. When the rise of stock price and the expansion of capital inflow become the mainstream of economic phenomenon, the bubble economy is on the horizon in China.

The formation of the bubble economy is self-reinforcing and is gaining support from more and more people, which is very difficult to curb by the voice of several economists with conscience and foresight. Moreover, it is hard for the increase of returns of the enterprises to keep up with the rising speed of the stock prices during the formation of the bubble economy. The direction of Chinese macroeconomic policy is highly dependent on the economic trend of developed countries and domestic real economy, and the room for adjustment is limited. Effort shall be made from outside the stock market to keep the stock market bubble away from the real economy.

The formation of bubble economy lies in the greed of people for wealth as well as the pursuit of wealth through shortcuts. Returns from the investments in real industry are no more than that in the stock market and have much weaker liquidity than stocks. But it brings people a sense of achievement when investing in the real economy, which is rather attractive for many people. In case the real economy lacks investment opportunities and the money of the public finds no satisfactory outlet, the stock market bubble is inevitable.

Make a general survey of the history of the bubble economies in all countries, we can find that compared with those countries and regions, the advantage of China is that investment saturation in the real economy is still far away, and there is still much room for investments in many fields of the national economy. In fact, due to administrative regulation, nongovernmental funds fail to enter into many investment fields; in addition, due to the unsound protection to investments, the channel between nongovernmental funds and real economy investments is still obstructed. If the funds of enterprise and residents fail to invest in real economy, they will enter the financial market for speculation, which are the lessons from Japan and China's Taiwan. If China deregulates the limitation of investment areas and strengthens the protection of nongovernmental investments, the nongovernmental funds may be transformed into investments in real economy, and the pressure of the bubble economy may be turned into an investment rush in the real economy, thus China can be pulled away from the bubble economy and brings its economy into a new phase of high-speed growth.

Research on the Relationship between Capital Market Development and Monetary Policy[5]

Since the 1970s, with the development of information technology, financial innovation, deregulation, and financial globalization, the capital markets of industrial countries such as the United States were able to develop in depth and in width, posing more challenges to the traditional targeting and operational framework of monetary policy. In the past twenty years, although central banks of all countries have made great achievements in terms of controlling inflation of goods and service, there are no good solutions to certain problems such as the transmission of monetary policy hampered by the development of capital market and asset price bubble. In practice, as early as in 1929, the slump of New York stock market caused long-term recession of the economies of United States and the world; the "bubble economy" of Japan triggered by the extreme inflation of asset price at the end of 1980s had long-term negative effects on its economy; the obvious deviation of the assets price in the Western countries, such as the United States, from the trend of the real economy since the 1990s have come to be the general concern of decision-makers. In China, the stock market was established in 1990, the scale and influence of which have been under enormous progress in width and in depth after development of more than a decade. The influence of the capital market on the monetary policy is increasingly obvious. The central bank must determine the operational framework of monetary policy based on the new financial environment under the conditions of a mature capital market, for the purpose of better utilizing the capital market to achieve the objectives of monetary policy and weakening the adverse effects on the development of the capital market in relation to monetary policy.

This article analyzes the influence of the capital market on monetary policy on four respects, that is, supply and demand of money, the transmission mechanism of monetary policy, objectives of monetary policy and the operational system of monetary policy, and in particular it is to analyze Chinese capital market, especially the influence of the rapid expansion of the stock market on the monetary policy of the central bank.

I. Influence of the Capital Market Development on Supply and Demand of Money

The impact of the capital market on the monetary policy is based on the changes of the function of money supply due to the development of the capital market, leading to the changes of the transmission process and internal mechanism in the financial system and the real economy upon the implementation of monetary policy tools by the central bank; accordingly, in practice, the central bank must take into account the objectives of monetary policy and adjust and reform the mechanism of monetary policy tools accordingly to allow monetary policy to align with the changes of financial system.

(I) Influence of the Capital Market on Money Demand

Assuming that the short-term real economy stays the same, that is, the income is not changed, the influence of the capital market on money demand is mainly manifested in three aspects: (i) wealth effect, that is, the fluctuation of asset price in the capital market will change the balance sheet of enterprises and individuals and so is the independent variable of the money demand function. The rise of asset price means the increase of nominal wealth of people, if people consider such wealth increase as regular income, the demand of money will increase accordingly. (ii) Capital effect. The exchange of stock, as a kind of financial instrument, will also need money as intermediary. With the development of the capital market and the corresponding increase of trading volumes, under the condition that turnover rate cannot be increased to an infinite amount due to the constraints imposed by practical conditions, it will inevitably lead to more money used as intermediary; as a result, the development of the capital market or the rise of asset price will raise the demand of money. (iii) Substitution effect. The rise of stock price will allow people to adjust their asset structure by holding more stocks and less money, thus reducing the percentage of money in asset portfolios and the demand for money. The net influence of stock price fluctuation on money demand is determined by these three effects altogether: wealth effect and trading effect increase the demand for money while the substitution effect reduces the demand of money. Generally speaking, the wealth effect must be greater than the substitution effect and the most obvious is usually the capital effect. As a result, the development of the capital market is almost accompanied by a growing demand for money. A scholar conducted an empirical analysis of the relationship between China's stock market and the demand for money through multiple linear regression model based on the data from Q1 of 1993 to Q3 of 2000 (Shi, 2001) and discovered the positive correlation between China's stock market and the demand for money. This means that among all forces resulting from the money demand by the stock market, including wealth effect, asset portfolio effect, capital effect, and substitution effect, the force that raises the demand for money (wealth effect, capital effect, etc.) is stronger than the force that lowers the demand for money (substitution effect); logically speaking, these new demands must be satisfied with a certain amount of money supply. The existing monetary policy of China must take into consideration such continuous growing demand of money as brought about by the development and prosperity of stock market to further improve the plan of money supply.

(II) Influence of the Capital Market Development on Money Supply

The influence of the development of the capital market on money supply is presented in terms of structure and quantity. On the one hand, the rise of asset price will strengthen the liquidity of money. With the rise of nominal value of virtual assets and its implied return, the return of money is relatively low, which leads to the increased preference of liquidity. Individuals and institutions are willing to hold more cash and demand deposit, resulting in an excessive growth in M0 and M1, and the money liquidity ratio (M1/M2) continues to go up. At the end of 2000, the money liquidity was 39.5 percent, increased by 1.3 percent compared to the end of 1999.

On the other hand, the continuous rise of asset price increases the opportunity cost of savings. The substitution effect between money and assets will bring down the growth of money supply. A scholar made a regression analysis of the relationship between securities trading volume and money supply from January 1996 to December 2000 (Yan and Li, 2001). In this period, the securities market had already made relatively great development, and the market value and trading volumes in stock market both witnessed a relatively significant increase. The conclusion of the regression analysis is that the effect coefficients of securities trading volumes on the M0 that lags behind one or two months are respectively -0.02 and -0.03, and the sum of the two is the negative effect coefficient of -0.05; the effect coefficients of securities trading volumes on the M1 that lags behind one or two months are respectively -0.0035 and -0.0039, and the sum of the two is the negative effect coefficient of -0.0074; the effect coefficients of securities trading volumes on the M2 that lags behind one or two months are respectively -0.0025 and -0.0036, and the sum of the two is negative effect coefficient of -0.0061. It shows that the securities trading volume reduced the growth rate of money supply at all levels. The trading at the stock market of China is always active, with the acceleration of financing by means of stock issue and allotment, while a large amount of frozen capital used for purchase of stocks (according to the statistics of the exchange, it is usually RMB300–500 billion). In the meantime, stock issue and allotment becomes one of the important sources of enterprise financing, leading to a change of money structure. It mainly shows that a large amount of active trading capital is held up in circulation and money liquidity is strengthening. In recent years, the growth rate of M1 is always higher than the planned growing rate while that of M2 is ower, which is a proof that the capital market improves money liquidity.

The PBC included the deposit of security exchange into the scope of M2 in 2001. With the development of the capital market and financial deepening, the scope of money supply is gradually expanding. The substitution effect of the capital market will mainly affect the structure of money supply, that is, the distribution of the money supply at different levels, instead of the total amount of money supply; therefore the development of the capital market will boost the continuous and rapid growth of the money supply.

II. Influence of Capital Market on the Transmission Mechanism of Monetary Policy

The transmission mechanism of monetary policy goes from the central bank to the financial system and then to the real economy. The main channels may be the price channel and the quantity channel—the price channel being the interest rate channel and the quantity channel being the credit channel, which are also mutually affected. The interest channel means that the policy adjustment from the central bank will first affect the short-term interest rate in the market and then be transmitted to long-term interest rate to affect investments and then influence the real economy. The credit channel is the process in which the central bank adjusts base money and commercial banks accordingly change the credit so that the real economy is affected through the adjustment of money supply. The development of the capital market and the rise of stock price will affect consumption through wealth effect, and affect the borrowing costs and borrowing capability of enterprises through the change of the net value of enterprises so that the social credit scale and real economic activities are affected.

Monetary policy has a bearing on domestic asset price—bond price, stock price, and real estate price through the capital market—and then affects the behavior of individuals, enterprises, and banks and finally affects economic growth and price level. The short-term interest rate determined by the central bank and the change of short-term interest rate affects the structure of supply and demand of capital through changing the relative price level of all financial tools in the money market and capital market; in the meantime, the change of short-term interest rates will usually have homodromous impact on the long-term bond yields (although the degree of such influence is uncertain). The long-term interest rate also reflects the investors' expectation of future inflation rate and economic growth; so the change of interest rate will, serving as a policy signal, change the investors' expectation of the economy, and such change of expectation will be reflected in the current price, that is, the instant adjustment of asset prices. The influence of monetary policy operations on the asset prices in the capital market will further transmit the intention of monetary policy to the real economy by changing the balance sheets of individuals, enterprises, and banks. On the one hand, wealth effect brings more cash flow into the balance sheet of the general public, affecting the income and expenditure so as to change the consumption and investment demand. On the other hand, under modern economic conditions, the capital market is the main venue of resource allocation of the whole society, and the signal of asset price movement will change social resource allocation so as to enhance total supply, and if there is any inconsistency between total supply and total demand, the inflation rate will go up or go down.

The influence of the capital market on monetary policy is subject to the following factors:

1. Scale of Capital Market in National Economy

The major influence of the capital market on the macroeconomy originates from the impact of the capital market on the balance sheet of the whole society. If the relative value of bank credit is high in the balance sheet, the influence of capital market will be relatively weak, or otherwise it will be relatively strong.

2. Degree of Competition in Capital Market Compared with Other Financial Markets

A capital market with width, depth, and efficiency has greater flexibility and responsiveness to the transmission of monetary policy of the central bank. The monetary policy may promptly be transmitted via the capital market; the strength of the capital market compared to bank credit market is that, if monetary policy is transmitted via the bank credit market, it must first go through the lending behaviors of commercial banks and then to the nonbank public and the real economy, which means the bank has to work as the intermediary; whereas, because the capital market has various participants, not only may all banks and the nonbank public directly be influenced by the monetary policy of the central bank but also the signals of monetary policy may also reach all residents more easily and directly, thus the efficiency and effect of transmission is greatly enhanced. Within the financial system, if the degree of competition is relatively great, the transmission of monetary policy of the central bank will be strengthened. Of course, the transmission channel and the mechanism of monetary policy become more complex.

3. Degree of Liberalization of Monetary Policy Tools of the Central Bank

The central bank can directly control the assets of commercial banks through monetary policy operations so as to control the liabilities of commercial banks, namely to control the supply of money, but such influence on the capital market is somewhat indirect. On the contrary, the indirect monetary policy operation of the central bank is to change its own assets by means of economic transactions so as to determine its own liabilities, that is, the reserve fund, which is in turn the assets of commercial banks;

changing base money will adjust the balance sheet of commercial banks so as to indirectly determine the supply of money. The representative method of indirect monetary policy operation is open market operation. Indirect operation affects the liabilities of banks in an indirect way but affects the capital market directly. The central bank conducts open market operations in the bond market, which has a direct influence on the market. In case a country adopts such indirect method (mainly open market operation), the influence of the capital market on the monetary policy will be enhanced; as a result, the central bank will pay more attention to the capital market.

4. Efficiency of the Capital Market

The operational efficiency of the capital market mainly refers to the degree of responsiveness of investors to economic information, that is, whether asset prices reflect the economic elements and investors' expectation of the future timely and sufficiently. The more sophisticated the price formation mechanism of the capital market, the higher the efficiency of the capital market and the larger the influence on monetary policy.

III. Influence of Capital Market on the Objectives of Monetary Policy

(I) Influence of Capital Market on the Ultimate Goal of Monetary Policy

With the practice of the monetary policies of central banks, academic circles and central banks have come to a consensus that the ultimate goal of the central bank is to maintain the stability of the monetary system. With the development of the securities market, the fluctuation of stock price has caused greater volatility on the general price level. On the one hand, the rise of stock price will improve the balance sheets of enterprises and residents, which leads to the inflation of general goods and service price level through wealth channels; at the same time, stock price inflation and consumption goods inflation will distort price signal and mislead investments and decisions on the real economy, thus giving rise to misallocation of resources in the real economy. The surge of stock price may also lead to overinvestment of enterprises or excessive loans by investors to invest in stocks, fueling the stock bubbles. On the other hand, once the stock price experiences a dramatic drop, the wealth of enterprises and individuals will shrink substantially, denting confidence, and thus cutting investments and consumption expenditure to a large extent; at the same time, the fall of value in bank collaterals will place banks into a financial crisis and induce a credit crisis, which may give rise to severe deflation in extreme cases.

With respect to the issue of whether the central bank will treat the asset price represented by stock prices as conventional regulation and control objective, or under the situation of a relatively stable price level, whether the central bank will intervene given the extreme volatility of asset prices, there are two standpoints. One holds the opinion that no matter theoretically or practically, monetary policy must promptly respond to the dynamics of the capital market. The opposite opinion is that monetary policy must put more emphasis on controlling the inflation of goods and service prices other than intervening in the capital market (excluding bond market), or otherwise the stability of the monetary policy will be affected. The key problem here is whether to pay attention to asset price because it is indeed an important element of affecting goods and service prices, or should the PBC even treat the asset price as an observation index or an intermediary objective. Or should PBC take the ultimate goal as to maintain economic stability, thus the asset price, along with the goods and service prices, are all "ultimate objectives." Asset price obviously does not have controllability, so it is difficult to be the ultimate goal, but it can be taken simply as an observation objective of the central bank. The reason is that, first of all, the central bank is usually deemed to be unable to calculate the amount of bubble in the capital market, but in practice, this is not important. It is true that the central bank fails to calculate how much bubble would be in the capital market, but when the asset price becomes so abnormal that it cannot be explained with existing economic theory, the central bank could at least tell there is a bubble. Just as it is difficult for us to say that a man is a fat person when his weight exceeds a given number, but if we meet someone that weighs over 150 kilograms, we could definitely say he is obese.

However, the problem is that even if the central bank thinks there is bubble, it is difficult to take any meaningful action; the bubble is welcomed by the general public, and it is relatively safe for the central bank (not the economy) to let the bubble burst in its own way. That is to say, it is hard for the central bank to assume moral risk. In practice, the excessive rise of the asset price generally occurs in the period with a relative steady price level, and the deviation of the stock price and the price level of the real economy generally put the monetary policies of the central bank in a dilemma, which increases the difficulty in regulation and control of asset prices by monetary policy.

(II) Influence of Capital Market on the Intermediate Target of Monetary Policy

The effectiveness of money supply as the intermediate target of monetary policy is being weakened. In an open market economy, the controllability, predictability, and relevance of aggregate money supply as the intermediate target of monetary policy is becoming more dissatisfactory. The development of the stock market brings about changes to the money demand function and results in the relatively large difference between the actual money demand and the quantity target of monetary policies. If the intermediate target of the monetary policies only considers the relationship between the money aggregates and general price level without full consideration of the demand on money resulting from market development, it is very difficult to see the whole picture of the economy. From the perspective of money supply, the money supply quantity is jointly determined by the activities of the central bank, financial institutions, enterprises, and individuals, and the influence of the latter three activities on credit creation has become increasingly stronger, and the development of the stock market is also an important factor that will affect the latter three activities. The development of the stock market changes the demand and supply of money and poses challenges to the practice that takes money supply as the intermediate target. Since 1990s, most Western countries have made corresponding adjustment to the intermediate targets of their monetary policies, for example, replacing money supply with interest rate as the intermediate target or adopting the inflation targeting. For countries that continuously exercise money supply as the intermediate targets for their monetary policies, they also undertake certain reforms; for instance, Germany included interest rate and inflation as well as other variables in the targets of monetary policy.

IV. Influence of Capital Market Development on the Operational System of Monetary Policy

Over the past decade, in developed countries and emerging market economies, the financial deepening, the diversification of financial institutions and globalization of the financial market as brought about by the development of the capital market has prompted central banks to develop new monetary policy operation procedures and tools to more effectively and timely influence the activities of all market participants and change the formation of different financial market prices.

(I) The monetary policy tools focus more on open market operations and other market-oriented measures.

As for the transformation of the monetary policy operation system, on the one hand, the monetary policy frameworks of transition countries transform from direct to indirect management; on the other hand, the monetary policy operation systems of developed countries and emerging economies become more market oriented, embodied in the reinforcement of the market status of the central bank. The central bank has a dual identity, first as the representative of the government with statutory power; for example, it may formulate the reserve requirement system, but it is also a bank that would trade in the market. In the market-oriented monetary policy system, there are tools that may be applied on a mandatory basis given the government identity of the central bank, for example, the reverse requirement system, etc. However, these tools have been weakened continuously and tend to disappear. The importance of some tools lies in between, for example, the central bank lending for commercial banks is on a continuous drop, because on the one hand it works as the economic transaction between the central bank and commercial banks, and on the other hand it is based on the government's intention as the lender of last resort. Fully liberalized monetary policy tools as represented by open market operations are merely economic transactions, with the advantages of openness and transparency, and therefore are under rapid development.

Reserve requirement system, rediscounting, and open market operations are the three essential instruments of the traditional monetary toolkit of a central bank, which can effectively influence the credit scale of commercial banks by influencing the financing cost of commercial banks and therefore influencing the consumption, investment, and even the whole economy. With the intensification of the depth and width of the securities market in recent years, the stock market becomes another important channel to influence monetary policy other than the bank's credit channel, and central banks place a great weight on open market operations due to the fact that it is more flexible and market oriented. Moreover, in the formulation and operation of the monetary policies, the central bank has a better understanding of the important role of the psychology and expectation of the general public, which means that the central bank will to a greater extent depend on market information, increase the transparency, and pay attention to the strategy of sending policy signals to the market in its monetary policy decision-making and operations. Under the rapid development of the capital market, the financial environment faced by the central bank becomes more uncertain; therefore, the central bank prefers flexible monetary policy tools. Open market operations can provide a more flexible, market-oriented, and independent monetary policy tool for the central bank. The precondition for open market operations to play its role is a sound capital market, and only a developed bond market can provide sufficient liquidity for the operations of the central bank to allow the operations to fulfill the quantity and price targets without causing too much impact on the market. The efficiency of the market will also guarantee the rapid and balanced transmission of the operational effects of open market operations in the financial system and real economy. Therefore, it could be said that the development of the capital market results in a prominent role played by open market operation as the monetary policy tool.

(II) The Development of Monetary Policy Operation Target Is Directed toward the Short-Term Market Interest Rate

It was a trend for monetary policy changes in the 1990s to adopt interest rate as the operational target of the monetary policy and the term of targeted interest rate was getting shorter. The main reason was the development of the capital market; therefore the status of interest rate in the transmission of monetary policy is strengthened. Generally, the following factors need to be considered in the choice of the interest rate as the operational target of the central bank: (i) relatively low volatility of interest rate; (ii) status in the interest rate system, that is, influence on other interest rates; and (iii) the central bank's control over such interest rate. In view of the increasing development and scale of the capital market, the central bank's influence on the price of long-term bonds weakens, and the central bank can only impose decisive influence on the short-term interest rate of the money market. As to the long-term bond market, central banks in developed countries will minimize intervention as much as possible so as to allow the long-term yield embodied in the long-term bond price to be fully reflected in the inflation expectation of the public to serve as a reference for the central bank to make decisions on monetary policies. Another reason for the central bank's inactive intervention lies in that the central bank has limited influence on the long-term bond market. The money market is an interbank lending market on which the banks open accounts at the central bank to engage in reserve trading and is therefore a fundamental money trading market, so the central bank has comparatively strong control over that market, and long-term bond market falls into the scope of the capital market, because of its many participants, including banks, investment funds, insurance companies, manufacturing enterprises, individuals, etc., the trading fund of which includes base money and money, and the central bank's influence on it is very limited. As a result, the central bank will usually and indirectly influence the long-term interest rate by influencing the short-term interest rate, without direct intervention in the long-term interest rate level. Another reason for choosing short-term interest rate as the operational target is that, comparing with short-term interest rate, the long-term interest rate level formed by the capital market is subject to the influence of many more factors, especially the influence of the public's expectation of future economic trend, and therefore are highly volatile, which makes it inappropriate to be the operational target.

(III) Diversification of Open Market Operation Tools

The tools of open market operations of the central bank actually refer to the collaterals used. The central bank usually has to sell or use collaterals to make repurchase in the recovery of the base money via open market operations. In most Asian countries, the major significance of the central bank holding collaterals lies in recovering the liquidity of the banking system. Japan, China, and other non-Asian countries have long-term fiscal deficits; however, Asian countries other than Japan and China all have periodical fiscal surpluses with a acute problem of collateral shortage. The first alternative to treasury bonds is the bonds issued by the central bank. Some countries believe that it is better for the central bank to issue treasury bonds than its own bonds, because it is conducive to forming a unitary treasury bond market. Countries with fiscal surpluses are trying to develop the treasury bond market. The Federal Reserve is studying the possibility of purchasing institutional bonds and other financial instruments other than treasury bonds.[6]

Since the twenty-first century, the influence of the capital market on the monetary policy becomes greater. Monetary policy is the activity of the central bank to adjust its own balance sheet. The credit channel implemented by traditional monetary policy is that the central bank changes its liabilities via credit transactions with commercial banks, and open market operations represent the market channel for the implementation of monetary policy, through which the central bank changes its liabilities via trading in the bond market and other open markets. Market channel is advantageous in terms of flexibility, efficiency, and convenience in implementation, and the key reasons for such advantages are that since commercial banks assume the payment and clearing function, when the central bank trades with non-commercial-bank financial institutions or the nonbanking public may also change commercial banks' reserves at the central bank. This type of trading will not be subject to the influence of commercial banks' demand. This will overcome the fundamental drawback to the implementation of traditional monetary policy. Under the traditional credit channel for the implementation of monetary policy, it would require the coordination of the credit needs of commercial banks if the central bank wishes to change its own liabilities. Even though the central bank may adjust interest rate to influence the credit demand function of commercial banks, the implementation of monetary policies will eventually require the consent of commercial banks before it can go ahead. While the operation of the capital market shows a different picture, and the counterparties of the central bank include all market participants, commercial banks merely account for a small portion. In developed countries like the United States, the major power of the capital market is investment banks, and 22 primary dealers of open market operations of the Federal Reserve are all investment banks. In this case, the central bank conducts trading with investment banks and other counterparties, and as a result, the liabilities of the central bank change. Nevertheless, this process has nothing to do with the decisions of commercial banks. Through this sophisticated institutional design under the modern financial system, the effectiveness of monetary policy will be greatly enhanced. To my understanding, this is the root concept of "implementing monetary policy operations via capital market" as put forward and studied by the Federal Reserve recently. The trend of monetary policy operations of developed countries is to simplify the balance sheet of the central bank as much as possible, reduce the types of monetary policy tools, specify monetary policy targets, and send a clearer signal of monetary policy operation. Therefore, we have reasons to believe that implementing monetary policy operation via capital market will gradually substitute the current credit channel and become the mainstream of monetary policy operation.

Does the Expansion of Consumer Credit Sector Affect the Effectiveness of Monetary Policy[7]

In this section, we argue that as China's consumer credit sector is expanding, the central bank's role in smoothing economic fluctuation and promoting economic growth becomes more important. We build a general equilibrium model with durable and nondurable goods to analyze how the consumer credit sector affects the transmission mechanism of monetary policy. The model finds that an expanding consumer credit sector improves the efficiency of the monetary transmission mechanism. Two policy implications derived suggest China's central bank should encourage the development of the consumer credit sector and liberalize market-based monetary policy tools such as interest rate tools.

I. Introduction

Post-Mao economic reforms have created a market-oriented economy in China while the government continues to play a very important role. With decades-long economic growth, stable incomes, declining birth rates, and household sizes, China is following much of Asia into a consumer revolution. The ability to buy on credit is transforming China and meanwhile poses a challenge for China's economic policymakers.

This research project is motivated by the astonishing development of China's consumer credit market. After the welfare distribution of houses ended in China in July 1998, all housing units entered the market for sale.

Accompanying this housing reform, the PBC launched the personal consumer credit policy and introduced "consumer credit" to Chinese households. Auto ownership, fueled by credit, has also been exploding since 2002. The ability to buy on credit forces financial systems to cater to new consumer demands, which has resulted in a consumer borrowing increase of 125 percent annually since 1998.[8]

Housing lending from commercial banks has become the principal channel of raising funds for housing reform in China, and it also becomes an important macromonitoring means of the government over housing and real estate markets. China's housing loans amounted to 1.65 trillion Yuan by March 2005, making up 81 percent of total consumer loans outstanding. China's personal consumer loans and housing loans have experienced triple and double digit growth since 1998. Although China's consumer credit has recently been increasing quickly, its percentage out of the total credit market debt outstanding is much lower than those in developed economies. Consumer loans only accounts for 8 percent of total loans issued by all domestic financial institutions in China by March 2005 compared to that over 25 percent in the United States. We expect the consumer credit sector in China will continue growing fast in the next decade.[9]

In this section, we will explore how an expanding consumer credit sector will affect the effectiveness of monetary policies in China and how China's central bank, the PBC, should adapt to expanded consumer borrowing and improve its ability of using monetary policies to stabilize the economy.

Our investigation is related to two important questions in the literature. Does monetary policy affect the real economy? If so, what is the transmission mechanism by which these effects pass through? While there is no single prevailing view of the monetary policy transmission mechanism, it is widely accepted that the interest rate channel and the credit channel are two key components of how a central bank's monetary policy effects are transmitted to the economy.

According to the interest rate channel, the central bank uses monetary policies to affect real economic activities through changing the interest rate level and then the businesses' investment demand and consumers' spending on housing and durable goods. The credit channel concentrates on the direct influence of the central bank's policy on the supply of bank loans and on those businesses and consumers whose spending is dependent on bank lending.

The development of credit markets is believed to be important for both channels of the monetary transmission mechanism. Many studies argue that in advanced economies like the United States, a more efficient credit market may make monetary policy less effective when the interest rates on credit instruments becomes less sensitive to monetary policy changes and the volume of bank credits drops after a monetary contraction. But this argument fails to address what is happening in China, an emerging economy, which has just begun the process of turning itself into a credit-driven economy.

To investigate how an expanding consumer credit sector will affect the effectiveness of monetary policies in China, we will develop a general equilibrium model to study the qualitative and quantitative relationship between monetary injections and the availability of consumer credit and real activity. The model is based on Fuerst (1992) and Li (2000) with the addition of distinguishing durable goods from nondurable goods and the assumption that the consumer credit sector finances the purchase of durable goods.

We distinguish durable goods from nondurable goods for two reasons. First, capital is assumed away in our model. To capture the effect of monetary policy transmitted through the credit channel, we need to separate durable goods from nondurable goods and assume that durable goods consumption must be financed only through the consumer credit market while nondurable goods are purchased using cash. Such a distinction will make monetary policy affect the consumption and production of durable goods through the credit channel. Second, the durable goods sector is more interest rate sensitive than the nondurable sector, and these sectoral differences have important implications for the interest rate channel.

To quantify the two channels of the monetary transmission mechanism, the liquidity effect (the effect of monetary policy through the interest rate channel) and the loanable funds effect (the effect of monetary policy through the credit channel) are computed from the model. The results show that the introduction and expansion of the consumer credit sector in China improves the efficiency of the monetary transmission mechanism through both channels. Therefore, monetary policy becomes more effective in stabilizing economic fluctuations in an economy with a larger consumer credit sector.

We derive two policy implications for China's central bank. First, the PBC should encourage the growth of the consumer credit sector. Second, the PBC should focus on developing and liberalizing market-based monetary policy tools, in particular speeding up its ongoing interest rate reforms.

The paper is structured as follows. First, a literature review is conducted to relate the current study to previous research. Second, a theoretical model with both durable and nondurable goods will be elaborated to study the effect of consumer credit expansion on the monetary transmission mechanism. Then, our model results will be related to China's reality to derive the policy implications for the PBC. The last section concludes and suggests the future empirical implementation of the paper.

II. Literature Review

A large body of literature has examined the process of monetary transmission in general, but the relevance of each specific channel remains an open question.

The conventional transmission mechanism of monetary policy is through the interest rate channel: money expansion (contraction) will push down (up) interest rates and stimulate (discourage) demand and aggregate economic activity. Although Keynes originally emphasized this channel as operating through businesses decisions about investment spending, later research recognized that investment decisions include consumer choices about housing and consumer durable goods. Wilcox (1992) discovers that nominal interest rates are equally important in explaining both durable and nondurable consumption.

Research on the credit channel is plentiful, including Bernanke and Blinder (1992), Kashyap, Stein, and Wilcox (1993), Bernanke and Gertler (1995). The credit channel exists based on the assumption that bank loans and other bank assets are imperfect substitutes. When the central bank reduces money supply, banks will not be able to lend as much as before even after selling other bank assets, and therefore spending by customers who borrow from banks must fall, and so must aggregate demand; when the central bank increases money supply, and therefore loans, individuals or firms whose spending is dependent on bank loans will be able to borrow more and increase consumption and investment.

Gertler and Gilchrist (1993) argue that in today's financial markets, borrowers are no longer bank dependent because they are more likely to access alternative forms of finance. After a monetary contraction, banks can also offset a decline in reserves with other sources of funds, such as CDs or new equity issues, so the credit channel is not prominent.

But the credit channel is not entirely dead. Kashyap and Stein (2000) find that small banks and small borrowers are closely connected in credit markets. Ludvigson (1998) provides evidence that consumer credit is a significant predictor of consumption.

Surprisingly there are very few studies on consumer credit markets and the monetary transmission mechanism. Li (2000) extends Fuerst (1992) to evaluate the role of household credit markets in the transmission of monetary policy. He focuses on the effect of household credit markets on the traditional interest rate channel. The paper reveals a positive contemporaneous correlation between monetary shocks and consumption that helps to explain the negative correlation between the nominal interest rate and monetary policy. He explains why the liquidity effect may dominate the anticipated inflation effect in the short run so that the nominal interest rate will fall after a monetary injection. But Li (2000) does not discuss the impact of consumer credit markets on the credit channel of the monetary transmission mechanism.

III. The Model

In this section, we will build a theoretical model to show an expanding consumer credit sector makes the central bank's monetary policy more effective. The model focuses on analyzing how a consumer credit expansion will affect the transmission mechanism of monetary policy.

To evaluate the role of consumer credit sector in the transmission of monetary policy, we will follow Fuerst (1992) and Li (2000) to construct a model with both durable and nondurable goods where durable goods consumption must be financed through household credit markets.

In our model, there are two sectors in the production side of the economy. Sector one is the consumer goods producing sector, and goods-producers hire labor to produce durable and nondurable goods. Sector two is the finance sector consisting of both financial intermediaries and credit-service producers. Financial intermediaries do not hire any labor but channel the funds between households and credit producers. Credit producers in sector two employs labor to produce a flow of credit services.

We assume that in the economy, there are an infinite number of identical households and an infinite number of homogenous firms residing in the goods producing and financial sectors; the central bank controls the money supply. We study a deterministic model instead of a stochastic one so that the model solution can be calculated directly without resorting to numerical methods.

Preferences

All households in the economy last in perpetuity and have identical preferences regarding consumption and leisure. The maximization problem of a representative household is shown here as:

$$U_0 = \sum_{t=0}^{\infty} \beta^t [u(c_t) + v(1 - n_t)] \tag{4.1}$$

Where n_t is work effort at time t, c_t is consumption at time t. u (.) and v (.) are the utility functions of consumption and leisure, respectively. Consumption c_t is the sum of durable and nondurable goods consumed:

$$c_t = (g_t + q_t) \tag{4.2}$$

Where g_t represents nondurable goods purchased by cash and q_t represents durable goods purchased by credit. In this simple model, we assume goods purchased by cash and goods purchased by credit are perfect substitutes as in Fuerst (1992) and Aiyagari and Eckstein (1994). The price of goods is given by P_{gt}.

Production

On the production side of this economy, there are two sectors. Sector one, the goods producing sector, employs labor n_{1t} to produce output y_t.[10]

$$y_t = F(n_{1t}) \tag{4.3}$$

Following Aiyagari and Eckstein (1994) and Li (2002), we assume sector two, the financial sector, consists of both financial intermediaries and credit-service producers. The representative financial intermediary does not hire any labor but channels the funds between households and credit producers. It accepts cash deposits D_t from households at the beginning of period t, receives monetary injections X_t from the central bank during period t, and provides loans to credit producers. The nominal interest rate the financial intermediary charges for loans and pays on deposits are given by R_t.

The representative credit producer in sector two employs labor n_{2t} to produce a flow of credit services $Q(n_{2t})$. The household can purchase one unit of credit services to purchase one unit of goods. To finance goods consumption purchased with credit q_t, credit producers need to provide q_t units of credit services. To provide $Q(n_{2t})$ units of credit services, σ fraction of such credit services must be provided in form of cash, so credit producers must borrow cash B_t from financial intermediaries to produce credit services.

Cash-in-Advance Constraints

Two cash-in-advance constraints exist in this economy. First, the household brings in money balance M_t to period t, puts aside D_t out of M_t in the financial intermediary, and then starts supplying labor n_{1t}, n_{2t} to the sector one and two producers. The household consumes g_t units of nondurable goods using the cash on hand, so the first cash-in-advance constraint for this model is

$$P_{gt} g_t \leq (M_t - D_t) \tag{4.4}$$

Second, the household also buys q_t units of credit services to consume q_t units of durable goods. The $Q(n_{2t})$ units of credit services, in equilibrium equal to q_t, are produced by the credit-service producer using n_{2t} units of labor supplied by the household and B_t amount of cash borrowed from the financial intermediary. Since only σ fraction of durable goods consumption must be supplied in form of cash, the second cash-in-advance constraint is the constraint faced by the credit-service producer when producing $Q(n_{2t})$ units of credit services,

$$\sigma P_{gt} Q(n_{2t}) \leq B_t \tag{4.5}$$

Money Supply Process

The money supply process is controlled by the central bank and follows

$$M_{t+1}^s = M_t^s + X_t \tag{4.6}$$

Where M_t^s is the money supply at the beginning of period t+1, and X_t is the monetary injection during period t. As in Lucas (1990), we assume that D_t is determined before X_t. Thus D_t is not a function of the current-period's monetary injection but can be a function of the past $\{X_s\}_{s=0}^{t-1}$

Individual Budget Constraints

The household supplies n_t units of labor in which goods producers hire n_{1t} units and credit-service producers employ n_{2t} units. The nominal wage rate is given by W_t. At the end of each period, the family receives labor income and pools its cash receipts and enters period t+1.

$$\begin{aligned} M_{t+1} = &[M_t + D_t R_t + W_t n_t - P_{gt}(g_t + q_t) - P_{gt} q_t] + X_t(1 + R_t) \\ &+ [P_{gt} F(n_{1t}) - W_t n_{1t}] + [P_{qt} Q(n_{2t}) - W_t n_{2t} - B_t R_t] \end{aligned} \tag{4.7}$$

The left hand side is the end-of-period t (also the beginning-of-period t+1) cash holdings. On the right hand side, the first term in brackets represents the cash receipts of the household. The second is cash holdings of the financial intermediary. The third is the profits of the goods producing firm, and fourth is the profits of the credit producer minus loan interest payments to the financial intermediary.

The optimization problem thus becomes choosing a sequence $\{g_t, q_t, n_{1t}, n_{2t}, D_t, B_t, R_t, n_t \text{ and } M_{t+1}\}$ to maximize (4.1) subject to (4.4), (4.5), and (4.7). After solving the model, we will calculate the liquidity effect (the effect of monetary change on the economic activity through the interest rate channel) and the loanable funds effect (the effect of monetary change on the economic activity through the credit channel) to evaluate how the introduction and expansion of the consumer credit sector will affect the transmission mechanism of monetary policy.

The Liquidity Effect of Money Growth

Appendix 2 solves the liquidity effect after an unanticipated monetary injection. We find that the nominal interest rate and the relative price of durable goods to nondurable goods falls $\left(\frac{\partial R_t}{\partial X_t} < 0, \frac{\partial (1+R_t)}{\partial X_t} < 0\right)$; both the goods producer and the credit-service producer will hire more labor $\left(\frac{\partial n_{1t}}{\partial X_t} > 0, \frac{\partial n_{2t}}{\partial X_t} > 0\right)$; Both the output and consumption level of total goods and the credit-service increases $\left(\frac{\partial y_t}{\partial X_t} > 0, \frac{\partial q_t}{\partial X_t} > 0\right)$. In conclusion, due to the liquidity effect, employment, and output in both sectors respond positively to monetary injections.

Compared with Li (2000), our model explicitly solves the liquidity effect. Furthermore, we show how the existence and expansion of the consumer credit sector influences the liquidity effect: the greater, the slower R_t responds to the exogenous monetary injection. The intuition here implies that the smaller proportion of goods is financed by consumer credit, the less sensitive the nominal interest rate is in response to the central bank's monetary policy.

The Loanable Funds Effect of Money Growth

In our model, the production and consumption of goods and credit services increase not only due to the drop in the nominal interest rate. The model also exhibits the loanable funds effect of money growth through the credit channel of the monetary transmission mechanism. The credit channel magnifies the effect of monetary injection on the economy.

This magnifying effect takes place through the financial intermediary. When the central bank injects cash into the financial intermediary, the total amount of cash available for the credit-service producer to borrow, $(D_t + X_t)$, increases. Since the household purchases credit services to consume durable goods, the amount of credit services produced directly relates to how much cash the credit-service producer can borrow from the financial intermediary. Thus, when more cash B_t can be borrowed, the credit-service provider produces more units of credit services; the household purchases more units of credit services and consumes more units of durable goods.

In equation (28) listed in appendix 1,

$$q_t = \frac{D_t + X_t}{\sigma(M_t - D_t)} g_t$$

We see that when X_t increases, the proportion of nondurable goods consumption out of total goods consumption, $\frac{D_t + X_t}{\sigma(M_t - D_t) + D_t + X}$ will increase. After finding that as money is injected into the economy, not only does the total goods consumption increases $\left(\frac{\partial c_t}{\partial X_t} > 0\right)$ but also the nondurable goods consumption increases even more $\left(\frac{\partial q_t}{\partial X_t} > \frac{\partial c_t}{\partial X_t}\right)$; we conclude that the credit channel of the monetary transmission mechanism is amplified after the introduction of consumer credit since the monetary injection has a greater impact on demand for credit goods than for cash goods.

Summary and Analysis of Model Results

The model solutions suggest that a consumer credit expansion can make a central bank's monetary policy more effective. Prior to the consumer credit sector, monetary policy affects consumption through the relatively narrow and indirect interest rate channel. The development and expansion of the consumer credit sector changes and magnifies the effects of monetary policy on the consumption demand and total output in two aspects.

First, the consumer credit sector improves the efficiency of the interest rate channel. We show that when there is no consumer credit sector in the economy, the interest rate change has only a small and indirect effect on the current period's consumption. After introducing the consumer credit sector into the model, the changes in the interest rate directly affect consumers' behavior and subsequently affect consumption demand and aggregate output. Moreover, the expansion of the consumer credit sector increases the money elasticity of interest rate that implies that an unexpected money injection will push the interest rate even lower and stimulate aggregate demand and output more as the consumer credit sector grows larger.

Second, our model shows the existence of the consumer credit sector amplifies the credit channel. The credit channel provides an additional channel of transmission for the central bank's policy to affect the real economy. When all consumption is purchased by cash, the central bank is only able to affect firms' borrowing through the credit channel. In a model like ours, assuming no capital and no firms' investment, the effect of monetary policy through the credit channel is just zero. After the introduction of consumer credit, an unanticipated monetary injection causes credit service producers to hire more labor and increase the production of consumer credit. Thus monetary injection affects the consumption and production of both durable and nondurable goods. So the loanable funds effects are amplified in the economy with a growing percentage of consumers relying on financial intermediaries to finance consumption.

IV. Policy Implications

Our model results prove that the introduction of the consumer credit sector would improve the efficiency of the monetary transmission mechanism through both the interest rate channel and the credit channel. Such an introduction also makes monetary policies more effective in stabilizing economic fluctuations.

We derive two major policy implications for the PBC from the model. First we recommend the PBC adopt policies to encourage the development of the consumer credit sector so that the PBC is able to control consumer credit[11] in addition to business credit it traditionally manages.

For a central bank, money aggregates and interest rates are two main monetary policy instruments. The interest rate tool is rarely used by the PBC since state-owned firms in China unanimously face soft budget constraints and do not respond to interest rate changes. Most deposit and loan rates set by the PBC rarely fluctuate.

When the PBC uses its monetary policy to affect the real economy, the credit channel dominates. The PBC has been using the market-based liquidity management (or through administration of guidance planning before abolishing the quota control on credit in 1998) to control loan availability and then to affect firms' investment demand and aggregate output.

The liquidity management has its limitations such as that it usually works better during a monetary contraction. When the PBC injects money to the economy to stimulate the aggregate demand, it may face the problem that the increase in loan availability does not necessarily lead to a significant increase in the actual loan activity or the investment demand. Another concern about the liquidity management is that the investment demand is much more volatile than the consumption demand.

Thus, when the central bank's policy affects real economic activities through its influence on the investment demand, the macroeconomy unavoidably will experience higher volatility. The introduction of consumer credit sector can help to relieve both concerns since the consumption demand is complementary to the investment demand and usually less volatile than the investment demand.

To stimulate the consumer credit sector to grow, the PBC could lower consumer credit interest rates and extend pay-off terms and guide commercial banks to simplify the consumer loan application process. The PBC should also play an important role in encouraging more consumer loans directed to education, affordable housing in the city, farming equipment and fertilizer in the countryside.

The second policy implication we derive from the model is that as the consumer credit sector expands and its importance increases in the total loan structure, China's central bank should focus more on market-based monetary policy tools instead of regulative monetary policy instruments. In particular, the PBC should take actions to liberalize interest rates.

Most of China's banks and firms are wholly or partially state owned, and their decision making is more or less under regulation. Therefore these firms' investment demand is not responsive to interest rate changes. But the interest rate channel will become an important monetary transmission mechanism when China's consumer credit sector is expanding. The reason is that in China consumers' decision-making is market based. After interest rates are liberalized, any change in the interest rate will directly affect consumers' cost of borrowing, and it therefore influence consumers' demand for bank loans and eventually affect the consumption demand and aggregate output. Thus we recommend as the consumer credit sector is growing in China, the central bank should speed up its ongoing interest rate reforms and make the interest rate an effective monetary policy tool as in most developed economies.

V. Conclusion and Future Research

In this section, we use a general equilibrium model with durable and non-durable goods to explore the role of an expanding consumer credit sector in the monetary transmission mechanism. We assume the purchase of durable goods can be only financed by the consumer credit sector, and there is a one-to-one relationship between the consumption of durable goods and the amount of consumer credit.

Our model finds the expansion of the consumer credit sector amplifies the credit channel of the monetary transmission mechanism and improves the efficiency of the interest rate channel. When the central bank injects money to the economy, liquidity and consumer loan availability increases. Thus, monetary policy directly affects the consumption demand through the consumer credit sector. At the same time, since consumer credit is more interest rate sensitive, consumer credit and consumption expenditure will be affected to a greater extent than business credit and firms' investment expenditure after the interest rate changes.

The two policy implications derived from the model suggest that the central bank should encourage the development of the consumer credit sector and rely more on market-based monetary policy tools, especially interest rate tools.

In the future, it will be interesting to conduct an empirical investigation to establish the quantitative evidence of the consumer credit sector in monetary transmission. The empirical examination will be closely related to the theoretical model in this section. A vector auto-regression (VAR) model will be used to analyze how the change in monetary policy will affect interest rates, mortgage rates (the conventional interest rate channel), and the supply of bank consumer loans (the credit channel). The VAR model will also help to discover how monetary policy will affect real economic variables such as consumption and output, and what significant importance of each monetary transmission channel will exhibit.

Notes

1 Money Market

1. This article was originally compiled based on the speech delivered by the author at the first anniversary symposium of the establishment of interbank bond market on June 16, 1998.
2. This article was originally written in June 1999 and awarded the first place of second-class awards from China Youth Finance Forum Writing Award.
3. The article was originally completed in May 2000.
4. This article was originally completed in May 2011.
5. Take Japan as an example, generally speaking, an enterprise wishing to issue short-term commercial papers in the money market for financing requires a good reputation, and it is difficult for SMEs with a poor reputation to finance directly through commercial papers, whereas bank acceptance bills are based on the dual reputation of the borrowing enterprise and the associated bank, which provide greater convenience to the financing activities of SMEs in the money market. The borrower using bank acceptance bills to finance must pay a commitment fee to the bank, in addition to the payment of principal and interest to the lender, so the cost of loan is higher than that of commercial papers in general.
6. From 2002 to 2006, the balance of discounted bills accounted for 70–80 percent of the balance of acceptance, but after 2007, the proportion of the balance of discount to the balance of acceptance fell to 50–60 percent, or even 26 percent in 2010. Such data is caused by banks' intentional manipulation of making balance of discount low at a certain time point to cope with the examination on the one hand, and on the other hand, bills transfer off balance sheet through financing.

2 Bond Market

1. This article was originally published in the *Capital Market* in August 2001.

2. This article was originally the first section of the cover article "Launch of Bond Market" of the *Caijing* Magazine, No. 5, 2002 that was published on March 5.
3. This article was originally the second passage of the cover article "Launch of Bond Market" of the *Caijing* Magazine, No. 5, 2002.
4. This article was originally the third piece of the cover article "Launch of Bond Market" of the *Caijing* Magazine, No. 5, 2002.

3 Foreign Exchange Market

1. This article was originally completed in March 1997.
2. This article was originally completed in July 2003.
3. This article was originally completed in July 2004.
4. This article was completed in August 2007.
5. Compiled from the speech of the author delivered on the Interbank Foreign Exchange Member Commendation Meeting in April 2009.
6. Compiled from the speech of the author in the 21st EMEAP/BIS Foreign Exchange Market Conference.
7. Complied from the speech delivered by the author on the biweekly roundtable seminar of the China Finance 40 Forum, the "Euro-American Debt Dilemma and Chinese Financial Strategy," which was held on May 29, 2011.

4 Stock Market

1. This article was originally published in the *Chinese Securities* in July 1998.
2. This article was originally published in the *Caijing* Magazine No. 9, 2000.
3. This article was originally published in the *Listed Company*, No. 9, 2000.
4. This article was published in the *Caijing* Magazine, No. 7, 2001.
5. This article was completed in June 2003.
6. The Federal Reserve has conducted the unconventional policy of purchasing large quantities of long-term securities, including agency securities and agency mortgage-backed securities (MBS). As the result, the large reductions in mortgage rates due to QE1 appeared to be driven partly by the fact that QE1 involved large purchases of agency-backed MBS.
7. Compiled from the speech of the author delivered on the Peking University and University of Virginia Joint Conference "China's consumer credit policy" in August 2004. American Economic Association (AEA) Annual Meeting 2006 paper. This paper was published in the *Journal of Financial Research*, November 2011. The coauther is Zhang Yanchun.
8. The data is collected from the Quarterly Monetary Policy Report published by the PBC.
9. In 2015, a decade later, the consumer credit sector has continued to grow quickly.

10. We assume it is an economy without capital to simplify the analysis. This simplification does not affect the major findings of our paper. In our model, even without capital, the production of consumer goods will be affected by the monetary policy through the relative price movement of nondurable goods versus durable goods. The demand for credit services and thereafter the reallocation of labor between the goods producer and the credit service producer will adjust.
11. Although how significantly monetary policy affects the supply of bank loans in the United States generates controversy, this channel provides valuable information for analyzing China's current situation since commercial loans remain the most important source of funds, and commercial banks in China cannot easily replace lost (retail) deposits with other funds.

References

Bernanke, Ben and Alan Blinder, "Federal Funds Rate and Channels of Monetary Transmission," *American Economic Review*, 82 (1992): 901–921.

Bernanke, Ben and Mark Gertler, "Inside the Black Box: The Credit Channel of Monetary Policy Transmission," *Journal of Economic Perspectives*, 9 (1995): 27–48.

Demsetz, Harold, "The Cost of Transacting," *The Quarterly Journal of Economics*, 82, 1 (February 1968): 33–53.

Earl, Dennis and Margret Kurz, *Risk in Clearing and Settlement of China's Treasury-Bonds and Plan for Reducing Risk*. Report of World Bank on China's Treasury-Bond Market Risk Control Mechanism and Information Management Consultancy Project, No. 9, 1997.

Fuerst, Timothy S., "Liquidity, Loanable Funds, and Real Activity," *Journal of Monetary Economics*, 29 (1992): 3–24.

Genyou, Dai, *China Monetary Policy Report*. Beijing: China's Finance Press, 1999.

Gertler, Mark and Simon Gilchrest, "The Role of Credit Market Imperfections in the Monetary Transmission Mechanism: Arguments and Evidence," *Scandinavian Journal of Economics*, 95 (1993): 43–64.

Greenspan, A., "Global Challenges," remarks at the Financial Crisis Conference, Council on Foreign Relations, New York, July 12, 2000.

Guofeng, Sun, *Study on China's Monetary Policy Transmission Mechanism*, master thesis of the Graduate School of the People's Bank of China, 1996.

Guofeng, Sun, "Reform in New Shares Issuance Mechanism Is Imperative," China Securities Journal, July 12, 1998.

Guofeng, Sun, "Development of Interbank Bond Market and the Regulation and Control of the Central Bank's Monetary Policies," *Journal of Financial Studies*, 9 (2000): 76–83.

Jianmin, Shi, "The Stock Market, Demand for Money and Aggregate Economy: General Equilibrium Analysis," *Economic Research Journal*, 5 (2001): 45–52.

Kashyap, Anil and Jeremy Stein, "What Do a Million Observations on Banks Say about the Transmission of Monetary Policy," *American Economic Review*, 90 (2000): 407–428.

Kashyap, Anil, Jeremy Stein, and David Wilcox, "Monetary Policy and Credit Conditions: Evidence from the Composition of External Finance," *American Economic Review*, 83 (1993): 78–98.

Li, Victor E., "Household Credit and the Monetary Transmission Mechanism," *Journal of Money, Credit and Banking*, 32 (2000): 335–356.

Lin, Justin Yifu, *Economic Theory on Institutional Change: Induced Institutional Change and Imposed Institutional Change, Property Rights and Institutional Change*. Shanghai: Shanghai People's Press, 1994.

Lucas, Robert E., Jr., "Liquidity and Interest Rates," *Journal of Economic Theory*, 50 (1990): 237–264.

Ludvigson, Sydney, "The Channel of Monetary Transmission to Demand: Evidence from the Market for Automobile Credit," *Journal of Money, Credit and Banking*, 30 (1998): 365–383.

North, Douglas G., *Institutions, Institutional Change and Economic Performance*, translated by Liu Ruihua. Shanghai: Shanghai SDX, 1994.

Rao Aiyagari, S. and Zvi Eckstein, *Interpreting Monetary Stabilization in a Growth Model with Credit Goods Production*, Working Paper 525, Federal Reserve Bank of Minneapolis, 1994.

Ruilong, Yang and Yang Qijing, "Models for Tiered Progressive Institutional Change," *Economic Research Journal*, 3 (2000): 24–31.

Stigler, George J., "Public Regulation of the Securities Markets," *The Journal of Business*, 37, 2 (April 1964): 117–142.

Wenjun, Gou, "The Development of the Capital Market and Reform of Monetary Policy," *Journal of Financial Research*, 5 (2000): 64–70.

Wilcox, David, "The Construction of US Consumption Data: Some Facts and Their Implications for Empirical Work," *American Economic Review*, 82 (1992): 922–941.

Yan, Qingmin and Muxiang Li, "The Impacting Effect of China's Money Supply on Economic Growth," *Chongqing Finance*, 3 (2001): 11–14.

Yuyan, Zhang, "Interest Group and Non-Neutrality of Institution," *Reform Journal in China*, 2 (1994): 97–106.

Index

About the Author

Sun Guofeng, Deputy Director General, Monetary Policy Department, People's Bank of China.

Sun Guofeng graduated from the Graduate School of the People's Bank of China in 1996, before joining PBC's Planning and Central Bank Lending Department in the same year. He then worked in the Bank's Monetary Policy Department, where he served as Deputy Director of Open Market Operations and subsequently Director of Foreign Exchange Transactions. Mr. Sun has held the office of Deputy Director General of Monetary Policy Department since 2010, primarily engaged in the establishment of the interbank bond market, the development of China's money market, the launching of open market operations, the reform of RMB exchange rate regime, and the innovation of monetary policy tools. During 2003–2004, he was invited to do research as a visiting scholar at Stanford University. Mr. Sun is currently a professor at People's Bank of China, part-time professor at the University of International Business and Economics in China, a graduate tutor at the Tsinghua University of China, and a distinguished member of the China Finance 40 forum.

Sun Guofeng holds a Ph.D degree in economics from Chinese Academy of Social Sciences, and has for many years studied topics such as credit money theory, central bank monetary policy, RMB exchange rate, the bond market, the money market, and international financial markets. He is the author of 2 books and more than 70 academic papers published in academic journals, including "Economic Research" (China), "Financial Research" (China), and "Journal of Chinese Political Science" (US), and has been a guest speaker at various colleges and research institutions including Stanford University, University of California, Berkeley, the Bank for international Settlements, Peking University, China Academy of Social Sciences, and China Society for Finance.

Printed and bound by CPI Group (UK) Ltd, Croydon, CR0 4YY